FRONT-LINE STALINGRAD

The grim story of the defence of Stalingrad, for the Russians the bloodiest battle in the whole of World War II. Day after day through the glorious Indian summer of 1942 they hung on, battered, hungry, exhausted, longing for the harsh Russian winter to herald a German retreat.

The author himself was in the thick of the fighting – as a sapper in the hard-pressed trenches outside the city. He has drawn on his own personal experiences in this vivid but sombrely realistic account. Here is heroism, comradeship and humour, but here also is violence, injustice, the anger of men whose nerves are frayed to breaking point.

VICTOR NEKRASOV

Front-Line Stalingrad

Translated by
David Floyd

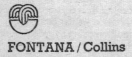

FONTANA / Collins

First published by Harvill Press 1962
First issued in Fontana Books 1964
Second Impression December 1975
Third Impression December 1978

© in the English translation with Harvill Press 1962

Made and printed in Great Britain by
William Collins Sons & Co Ltd, Glasgow

I

The order to retreat was quite unexpected. Only the previous day Divisional HQ had sent down an elaborate scheme for new defence works—reserve positions to be designed, roads to be repaired and bridges to be built. They had wanted to take three sappers away from me to fit out a club-house for the division. In the morning there had been a call from Divisional HQ—to be ready to receive a front-line song and dance troupe. What could be more relaxed? Igor and I even went to the trouble of getting shaved and of trimming and washing our hair, and we washed out our vests and pants. And as we waited for them to dry we lay on the bank of a little stream and watched my sappers knocking together rafts for the scouts.

It was then that Lazarénko, the staff runner, appeared. I had noticed him a long way off. He came running across the fields and I could smell at once by the speed at which he moved that it was not the concert that brought him.

Probably another inspection or something from Army or Front HQ . . . It would mean clambering up to the front line again, demonstrating the defences and listening to comments. Another night wasted. And the engineer had to answer for everything.

There's nothing worse than being on the defensive. Every night an inspection. And every inspector with his own likes and dislikes. For one the trenches are too narrow—difficult for transporting wounded and moving machine-guns. Another thinks them too wide—they'll catch the shrapnel. A third finds the breastworks too low—should be forty centimetres, and yours, as you can see, are not even twenty. A fourth will tell you not to dig trenches at all—anything to deceive the enemy! Just try and please everybody! Meanwhile the divisional engineer commander doesn't give a damn. Only once in the last fortnight had he turned up, and then only to rush along the front line at the gallop without saying anything that made sense. And I was continually starting everything over again and standing to attention to receive the regimental commander's lecture:

" When on earth will you learn, my dear comrade engineer, to make decent trenches . . ."

Lazarénko hopped over the fence.

"Well? What's the matter?"

"The Chief of Staff wants you," he beamed, revealing a fine array of teeth and wiping his perspiring brow with his cap.

"Who? Me?"

"You and the anti-gas officer. You're to be there in five minutes, he said."

No, not an inspection, then.

"But what's on? Don't you know?"

"I'm damned if I do." Lazarénko shrugged his sweating shoulders. "You can't make out a darned thing . . . They chased all the orderlies away. The captain had just gone to rest when a liaison officer suddenly arrived with a message."

We had to put on our vests and pants while they were still wet and go to HQ. Platoon commanders were also summoned . . .

Maxímov, the Chief of Staff, was not there. He was with the regimental commander. In the HQ dug-out we found commanders of supporting units and staff officers. Of the battalion commanders there was only Sergíenko, of the third battalion. Nobody knew what was going on. The liaison officer, lanky lieutenant Zvérev, was fussing with a saddle, puffing and swearing, quite unable to tighten the girths. "Div. HQ are packing up. That's all . . ." He knew no more.

Sergíenko was lying on his stomach, hacking away at a piece of wood, and grumbling as usual.

"No sooner have we got the delousing chamber fixed up than we have to get the hell out of it again. Damn soldiering for a life. The men scratch till they draw blood. You can't get rid of the things."

Samúsev, the fair-haired, watery-eyed commander of an anti-tank gun, smiled scornfully.

"You should worry about a delousing chamber! Half my men are down with swollen backs. From injections. Each one had about half a pint of something stuck into him. Nothing but grunts and groans."

Sergíenko sighed.

"Perhaps we're going back to re-form, eh?"

"Oh, sure," said Goglídze, the scout, with a wry grin. "The day before yesterday they surrenderd Sevastópol, and *they* were just about to re-form. They can't wait to see you in Tashkent!"

The rumbling continued in the north, and above the

6

horizon, far, far away, German bombers, an uneven drone, were still heading in that direction.

"They're making for Valúiki, the sods," Samúsev spat out in a burst of temper. "Sixteen of them."

"They say they've already flattened Valúiki," announced Goglídze, who always knew everything.

"*Who* says?"

"I heard it yesterday from the eight-fifty-twos."

"A fat lot they know."

"Whether they do or not, that's what they say."

Samúsev sighed and turned on his back.

"Anyway, you wasted your time digging yourself a fox-hole, scout. You'll have to leave it for the Jerries as a souvenir."

Goglídze laughed.

"It's always the bloody same. It never fails. Every time I dig in, off we go. This is the third time I've made a hole and I still haven't managed to spend the night in one."

Maxímov eased his way out of the major's dug-out. He approached us with firm steps, as if on the parade ground. You could tell him a kilometre away by his stride. He was obviously out of spirits. He asked who was missing. There were two battalion commanders and the chief liaison officer absent: they had been sent for yesterday by Divisional HQ.

With his arrival everyone fell silent. And so as not to appear idle—the desire to look busy when the chief of staff is about is instinctive—everyone began to fumble in his map-case or look for something in his pockets.

A second wave of German bombers crossed the horizon.

Then the battalion commander arrived. Kappél, commander of the second battalion, thick-set, like a thoroughbred bulldog, but no longer young. And Shiryáev, the dashing commander of the first battalion, with his golden forelock and his cap cocked in an impudent manner over his left eye. In the regiment he was known as Kuzmá Kryuchkóv.[1]

They both saluted. Kappél did it like a civilian, with the palm of his hand half-closed and facing forward, Shiryáev saluted in the specific manner of an experienced front-line officer, flicking open the fingers of his hand as they reached his cap.

Maxímov stood up. We did the same.

"Do you all have your maps?" His voice was sharp, disagreeable. "Take them out, please."

[1] Kuzmá Kryuchkóv: a Cossack sergeant, hero of World War I.

We took them out. Maxímov opened out his own crumpled, much-fingered large-scale map. A thick red line stretched right across it from left to right, from west to east.

"Take a note of the route."

We wrote it down. It was a long march, of a hundred kilometres or so. The destination was Nóvo-Bélenkaya. There we had to reassemble in sixty hours, that is to say, two and a half days.

"Is the picture clear?" Maxímov asked.

Nobody answered.

"I think it should be. We set out at 2300 hours. The first stage will be 36 kilometres. The day will be spent resting in Vérkhnyaya Duvánka. We shall move, of course, with scouts and rear guards. You will receive the movement order in about thirty minutes from Kórsakov. He's working on it now."

Every word of Maxímov's was clearly articulated. He wouldn't have made a bad radio announcer.

"The first battalion will stay where it is. Do you understand? It will cover the move. I warn you—everything must be taken along. There must be no stragglers. It's a long march. Pay attention to footwear . . ."

Holding his pipe in his slender, pale fingers, he ejected short, sharp streams of smoke. Then, screwing up his eyes, he looked at Shiryáev.

"And what have you got, battalion commander?"

Shiryáev straightened up his tunic. "Able-bodied fighting men—twenty-seven. Altogether, counting horsemen and sick, about forty-five men."

"What armament?"

"Two Maxims, two Degtyaryóvs and two eighty-two milli-metre mortars."

"Mortar shells?"

"About a hundred."

"And fifties?"

"Not one. And very little machine-gun ammo. Two belts for each fixed gun and five or six discs each for the portable ones."

Shiryáev spoke quietly, without haste. You could tell he was worried and was trying not to show it. He cut quite a figure, with his tightly buckled belt, his broad shoulders, his powerful calf muscles, his arms straight down at his sides and his fists lightly clenched. Through the open collar of his tunic a blue triangle of vest was showing. It was odd that Maxímov did not tell him off about it.

"So . . ." Maxímov carefully folded his map and put it into his case. "Everything's clear . . . Kérzhentsev, the engineer, will stay behind with you. Understand? Hold on for a couple of days. On the eighth, as it gets dark, start your withdrawal."

"By the same route?" Shiryáev asked quietly. He did not take his eyes off Maxímov.

"The same. If you don't find us . . . Oh well, you know what to do then . . . That's all."

Shiryáev inclined his head in understanding. Everybody remained silent. Somebody, Kappél I think, drew a sharp breath.

"That's all, I said." Maxímov turned sharply in his direction. "Back to your jobs."

We all stood up, shaking off sand and bits of grass.

"I want to see you two."

This was directed at me and Shiryáev.

It was cramped and damp in his dug-out and it smelt of earth. On the table lay the plans of our defences—my work. I had spent the whole morning drawing them up, hurrying to get them off to Div. HQ. The deadline had been 2000 hours.

Maxímov carefully put the sheets of paper together and set light to them by the lamp. The paper shrivelled up, came momentarily to life and then turned black.

"The Germans have got to Vorónezh," he said in a colourless voice, trampling the black, brittle ash into the ground with the toe of his boot. "Last night."

We remained silent.

From under the table Maxímov drew out a cloth-covered aluminium flask with a screw-cap. We each drank in turn from the cap. It was a strong home-made vodka, of about sixty per cent. It caught our throats. We ate some salted gherkins to counteract the drink, and then took another shot each.

For a long time Maxímov sat rubbing the bridge of his nose with two fingers.

"Were you in the forty-one retreat, Shiryáev?"

"I was. Right from the frontier."

"Right from the frontier . . . And you, Kérzhentsev?"

"No," I said. "I was in the reserve."

Maxímov absently crunched a gherkin.

"In general the situation's lousy. We can't escape encirclement." He looked at Shiryáev straight in the eyes. "Save your bullets. While you are sitting here these couple of days, don't do a lot of shooting. Just enough to keep up appearances.

9

And don't get mixed up in any battles. Try and find us. We shall be somewhere or other. If not in Nóvo-Bélenkaya, then nearby. But do remember—you, too, Kérzhentsev," he looked at me sternly, "you don't budge from here until the eighth. Understand? Even if the very ground gives way beneath you. That's what the major said: 'Leave Shiryáev and give him Kérzhentsev to help him.' That means something ... Ah, yes. What have you decided about the trucks?"

Shiryáev grinned:

"Oh, to hell with the trucks! Take the lot! I'll hang on to three carts for the ammunition. That'll be plenty . . ."

"All right. We'll take them then."

"Do you believe in dreams, Kérzhentsev?" Maxímov asked suddenly, and without waiting for an answer added: "Last night I dreamt that two of my front teeth fell out."

Shiryáev laughed. His teeth were packed closely together and very regular.

"The old women say it means some close relation is going die."

"A relation?" Maxímov was drawing curly lines on a piece of newspaper. "Are you married?"

"No," we replied, almost in unison.

"You should be. I'm not married either, and now I'm sorry. A wife is a necessity. As necessary as the air we breathe. Especially now . . ."

The curly lines turned into a woman's head. Long eyelashes and a small mouth, shaped like a heart. Over the left eyebrow was a birth-mark.

"You're not from Moscow, Kérzhentsev?"

"No, why?"

"Oh, only . . . There was a woman I knew before the war —Kérzhentseva, Zinaída Nikoláyevna. No relation?"

"No. I've got no one in Moscow."

Maxímov paced up and down the dug-out. I had the impression he had something he wanted to tell us, but that he was either embarrassed or couldn't make up his mind.

Shiryáev glanced at his watch. Maxímov noticed this and came to a stop.

"Yes, of course. Off you go, there's not much time."

We left the dug-out and he followed us out. There was no gunfire to be heard. Only the croaking of frogs.

We stood for a few minutes, listening to the frogs. The shadows of the fir-trees reached right up to the dug-out. A couple of mortar bombs whistled one after the other over our heads and exploded somewhere a long way back. From the battalion evidently. Shiryáev grinned.

"They're turning the heat on the round wood. But it's three days since there was a battery there."

We listened carefully. No more firing.

"Well, off you go," said Maxímov. "Watch your step."

He shook us firmly by the hand and made a move as if he wanted to embrace us. But he didn't. He just shook hands again.

"Save your bullets, Shiryáev, don't waste them."

"Very good, comrade captain!"

"Mind you . . ." and he walked off with his firm, stiff gait towards the bushes, where some signals men could be seen rolling up wire.

I agreed with Shiryáev to join up with him again in about an hour and a half when I had got all my affairs in order.

II

Our regiment had no luck. For something like six wretched weeks we had been fighting and then finished up without men or guns. Two or three machine-guns to a battalion. And it wasn't so long since we had first gone into battle—May the twentieth, before Ternóvaya, near Khárkov. Straight in, just as we were. Utterly inexperienced, we were always being switched from place to place, thrown into the defence, withdrawn, moved elsewhere, and again put into a defensive position. This was at the time of the Khárkov spring offensive. We would get lost and confused and would confuse others and just couldn't get used to being bombarded. In short, we weren't much use.

Then they shifted us to the south to Bulatsélovka, near Kupyánsk. There we hung about for another couple of weeks. We dug escarpments and counter-escarpments, laid mines and built bunkers. But then the Germans went over to the offensive. They sent swarms of tanks and showers of bombs at us. We completely lost our heads, got scared and started to move back. To cut a long story short, we were withdrawn from the battle altogether, replaced by a guards unit and packed off to Kupyánsk. There we built more bunkers and more escarpments and counter-escarpments until the Germans caught up with us again. We didn't defend the town for long

—just a couple of days. The order came to retreat to the left bank. We blew up the railway and the floating bridges and dug ourselves in among the reeds on the other bank.

And here at last we're going to hang on for a long time, we thought. We'll not let any damn Germans over the Oskól!

They simply aimed a few mortars at us from time to time. We did the same. That was all the war there was. In the mornings the "crate" would appear—a Focke-Wulf reconnaissance plane with double fuselage. We made great efforts to shoot it down with hand machine-guns, always without success. And, humming away undisturbed, flocks of Junkers would pass over in the direction of the rear.

My sappers dug shelters for the HQ, while village girls dug a second line of defence beside Petropávlovka. Meantime we, the staff officers, drew up reports, sketched out plans and from time to time went to divisional HQ for training exercises.

Life went on peacefully and evenly. Even the Moscow *Pravda* started to reach us. There were no casualties.

Then like a bolt from the blue, at 2300 hours, quick march!

And without a fight, that was the worst thing, without a fight. At Bulatsélovka we also had to leave well-established trenches, but at least the Germans made us do it, whereas here . . .

Could the Germans possibly have driven in so far? Vorónezh . . . If they had really got through to there our position was not entirely enviable . . . But they *had* apparently got through, otherwise they wouldn't be withdrawing us without a fight, especially from such a line as the Oskól. But between us and the Don there were no other rivers on our sector, it seemed. Were we really going back to the Don?

"Comrade lieutenant, what shall we load the cart with?" The platoon commander, very young, freshly promoted, with a faintly discernible moustache, looked at me inquiringly. "Shall we load up the mines?" he asked.

"Div. HQ have given us no lorries?"

"None."

"Bury them then. Are there still some left on the bank?"

"Yes. About a hundred."

"All right. Take a couple of dozen with you, just in case, and dig the rest in."

"Very good."

"Have you got all the spades?"

"There are thirty with the third battalion."

"Go and get 'em, quick!"

Turning smartly he ran to the cart, his map-case in his hand. A fine lad, and very keen, but a bit too scared of his superiors.

At midnight, with their mess-cans faintly rattling, the last company of our regiment moved off in the direction of Petropávlovka.

Shiryáev and I spent the whole night crawling round the front line. The machine-guns would have to be arranged quite differently. The day before, the men manning the strong-point had pulled out and taken all their machine-guns with them. There had been fifteen on our sector, now there were only five left—two Maxims and three Degtyaryóvs. They wouldn't go far. We would put the Maxims on the flanks and the hand-operated guns between them. The men would also have to be distributed differently—the battalion's front had increased in size by more than three times. That meant ten or twelve men to the kilometre, with 80 or 100 metres between each. Not what you might call crowded.

The next day passed quietly. The silly Germans didn't guess what was going on: they continued to strike at the road and the northern edge of Petropávlovka from time to time and without much enthusiasm. Two or three mortars exploded in our yard—Shiryáev's command point was in the cellar of a four-storey, badly shelled house, which appeared to have been some kind of hostel in the past. A tortoiseshell cat living with her kittens in our cellar had been wounded by a bit of shrapnel. The medical orderly bandaged her up. She miaowed, stared at us with frightened yellow eyes and quietly settled down in a box with her kittens. They squeaked, clambered on top of one another, poked their little noses into the bandage, but couldn't find her teats.

III

We spent the night mining the river bank. Valéga, my orderly, dug the holes. Bóiko, the sergeant, laid the mines and covered them up. They were set by a lively little soldier from the battalion, who looked like a beetle and had been a sapper in the past. Shiryáev had given him to me.

I lay among the burdock. It had a pleasant smell of the dampness of the night and of the earth itself.

Neither Valéga nor Bóiko were to be seen. Occasionally

13

a soldier would go past with mines, rustling cautiously through the reeds. He would be carrying four at a time, held together by a strap.

I was looking towards the other bank at groups of overhanging willows lit up by the fitful glare of the rockets . . .

Our street came into my mind—an avenue of mighty chestnuts. The trees stretched up and formed an arch. In the spring they were covered with white and pink blossom, just like candles. In autumn the roadsweepers burnt the leaves and children stuffed their pockets with conkers. I also gathered them in my day. We carted them home by the hundred. So beautifully clean and polished, they filled up all the drawers, got in everyone's way and for long afterwards they would be brushed out from under cupboards and beds. There was an especially large number of them under the big divan. It was a very comfortable divan, soft and wide. I used to sleep on it. There were plenty of bugs in it, but we didn't bother each other and they left me alone. After lunch grandma used to rest on it. I would cover her up with an old overcoat and hand her somebody's memoirs or *Anna Karenina*. Then I would look for her glasses. They would turn out to be in the drawer with the spoons or in the sideboard. By the time I found them, grandma would already be asleep and Fracas, the old cat with singed whiskers, would be looking out through slit eyes from under the worn coat collar.

Good Lord, how long ago that was! Perhaps it never was at all and only seemed to have been . . .

On the right there was a big wardrobe. We used to hide in it as children when we played hide-and-seek. In those days it was still standing in the corridor. Later it was brought into the room. On top of the wardrobe there were cardboard boxes with hats. On them was a lot of dust which was cleaned off only for the New Year, May Day and my mother's saint's day—the twenty-fourth of October.

Next to the wardrobe was a chest of drawers with an oval mirror and innumerable bows and little flasks. I couldn't recall when those flasks contained perfume, but for some reason or other it was not permitted to clear them away. If you took out the stopper and had a good sniff you could still detect the faint aroma of scent.

Beyond that there was a bedside table . . . No—a blue armchair with one of its legs tied up. It was not to be sat in —guests were always warned about that. And then came the bedside table. It was full of soft check-patterned slippers and in the drawers were little boxes with grandma's powders and pills. Nobody could sort them out any longer. And there too was a bottle of valerian drops,[1] put away so that the cat couldn't get at them.

And now the Germans had got it all.

I had received the last postcard from my mother three days after the news of the fall of Kiev. It was date-marked August. My mother said the Germans had been driven back, that the shell-fire could hardly be heard, and that a circus and a musical comedy had opened their doors. And for the rest—" write more often, though I know you haven't much time, but even if it's only two or three words . . ."

Ten months had passed since then. I would sometimes take the postcard out of my side pocket and look at the fine, almost illegible letters. They had been smudged through rain and sweat. In one place, at the very bottom, it was no longer possible to distinguish the words. But I knew them by heart. I knew the whole postcard by heart. On the side with the address, on the left, was an advertisement for the Rubber Trust—some feet in high boots. On the right was a stamp, with a picture of the " Mayakóvskaya " Metro station. As a child I took up stamp-collecting and asked all friends and acquaintances to stick beautiful new stamps on their envelopes. And my mother had put on a very fine stamp, just as when I was a child. They were kept in a small long box on the left of the table. And I expect my mother had looked through them a long time before settling on this one, so green and handsome. She had stood at the table and, without her glasses, had looked through them with short-sighted and screwed up eyes . . .

Shall I really never see her again? Small and active, in her golden pince-nez, and with a tiny wart, like a bilberry, on her nose. I used to like to kiss it—the wart—as a child.

Shall we really never sit again at the boiling samovar with the bent side and drink tea with mother's much-loved raspberry jam? Will she never again run her hand through my hair and say: " You look a bit off-colour to-day, Yurka. Perhaps you'll go to bed a bit earlier?" And in the mornings will she never again cook me potatoes on the primus in big round slices, the way I liked them?

Shall I never rush round the corner again for bread, stroll along the streets of Kiev, heavy with the scent of lime-trees in blossom, or go in the summer to the bathing beach, to Trukhánov island . . .?

[1] Used in Russia as smelling salts.

15

Dear old Kiev! How I longed for its wide streets, its chestnut trees, the yellow brick of its houses, the dark red columns of the university. How I loved the slopes down to the Dnieper. In winter we skied on them, in the summer we lay in the grass, counted the stars and listened to the muffled sirens of the ships passing at night. Then we would walk back along the Kreschátik, now quiet and with no lights in the shop windows, and would scare the watchmen dozing quietly in the archways, even in summer wrapped in their shaggy sheepskin coats.

I still wandered sometimes along the Kreschátik. Wrapped in my ground-sheet, I would close my eyes and go from the Bessarábka to the Dnieper. I would stop near the Shántser. That was the best cinema in the world. That's how it seemed to me as a child. There were statues of figures blowing into long trumpets beside the screen, altars with red ribbons waving like flames, and a very specific, evocative cinema smell. How many happy hours did I pass in the Shántser! "The Indian Tomb", "The Thief of Baghdad", "The Mark of Zorro". Goodness, it took your breath away. And a bit further, near the Proreznáya, in the cramped "Corso", where the seats weren't numbered, there were cowboy films, chases, gun battles, mustangs, Colts, women in trousers and bad men with thin moustaches and sarcastic grins. And at the "Express"—later for some reason or other it became the more prosaic "Second State Kino"—you could see drawing-room films with Pola Negri, Asta Neilsen, and Olga Chékhova. These films we didn't like very much, but we knew a man in the ticket office in the "Express", so we went there every single Friday.

I would turn off into the Nikoláevskaya. This was the most European of all the streets in Kiev. Carefully trimmed lime-trees with little fences round them. Great milk-white lamps hanging from thick chains suspended across the street. Dazzling Lincolns outside the "Continental". And near the circus there would be crowds of children waiting for Jan Tsygan to come out and betting on the outcome of the day's encounter between Danílo Pásunko and the Mask of Death.

Further on was the Olginskaya, then Institútskaya and the built-on building of the bank with the Gothic—or were they Romanesque?—turrets on the corners. Then the quiet, sleepy Lípki, cool even in the noonday heat of July. Cosy little private houses with dusty windows. The hundred-year-old elms of the palace garden. The leaves that rustled beneath your feet. And then, stop—a sudden drop. Beyond there was the Dnieper, fading into the blue distance, the vast sky, Podól, flat and bristling with chimneys, the clear-cut outline of St. Andrew's church standing on the very edge of the cliff, the splashing of the paddle wheels of the boats, and the clanging bell of the tram to Dárnitsa.

Dear Kiev!

How far away it all seemed, and how long ago it had all been, oh God, how long . . . There had been college at some point and the tedious sketching and the drawing-boards, and short, sleepless nights, and all sorts of theories of architectural composition and twenty other subjects that I'd already forgotten.

There had been six of us, inseparable friends. Anatóli Sergéyev, Rudénsky, Vergún, Lusia Strízheva and the happy little Shúrka Grabóvsky. For some reason everybody called him " Chízhik ". We studied together and we went on excursions together. We took all the exams together. When we finished at the institute we all went to the same factory. We had only just started work, just bought new T-squares and drawing instruments—and . . .

Chízhik had been killed before Kiev, at Goloséyevo. My mother had managed to let me know that. He lay in her hospital, with both legs torn off. I could get no reliable news about the others. Vergún, it seemed, had got cut off. Rudénsky had not been called up because of his short sight and it seemed as though he had been evacuated. He was there to see me off at the station. Anatóli became a signaller, or so somebody had told me, I had forgotten who.

What about Lusia? Maybe she had been evacuated in the end? Hardly likely . . . Her mother was old and sick and I had written to her aunt in Moscow, but she knew nothing. Two years ago, on the fifth of June, as I recalled, on Lusia's birthday, I took her on the Dnieper. We took a skiff, light and swift, with sliding seats, and rowed far down beyond the Natálka and the Strategic Bridge. We had our favourite spot there—a wonderful little beach, quite hidden among the reeds and broom. Nobody else knew the place and nobody else ever came there. The water there was as clear as glass and it was great to take a running dive into it from the high bank. And then, tired and with hands blistered from the oars, we sat in the palace park and listened to Tchaikovsky's Fifth Symphony. We sat at the side, on a bench, and next to us were some bright red flowers, and the conductor also had a flower in his buttonhole . . .

" Shall we do a third row?"—somebody asked just above my ear.

I started.

Valéga, my orderly, sitting on his haunches, was looking at me inquiringly with his little eyes, sharp as a cat's.

" A third row? . . . No, we shan't do a third row. Go on to the fourth sector by the landing stage."

We carted the rest of the mines over to the landing stage and started to lay them. There were still about forty left.

I V

In the morning a Messerschmitt circled for a long time over our positions. We didn't open fire; we wanted to save ammunition. Two large groups of Heinkels and one lot of Junkers 88's went over at a great height towards the north-east.

About seven o'clock in the evening a young lieutenant, in a brand new cap with a red band, arrived at our command point. He was from our right-hand neighbour, the third battalion of the eight-fifty-second regiment. He inquired how things were going with us and what we were thinking of doing. All was quiet with them too. They had about fifty men and five machine-guns. No mortars. We gave him a meal and sent him back.

As darkness came on we started to pack up. We loaded up two carts and ditched the third. Shiryáev's sergeant-major, the one-eyed Pilipénko, couldn't bring himself to part with his stores—old boots and saddles and sacks of rags. He would cram them on to every side of the cart. Shiryáev would throw them off. Pilipénko would chew on his hand-rolled cigarette with an air of indifference until Shiryáev went away, and then he would quickly stuff the sacks under the boxes of ammunition.

" Fancy throwing away boots like that. For God's sake! We've got half Russia to wander over yet." He covered up the sacks that were sticking out from under the boxes with some tattered matting.

About eleven o'clock we began to withdraw the troops.

18

They came past one at a time and lay down on what had once been the green lawn of the courtyard. Stealthily lighting up their cigarettes they packed their things and readjusted their foot-cloths.

At exactly midnight we gave the last burst of fire. We moved off.

For some time the white outline of the house could be seen through the pine trees. Then it disappeared.

The defences of the Oskól no longer existed. Everything that yesterday had been full of life and of gunfire, bristling with machine-guns and rifles, that had been shown on the plan as little circles, zigzags and interweaving sectors, that had cost thirteen days and nights of work—everything had been dug up, covered with three or four layers of earth and carefully camouflaged with grass and twigs—it was no longer of any use to anyone. In a few days it would all become once again a home for frogs, covered with silt; it would be flooded with black, stinking water that would subside, and in the spring it would be covered with fresh green grass. Only children would some time wander knee-deep in the water to collect rusty cartridge cases in places where machine-guns firing from the flanks and the centre had once stood. We were leaving it all without a fight, without firing a single shot . . .

Petropávlovka was interminably long and dusty. The church had a hole in the belfry. There was a bridge half rotted away which according to the plan I was to have repaired the next day.

It was quiet, surprisingly quiet. Even the dogs did not bark. Nobody suspected anything. They were asleep. To-morrow they would awake to see Germans.

And we go quietly, as though acknowledging our guilt, looking downwards, never looking round, taking leave of no one and nothing—straight to the east, on a course of 45 degrees.

Valéga strode along at my side. He was small but as tough as a little donkey, and came from the Altái.[1] He carried a rucksack, two water bottles, a mess-tin, a map-case, a haversack and then another gas-mask bag stuffed with bread. Before we set off I had wanted to throw out some of the things to make it lighter to carry. But he wouldn't even let me get near the bag.

" I know better than you do what is needed, comrade

[1] Altái—mountainous region in Western Siberia.

19

lieutenant. You packed the last time and toothpaste, shaving brush and shaving mug all got left behind. We had to go along to the chemical boys."

It was no good objecting. Valéga had the character of a dictator—there was no point in arguing with him. Altogether he was a remarkable fellow.

He knew how to do everything. He never had to ask about anything and there was never a moment when he sat idle. Wherever we turned up, in five minutes the tent was pitched, comfortable and well arranged, and always carpeted with fresh grass. His mess-tin always glistened like new. He would never part with his two bottles, one of milk and the other of vodka. Where he got his supplies no one knew, but the bottles were always full. He knew how to cut hair and shave, mend boots and get a fire going in pouring rain. I had a change of underwear every week, and he darned socks so that you couldn't tell where the hole had been. If we stopped near a river, we had fish every day ; if we were in a wood, then it was strawberries, bilberries and mushrooms. And it was all done without a word, quickly and without any prompting on my part. In all the nine months of sharing life with him I never once had to be cross with him.

He never talked about himself. I knew only that he was only eighteen and had no father or mother. He had a married sister somewhere whom he scarcely knew at all. He had been before the courts for something or other, but for what he wouldn't say. He had been in prison and been released before the expiry of his sentence. He had volunteered to fight. His real surname was Volegóv, with the accent on the " o ". But everyone called him Valéga. And that was all I knew about him.

We seldom talked, for he was certainly not talkative. Only once did he open up slightly. That was in the spring, two or three months back. We had got horribly wet and tired, and were drying ourselves by a fire. I was wringing out my foot-cloths. He was cooking dehydrated cereals in a tin. We had already existed for a fortnight on that stuff and we could no longer bear the sight of it.

All around it was dark and cold. The soaked ground-sheet puckered up and gave no warmth at all. We were alone.

With his pipe in his mouth, lit up by the flame from the fire, he looked like a gnome, cooking a magic broth.

" When the war's over," he said, " I'll go back home and build myself a house in the forest. A real log house. I love the forest. And you'll come and stay with me for three weeks. We'll go hunting and fishing together . . ."

I smiled:

"Why exactly three weeks?"

"How many then?" He seemed surprised, but his expression did not change. "You won't be able to manage more. You'll be working. But you'll come for three weeks. I know places where there are bears and elks and pike that weigh fifteen pounds apiece. We have lovely forests in the Altái. Not like the ones here. You'll see for yourself." He took a spoon out and licked it. "And I'll give you pelméni.[1] I know how to make them. In a special way—in our way."

That was the end of our conversation.

So then I asked him:

"Well, Valéga, when are we going to try your pelméni?"

He didn't even smile.

"We haven't got the right meat. And I couldn't make them properly here."

"You mean we've got to wait till the end of the war?"

He didn't reply, but went on walking. His boots were far too big for him—the toes had turned right up—while his cap was too small and sat right on the top of his head. I knew he had three needles stuck in it—one with white, one with black and one with khaki thread.

About seven o'clock we made a long halt. According to the map the village was called Vérkhnyaya Duvánka, but locally it was called Vershílovka. It was twenty-two kilometres from Petropávlovka. Which meant that we had already done thirty. Not bad, considering the state of the road.

Unaccustomed to marching, the men were tired. They threw down their kitbags and lay in the shade of an orchard with their feet up. The more enterprising were fetching milk and sour cream in their mess-tins. Valéga had also got hold of a loaf of white bread from somewhere, as well as some honey.

I ate it and said how good it was, though I had no appetite. I couldn't offend Valéga.

My feet were stinging. The left heel was slightly blistered. Altogether we were in a bad way for boots and now goodness only knew when we would come across a stores. The regiment was probably already far away, seventy or eighty kilometres. They might have taken up a defensive position somewhere or be fighting their way through the German lines. The local

[1] Pelméni—a Siberian speciality; small meat pasties.

people were saying: "The soldiers went through early on Monday. And the guns went past in the evening." That must have been our divisional guns. "They stopped only for an hour, then on they went. They were so tired and so unhappy, the soldiers."

And where was the front? In front, behind, to the right or the left? Did it exist at all? On a map it's usually marked with a thick red line, the enemy's with a blue one. Only the day before the blue line had been on the other side of the Oskól. But now?

The Germans were at Vorónezh. Maybe they had already taken it.

Why was there no firing to be heard? Two days earlier the sound of the guns reached us from the north. Then it died out and the sound moved to the north-east. Now there was nothing at all to be heard. It was quiet everywhere.

The soldiers crowded around the fire with their stew. As always they were grumbling at the small rations. They were shaking the apple trees. I stood up and went over to Shiryáev, who was sitting down, cleaning his pistol. His foot-cloths were drying nearby.

"Shall we be on the move?"

With his eyes screwed up he was inspecting the barrel of his gun against the light.

"Let the boys have a bite to eat and we'll move. In about twenty minutes, not more."

"How far is it to Nóvo-Bélenkaya?"

"Sixty or seventy kilometres. There's the map over there."

I measured it on the map. It worked out at sixty-five kilometres.

The senior adjutant came up—his face was covered with freckles—Lieutenant Savrásov. He had an anxious air. He sat down with us and lit a cigarette.

"There are two men missing already."

Shiryáev put his gun down on his foot-cloth and turned to Savrásov.

"What do you mean, missing?"

"Sidorénko from the first company and Kvast from the second. They were still with us last night?"

"Where have they got to?"

Savrásov shrugged his shoulders.

"Maybe they got blistered feet?"

"I don't think so."

"Let's have the company commanders here."

Shiryáev quickly gathered up his pistol and put on his foot-cloths. The company commanders came up.

It turned out that Sidorénko and Kvast came from the same village. From somewhere near Dvuréchnaya. One of them even had his wife to visit him at the time when we were making a defensive stand. They had always been together, though they were in different companies. But no one had noticed anything wrong with them before.

Shiryáev listened in silence, his lips tight. Without getting up or looking at the company commanders, he spoke slowly, almost without expression:

"If even one more man gets lost I shall shoot the person responsible with this very pistol. Is that clear?"

The company commanders made no reply. They stood and looked at the ground. One had a twitching eyelid.

"We'll never find those two now. They're home, the little heroes. Their battle's over." Shiryáev cursed and stood up. "Get the men on the move!"

His eyes were narrow and sharp. I had never seen him like that. He straightened up his tunic, got rid of the creases in front, all with sharp, short movements.

"The rats are leaving the ship! They're on the run, the skunks!"

He put the catch on his pistol and placed it in the holster.

The line of men stretched along the road. They wound on their puttees as they walked. They carried tins of milk for the journey. Women stood at the gates—silent, with heavy, rough hands hanging down. They stood outside every house, staring at us as we went past. The children looked too. Nobody ran after us. Everybody stood and watched.

V

I ran into Igor, quite unexpectedly. He and Lazarénko, the staff runner, both of them on horseback, suddenly appeared in front of us, just as if they'd popped out of the ground. The horses snorted. Igor had no cap, he was black from dust and there was a scratch on his cheek.

"Water!"

He sucked greedily at the flask. With his head thrown back he took a long drink, his Adam's apple moving. We asked no questions.

23

"Bandage up the mare, Lazarénko."

Lazarénko led the horses away. The large chestnut mare—she looked to me like the commissar's—was lame. A bullet had gone through her left hind quarter. The blood had congealed and flies had stuck to it.

Igor wiped his lips with the palm of his hand, and sat down on the roadside.

"Things are pretty bad," he said; "the regiment has had it."

We stayed silent.

"The major was killed, and the commissar as well . . ."

Igor bit his bottom lip. His lips were absolutely black from dust, dry and cracked.

"Where the second battalion is we don't know . . . Of the third there's only bits and pieces left. There's no artillery. There's one 45-millimetre left, and that's got a broken wheel . . . Give us a smoke. I've lost my case."

We all three lit up. We had no newspaper for making cigarettes, so we ripped pages out of a notebook.

"Maxímov is now acting as commander of the regiment. He too is wounded. A flesh wound in the left hand. He ordered us to look for you, and turn you back."

"Where to?"

"Who can tell that? Have you got a map? I haven't a damned thing left. No map, no map-case, no orderly. Had to take Lazarénko with me . . ."

"What about Afónka—killed?"

"Wounded. Maybe he's already dead. It got him in the stomach. I sent him to the field hospital but that's also smashed to bits."

"The field hospital too?"

"Yes. And the divisional signals company and the auxiliary services too. Give me some more water!"

He took a few more swigs and washed his mouth out. It was only then that I noticed how very much thinner he had got in those two days. His cheeks had fallen in, his gypsy eyes glistened and his hair was stuck in ringlets to his forehead.

"In short, the regiment has now got about a hundred men, not more. Or, rather, there were a hundred when I left. That includes everybody, down to the storekeepers and cooks. Your sappers are complete at the moment. I think there's only one wounded. Is your cigarette still alight?"

He took a light off me, holding my cigarette with his

fingers. He drew in deeply. Then he expelled the smoke in a thick, dense cloud.

"Well, Maxímov said to find you and join up again with him."

Shiryáev pulled out a map.

"Join up with him? Whereabouts?"

"They've lost contact with Div. HQ." Igor scratched the back of his neck with his cigarette holder. "Maxímov took the decision himself. Seems as though Div. HQ is cut off from us. Its last fixed point was about twenty kilometres from Nóvo-Bélenkaya. But we never got to Nóvo-Bélenkaya."

"Where are the Germans now?"

"The Germans? They're guzzling omelettes ten or twelve kilometres from here. And washing them down with schnapps."

"Are there many of them?"

"Enough! We counted about forty vehicles. All five-tonners and six-wheelers. If you reckon sixteen men apiece, you've already got 650."

"Which way are they moving?"

"No idea. There are two roads from there. One leads this way and the other—a sort of main road—goes south."

"And which way did Maxímov order?"

Igor tapped the map with his finger.

"Towards Kantemírovka. Or rather, to the village of Khútorka. If we don't find them there, then due south, for Starobélsk."

We got the troops on the move. We turned off the main road and took to a country road.

It appeared that everything had happened completely without warning. They had arrived in some village and settled down. Igor was with the third battalion. The second was somewhere ahead, about five kilometres. They had started to cook a meal. Wounded men passing through the village said the Germans were far away—something like forty kilometres: it seemed as though they'd been held.

And then, all of a sudden, from the very place, from precisely the village where the second battalion had stopped, tanks appeared. Ten or a dozen of them. Nobody could understand a thing . . . Some firing started up and there was general confusion. From somewhere or other appeared German Sten gunners. In the course of the gun battle the major and the commissar were killed. Three tanks were put out of action. The Sten gunners were driven out of the village.

Our men took up a circular defensive position. It was at this point that Maxímov sent Igor for us. Just as he was leaving the village the Germans attacked—about twenty tanks and motorised infantry, around fifty vehicles. On the way Igor was fired at and his horse was wounded. Where he got the scratch on his cheek he had no idea. He had felt nothing.

We crossed an anti-tank trench. It stretched across the countryside in huge zigzags, disappearing somewhere beyond the horizon. The earth was still fresh—you could tell it had been recently dug. The trenches were tidy, clean-cut, arranged according to all the best rules and carefully camouflaged with grass. The grass was green and lush ; it had not yet had time to dry out.

Thus we marched the whole day long. From time to time we would rest somewhere in the shade of an oak tree. Then we'd get up again and stride along the dry, grey road. In one village the old women said that the Germans, about twenty lorry-loads, had gone through an hour before. And swarms of motor-cyclists in the evening. All going over there—towards the other side of the wood.

The situation was getting more complicated. We had to abandon the carts. We took the machine-guns off and distributed the ammunition to the men. We left some of the food behind too—there was no other way.

With the night came the rain—fine, persistent and nasty.

VI

With the dawn we came across some half-destroyed farm buildings. It had apparently been a poultry farm—there were lots of chicken droppings all over the place. The day dawned overcast and damp. We were shrammed with the cold, our boots squelched water and our lips were blue. But we couldn't light fires, because the buildings could be seen from a long way off.

I had hardly managed to go off to sleep with a ground-sheet drawn over me, when someone jogged my foot with the toe of his boot.

" Get on to the defences, engineer. Jerries."

" What Germans?"

" Come and have a look and you'll see."

Shiryáev handed me a pair of field-glasses. A little line of people was moving parallel with our buildings about a kilometre and a half from us. There were about twenty men, without machine-guns. Probably a reconnaissance group.

Shiryáev wrapped his ground-sheet round himself.

"And what brings them over this way? Haven't they got enough roads, or what? See, they're making their way over here to the barns."

Igor came up.

"We'll take up a tough defensive position, eh, battalion commander?"

He had also been sleeping, apparently. One cheek was red and covered with strips. Shiryáev stared through his field-glasses and did not turn his head.

"Already done . . . I was thinking about it while you were snoring away. The men are deployed and the guns are in place. That's it . . . they've stopped."

I took the glasses. The lenses had got wet and it was difficult to see; I had to keep wiping them. The Germans were conferring about something. They then turned in our direction.

"Don't open fire till I tell you," said Shiryáev under his breath. "I've set up two guns in the next barn, which is also a good position."

The men lay crouched along the wall of the building, at the windows and doors. Someone without a tunic, in a blue vest and a ground-sheet, had clambered up on the beams.

Igor dug me in the side.

"Look . . . do you see?"

In the same place where the first group of Germans had appeared, there was something else moving. But as yet it was difficult to make it out—the rain interfered.

And then suddenly, right next to my ear:

"Fire!"

The leading man fell heavily to the ground. His companion too. And a few more of them as well. The rest ran for it, falling, tripping up, getting up again and bumping into each other.

"Cease fire!"

Shiryáev lowered his gun. The bolts clicked. One German tried to crawl away. They finished him off. Even so he remained for a moment on all fours and then slowly collapsed on his side. Then there was nothing to be seen or heard. It lasted a few minutes.

Shiryáev straightened up his cap that had slipped to the back of his head.

"Shall we light up?"

Igor felt in his pocket for tobacco.

" Now they'll come again."

He drew out a round brown box of tobacco. The sort the Germans use for butter and jam.

" Never mind, we'll have time for a smoke. At least it'll be a bit more cheerful."

Shiryáev rolled himself a cigarette as thick as his finger.

" I wonder if they've got mortars. If they have, then . . ."

The explosion of a mortar a couple of yards from the barn did not permit the sentence to be finished. A second exploded somewhere the other side of the wall. The third landed right in the barn.

The bombardment lasted about five minutes. Shiryáev squatted down with his back resting against the wall. Igor was not to be seen. The mortars came in batches, five or six at a time. There would be a gap of a few seconds and then again five or six mortars. Nearby someone was howling in a high, almost feminine voice. Then suddenly there was silence.

Raising myself up on my hands I peered through the window. The Germans were running across the field, straight at us.

" Listen for my word of command!"

Shiryáev jumped up and in one great stride reached the machine-gun.

Three short bursts. And then a long one.

The Germans disappeared into the ditch. We withdrew the men from the buildings. They dug themselves in on the other side of the back wall. We left only two machine-guns in the barn for the moment. We already had four men wounded and six dead.

Then the firing opened up again. Under the cover of mortar-fire the Germans were scrambling out of the ditch. They managed to cover twenty metres, not more, at the run. The land was completely flat, offering them no cover. One by one they scurried into the ditch. But most of them stayed where they were. The little mounds formed by their bodies stood out clearly, green against the clay soil over-grown with burdock.

After the third attempt the Germans abandoned the attack. With his sleeve Shiryáev wiped his brow, wet from rain and sweat.

" Now they're going to surround us. I know them of old."

Savrásov clambered in through the window. He was terribly pale. It even seemed to me his knees were knocking.

" Practically everyone's been killed in the other barn . . ."

28

He had difficulty in getting his breath. "A splinter damaged the machine-gun. I reckon . . ." Savrásov glanced anxiously from the battalion commander to me and back again to the commander.

"What do you reckon?" Shiryáev asked sharply.

"Well, we ought to . . . that is . . . decide something . . ."

"Decide! Decide! I don't need you to tell me what to decide. How many men are out of action?"

"I haven't yet . . . that is . . . didn't count."

"You didn't count . . ."

Shiryáev stood up. He went across to the rear wall of the barn. Through the shattered window could be seen the even, featureless countryside without a single bush.

"Well, well. We better be on the move, eh? They'll give us no peace here."

He turned round. He looked rather paler than usual.

"What's the time? My watch has stopped."

Igor looked at his watch.

"Twenty past eleven."

"Come on then . . ." Shiryáev bit his lips. "Only we shall have to sacrifice one machine-gun. We must have some cover."

It turned out that the only one of the machine-gunners left was Filátov. Kruglikóv was dead and Sevastyánov wounded. Shiryáev cast his eyes round the barn.

"And Sedykh? Where's Sedykh?"

"There he is, sitting on the beams."

"Come here!"

The fellow in the vest swung agilely by his arms and leapt lightly to the ground.

"Can you handle a machine-gun?"

"I can," the lad replied quietly, hardly moving his lips. He looked straight at Shiryáev without blinking.

He had a pink complexion, with a golden fluff on his cheeks. His eyes were those of a child—laughing, blue, slightly squinting, with long eyelashes like a girl's. With a face like that he should have been keeping pigeons or fighting with the neighbours' boys. But what didn't go at all with his child-like appearance—just as though someone had mixed things up—were the strong neck, broad shoulders and the firm biceps that twitched at every movement. He had no tunic on. An old colourless vest was practically bursting from the pressure of his young muscles.

"Where's your tunic?" Shiryáev suppressed a smile, though he asked like an officer, in a threatening tone.

"I was killing lice, comrade commander. And at that very moment . . . the Jerries. It's over there, by the gun." In his embarrassment he fiddled with a corn on the broad, coarse palm of his hand.

"All right, do you know the German ones?"

"What? German machine-guns?"

"Of course machine-guns. That's what we're talking about at the moment."

"The German ones not so well . . . but I reckon, somehow . . ."

"Never mind, I know them," said Igor. "In any case one of the officers will have to stay behind."

He was standing, with his hands stuffed into his pockets, rocking gently from side to side.

"I was thinking of Savrásov. Oh well, all right." Shiryáev didn't finish and turned towards Sedykh. "Do you get it, my lad? You will stay here with the lieutenant. Lazarénko will also remain—they are fighting lads, can be relied on. You can see for yourself—there's only Filátov left. You will give us cover. Understand?"

"I understand," Sedykh answered quietly.

"What do you understand?"

"I shall remain to give cover along with the lieutenant."

"To your places then." Shiryáev buttoned up the collar of his tunic—it was getting quite cold. "Take over that one, only move it over here. Here, where the Maxim is, is better. Get the men ready, Savrásov."

Savrásov departed. I couldn't keep my eyes off his knees—they kept on shaking with a nasty little tremble.

"Don't hang about too long," said Shiryáev to Igor. "An hour, not more. Then hurry after us. Due east. Towards Kantemírovka."

Igor quietly nodded his head, swaying from one foot to the other.

"Throw the machine-gun away. Get rid of the bolt. Hang on to the ammunition belts, if there are any left."

In five minutes the barn was empty. I was also staying behind with Valéga. Shiryáev left with fourteen men, of whom four were wounded, one of them badly. They carried him, using a tent as a stretcher.

The rain had stopped. The Germans were silent. There was a stench of sodden poultry manure. Igor and I lay down near the left machine-gun. Sedykh had fixed up the gun and was peering through the window. Valéga was puffing on his

30

pipe. Then he pulled out some dried crusts and a vodka flask. We drank in turn from an aluminium mug. Then it started to rain again.

"Comrade lieutenant, is it true that Hitler has only one eye?" Sedykh, gazing at me with his bright, childlike eyes.

"I don't know, Sedykh. But I think he's got both his eyes."

"But Filátov, the machine-gunner, says he is short of an eye. And that he's even incapable of begetting children . . ."

I smiled. You could tell that Sedykh was very anxious that it should be like that. Lazarénko winked at me condescendingly.

"He was gassed in the First World War and he's not really a German but an Austrian and his name's not Hitler but some neat little name beginning with Sch . . . Isn't that right, comrade lieutenant?"

"Yes, that's right. His name is Schickelgruber. He's a Tyrolean . . ."

Sedykh put his tunic on.

"And do the Germans like him?"

I recounted how and why Hitler came to power. Sedykh listened attentively, his mouth slightly open, his eyes unblinking. Lazarénko had the air of a man who already knew it all. Valéga was smoking.

"Is it true that Hitler is only a corporal? That's what the political officer told us."

"It's true."

"How can that be? To be at the head of everything and only a corporal? I thought the political officer was lying."

He turned shy and fiddled again with his callus. His way of looking shy appealed to me.

"Have you been in the army long, Sedykh?"

"Ages. Since forty-one, September."

"How old are you?"

He wrinkled his brow.

"Me? Nineteen, I suppose. Born in nineteen twenty-three."

It turned out that he had been wounded with a piece of shrapnel in the shoulder-blade at Smolénsk. He had been three months in hospital and then sent to the South-Western front. He got his sergeant's rank after being posted to our regiment.

"Well, what about it, do you like fighting?"

Once again he seemed embarrassed and shrugged his shoulders with a smile.

31

"Not so bad, so far. Only running away like this isn't much fun."

Even Valéga smiled at this.

"Don't you want to go home? You're not pining?"

"What is there at home? Only girls. Nothing else."

"You mean you don't want to go home?"

"Of course I want to . . . Only not now."

"When, then?"

"What's the point of going home like this? Must go with lieutenant's tabs, like you."

Valéga suddenly got up and looked through the window.

"What's that?"

"Jerries, I think. There they are, behind that hill."

To our left the Germans were skirting our positions. In short dashes, one at a time. Igor bent over the machine-gun. A short burst. His back and arms shook. The Germans took cover.

"Now they'll make it hot for us with their mortars," said Lazarénko under his breath, as he crawled over to his gun.

In a couple of minutes the bombardment began. The mortars landed around the barn but none dropped inside. Again the Germans tried to run across. The machine-gun only raised a small line of dust. Further than that line the Germans would not go. This was repeated three or four times.

The ammunition was coming to an end. We fired off the last rounds and crept one after the other through the back window. Sedykh, Igor, Valéga and then myself. After me came Lazarénko.

As I was climbing down from the window a mine exploded close by. I flattened myself against the ground. Something heavy fell on me from behind and slowly slid to one side. Lazarénko was wounded in the stomach. I saw his face turning white at once and his tightly compressed lips.

"I'm finished, I reckon." He tried to smile. Something red dropped from underneath his shirt. He clutched at it convulsively with his fingers. Great drops of sweat appeared on his forehead.

"I . . . comrade lieuten . . ." He was trying to say something, but it was impossible to understand him any longer. Straining all his efforts, he tried to raise himself and then voices rang suddenly in our ears.

From his pockets we took his pocket knife, some newspaper ready for making cigarettes and a much-worn pocket-book with a red rubber band round it. In his tunic were his

32

16

Komsomol[1] card and a triangular letter with crooked, child's writing.

We put Lazarénko into a trench, covered him with a ground-sheet and threw earth on with our hands.

Then we ran one at a time across to a small hillock. From there to another one, a bit bigger. The Germans were still firing at the barn. For some time the rafters could be made out; then they disappeared too.

VII

In the night we ran into our chaps. Absolute darkness, rain and mud. Some motor vehicles and carts. And someone's hoarse, strained voice dominating the general murmur of voices rang suddenly in our ears.

"Whoa, pest! Steady! Giddup, parasite!"

This " pest " and " parasite ", pronounced in just the same way and with no expression at all, with brief pauses to take air into the lungs, sounded sweeter than any music. Some of our men!

It was a little bridge of some kind. A big, canvas-covered cart had gone through the planks with one wheel. Two wretched mares—just skin and bones, their flanks spattered with blood and their necks strained forward—were slithering all over the wet planking. Behind there were lorries. In the light of flickering lamps were sodden figures. A powerful lad in a padded jacket was whipping the horses about the eyes and mouth.

"Parasitic pest. Get up . . . You . . . get . . ."

Somebody was huddling over the wheel, swearing and grunting.

"Look, you don't get hold of that. Get that, that's it . . ."

"You and your get that. Can't you see, it's rotted through."

"Then get hold of the axle."

"The axle! Look how many boxes are piled on it. The axle . . ."

Someone in a hood jogged me with his shoulder.

"Ditch the whole damned lot!"

"I'll ditch you," said the young tough, turning round.

[1] Komsomol: Communist League of Youth, the political organisation of the Communist Party for adolescents.

"Then I'll ditch it. Are the lorries to be held up just because of you?"

"Aw, let 'em be held up."

"Seréga, start the lorries." The man in the hood waved his hand.

The young tough seized him by the shoulder. Three others scrambled out from beneath the cart. The light of the headlamps picked out the wet backs, tired muddy faces and the caps on the back of their heads. The fellow with the hood I recognised as the man in charge of our arms store, Kopyrko. The hood fell over his eyes and got in his way. Kopyrko did not recognise me.

"And what do you want?"

"Don't you recognise me? Kérzhentsev—engineer."

"For goodness' sake! Where'd you come from? On your own?"

Without awaiting an answer he again attacked the fellow with the whip. They all seized the shafts and with a shout and a crunch they hauled out the wheel. Valéga and Sedykh helped.

"Get into the lorry," said Kopyrko. "I'll take you."

"Which way are you going?"

"What do you mean, which way?"

"Where will you take me? I want to get to Kantemírovka. There are villages of some sort there."

"So's you can get a look at the Jerries, or what?" Kopyrko gave me a tired smile. "I only just managed to get the lorry out of there."

"And where are you making for now?"

"Where everybody else is. For the south . . . Míllerovo, I suppose. Come on, get in."

"I'm not alone. There's four of us."

He hesitated.

"Oh, all right, get in. The fuel will give out in any case. Who've you got with you?"

"Svidérsky and two men—orderlies."

"Get up on the back. On that Ford over there. But you and I will ride in the cab. Goodness knows whether this bridge will take us."

But the bridge did take us. It creaked but it held out. The lorry moved with difficulty, wheezing and spluttering. The engine was playing tricks.

"Did you come across Shiryáev?" I asked.

"No. Where is he?"

"He was with me, but I don't know where he is now."

"I heard the major and the commissar were killed?"

"I heard the same. What about Maxímov?"

"I don't know—I was in the rear."

Kopyrko put the brakes on hard. There was a hold-up ahead of us.

"It's like this all the time. Oh, damn. We go three steps forward and then stop for an hour. And look at the rain.'

I asked who else there was from the regiment.

"Nobody. You can't make anything out. Here you've got our own army and the ones next to it. Div. HQ has moved somewhere north. But the Germans are there. No maps and no compass."

"Goodness knows where *they* are at the moment. A couple of hours ago they were in Kantemírovka. The petrol was nearly finished. And on top of everything I caught cold. You can hear what a voice I've got." He drew his hand over his eyes. "I haven't slept for two nights. The driver and armourer got lost somewhere during a bombardment. Two cans of petrol pinched. In short—well, you understand."

In front, one of the standing lorries began to move. We went on our way. Towards the morning the petrol gave out. We only just managed to reach a village.

In the first cottage we threw ourselves on the floor, on snoring bodies and seed husks.

It dried out a bit during the day. The clouds drifted in ragged clusters somewhere to the east. Occasionally the sun peeped through, but briefly and unwillingly. We were sitting on the twisted trunk of a tree by the roadside, smoking our last tobacco. Valéga still had a packet of *makhorka*[1] in his knapsack, but that was all, and there were four of us. Kopyrko had vanished somewhere with his lorry. He had probably managed to get some petrol somewhere and had gone off without us. To hell with him. It was a good thing, at any rate, that he gave us a lift through the night.

"Well?" said Igor.

"Well, what?"

"What next?"

"Get going, obviously."

"Where to?"

I didn't know myself where, but still I replied:

"To look for our chaps . . ."

"Who of ours—Shiryáev, Maxímov?"

[1] *Makhorka*—a plant used as a substitute for tobacco.

35

"Shiryáev, Maxímov, the regiment, the division, the army . . ."

Igor did not reply, but started to whistle. He had lost a lot of weight in the last few days, his nose was peeling and his moustache, once rather affected, in a thin straight line, was now drooping. What had he in common now with that smart young man in the photograph which he had once shown me? Where were the silk shirt, the striped tie fastened in a huge knot and the excessively wide trousers? A graduate of the art institute. The photograph had shown him leaning casually against the edge of a table, a cigarette in his mouth and a palette in his hand, and behind him a big canvas with some highly dynamic figures all rushing in the same direction.

Another photograph was of a fine young woman with slightly slanting eyes, wearing a white pullover. On the back a touching inscription. Unformed, half-childish writing.

All that was gone . . . No regiment, no platoon, no Shiryáev and no Maxímov. Only a blistered heel, a tunic with white stains soaked through with sweat. A revolver at my side and the Germans deep in the heart of Russia, descending like an avalanche to the Don, and long lines of vehicles, and thoughts that kept turning round, heavy as a millstone.

Igor could have been a decent painter. He had a steady hand, a bold line and he sketched well. He once drew me and Maxímov, on the page of a notebook. I still had the drawing in my case.

A long column of vehicles went past, drawing little anti-tank guns that bounced up and down on the bumps. The transports looked unusually smart with big, clearly painted figures on the doors: D-3-54-27, D-3-54-26. They were not ours. We had D-1. There were legs hanging over the sides of the lorries and sunburnt, bearded faces peering out.

" Which army, lads?"

" Which one do you want?"

" The thirty-eighth."

" Wrong number. Try inquiries . . ." More laughter.

Meanwhile the lorries continued—one after the other, yellow, green, brown and variegated. There seemed to be no beginning or end to them.

" Well, shall we go?"

Igor stood up, trod his cigarette end into the ground with his heel.

" Let's go."

We joined the general stream.

VIII

"Hey, there, men."

Somebody was waving from a passing cart. It looked like Kalúzhsky, the second officer of supply troops.

"Come over here!"

We went over. It *was* Kalúzhsky. He smelt of vodka, his tunic was undone, his smooth face with trimmed eyebrows was red and shiny.

"Hop into my carriage! I'll get you home. No good waiting for the tram, anyway." He stretched out a hand to help us up. "Want some vodka? I can let you have some."

We refused—we didn't feel like it.

"Pity. It's a good vodka. And we've got something to eat—we didn't have time to give out the extra rations. There's butter, biscuits and tinned fish." He winked happily, giving us a friendly slap on the shoulder. "Get your men on to those trucks there. The whole stores are going with me—five cart-loads."

"Where are you making for?" I asked.

"Don't be so simple . . . Who asks questions like that now? We're on the way and that's all. Where do you want to get to?"

"I'm asking a serious question."

"And I'm giving you a serious answer. We'll get to Stalingrad somehow or other."

"To Stalingrad?"

"Why, doesn't that suit you? Where do you want to go—Tashkent or perhaps Alma-Ata?"

He gave an explosive laugh, flashing with gold stoppings. His laughter was fruity and infectious. Altogether he looked wonderfully tough and irrepressible.

"Have you not come across our chaps?" asked Igor.

"Only other ranks, and not many of them. They say the major and the commissar were killed. Maxímov seems to have been cut off. I'm sorry for the chap, he had brains. An engineer, anyway . . ."

"Where are your tabs?" Igor put in, eyeing his collar.

"They fell off. You know what this stuff is like nowadays," Kalúzzhsky screwed up his eyes. "You put them on to-day and in two or three days they're already off. Ersatz."

"And I seem to remember your belt had a star on it."

"It had, a good one, with a shoulder strap. I had to give it away. The divisional photographer begged it off me. You know him—lame, with a stick. It was awkward to refuse him, somehow. He begged so hard. Perhaps you'll have a glass now all the same?"

We refused.

"Pity. It's good, Moscow stuff." He took a swig at the bottle and swallowed some butter, without bread. "That's a wonderful thing. You never get drunk. It lines the walls of the stomach. Our doctor told me about it. He was also a smart chap. Had two degrees. From Khárkov. I even saw his diplomas."

"And where is he now, do you know?"

"I don't know. He probably got himself out of it. He's no fool, he won't get into trouble." Kalúzhsky winked again.

On the whole, his view of things was this: The whole affair was evidently coming to an end. The whole front was retreating—this he knew for sure. He had spoken to a certain major who had got it from a certain colonel. The Germans intended to finish it all by September. It was very sad, but it was to all intents and purposes a fact. Even if we had managed to hold the Germans at Moscow, you could bet they had now made such preparations that . . . They had an air force, and the air force to-day was everything . . . You had to look facts coldly in the face. The most important thing was to get across the Don. Véshenskaya, they said, was already occupied—a lieutenant had come back from there yesterday. There was only Tsymlyánskaya left. They said the bombardment was savage. At the worst we could abandon the carts and get across somewhere higher up or lower down. By the way—but this was in strictest confidence—in a village yesterday he had managed to get three civilian suits by barter: shirts, trousers and some boots. He could let us have two of them. Me and Igor. You never knew. Anything could happen. You had to take care of yourself—we might still be of use to the country. Apart from that he had yet another plan . . .

But he never had the chance to tell us that plan. Igor, who had been silently digging about in the sole of his boot with a knife, suddenly raised his head. His drawn, unshaven face had become dark brown beneath a layer of sunburn and dust.

"Do you know what I would like most of all at this moment, Kalúzhsky?"

"Fruit tart with cream, perhaps?" laughed Kalúzhsky.

38

"No, not fruit tart . . . But to punch you in the face. To let fly at your self-satisfied mug. Get me?"

For a few seconds Kalúzhsky didn't know how to react—to get cross or turn it all into a joke—but he quickly took a grip on himself and with his usual laugh slapped Igor on the knee.

"It's all nerves, nerves. That's what bombing has done to you."

"You know where you can go with your bombing and your nerves." Igor shut his knife with a click and put it in his pocket. "And you call yourself an officer. You and your 'we may still be useful to the country' . . . What the hell use to the country is a good-for-nothing like you? You might at least have been ashamed to say such things in front of the driver."

The driver made as though he did not hear. Kalúzhsky jumped down from the cart and ran off to curse a lorry driver—it was his good fortune that a big Dodge had blocked our road.

Igor and I moved over on to another cart.

IX

The main stream was getting a bit thinner. Part of it turned off for Véshenskaya, and part for Kalách, avoiding Morózovskaya, while the rest—and they were the majority—made for Tsymlyánskaya.

We kept on the move. Night and day we kept moving, stopping only to feed the horses and cook a meal. There were no Germans to be seen. A " crate " flew over twice, dropping leaflets. Once a wheel broke. It took us a long time to mend it. We changed the grey, blind mare for a little bay stallion. He gave us a lot of trouble, kicking and snorting and not wanting to pull us. We changed him in turn for a quiet, hard-working old thing with a wet, drooping lip.

The general mood was frightful. If only we could have got some kind of news bulletin from somewhere telling us what was going on on the other fronts. If only the Germans had appeared somewhere. But there were no Germans, no war, only a gnawing nostalgia.

A major of the signals—we helped him to drag his jeep out of a ditch—said there was fighting going on at the moment somewhere between Voroshílovgrad and Míllerovo, and that one word—"fighting"—consoled us for a fleeting moment. It meant that our armies were still in action.

"Anyway, try and get through to Stalingrad, if you don't find your own army. New units are now being formed there. You'll get to the front quicker that way." The major slammed the door and disappeared in a cloud of dust.

Cursing, we climbed up on to our carts, which we had come to loathe.

More steppe, dust and scorching sky.

The women asked where the Germans were and where we were going. Silently we drank cold milk and pointed to the east. Over there . . . Beyond the Don . . .

I couldn't bear to look at those faces, at their inquiring, bewildered eyes.

What was I to tell them? I had two tabs on my collar and a revolver at my side. Why was I not there, why was I here, why was I bumping along on a creaking cart and only brushing aside every question with a gesture of my hand? Where were my company, my regiment, my division? After all, I was an officer . . .

What had I got to say to that? Only that war was war, that it was all based on surprise and cunning, that the Germans had more aeroplanes and tanks than we had, that they were hurrying to finish the war before winter and that they were therefore going all out . . . And even if we were obliged to retreat, a retreat was still not a defeat—we had retreated in forty-one and yet later driven the Germans away from Moscow . . . Yes, yes, yes, that was all very well, but now, *now* we were certainly going east—not west but east . . . So I didn't reply, but simply pointed to the east and said: "So long, Ma, we'll see you again, believe me, we shall meet again . . ."

And I had that faith . . . That was all that was left us then—faith.

We skirted Morózovskaya—dusty, chock-full of transports, with the still smoking ruins of its railway station and endless lines of stranded trucks.

Then came the Don, narrow, yellow, lost among the wheels, radiators and bodies of cars and the naked, half-naked and clothed human bodies, among the dust, the hooting of horns and the din, that never ceased for a minute, of roaring engines and human voices. There was a solid cloud of dust.

In the pause between two bombardments we skipped across the bridge. We lost Kalúzhsky with two of the carts. Sedykh was grazed by a piece of shrapnel. Somebody pinched Valéga's rucksack on the sly. He cursed, scratched the back of his head and wandered among the craters and wrecked carts. Just think of it—it had a quite luxurious shaving set in it!

On the other side of the Don there were more dreary steppes. To-day was like yesterday and to-morrow was the same as to-day. Sun and dust. A stupefying heat.

Then appeared the first units moving towards the front —well turned out, equipped with Sten guns and helmets. The officers wore yellow, squeaking belts, with beautiful new map-cases flopping against their sides. They eyed us somewhat ironically. They were from Siberia.

We were held back in one village. A whole officers' school was moving up to the front and they were short of weapons. They were taking them from those going the other way. Two lieutenants—Georgians—in brand-new caps, wanted to take our Sten guns and revolvers. First we swore at them, then we accepted a smoke of light, real leaf tobacco.

" You making for the front?"

" Yes, for the front. Yesterday we were training, and to-day we're already in battle." They both laughed.

" Well, not quite to-day. You've still got to get to the Jerries."

" And where are the Jerries?" the lieutenant asked cautiously, just in case anyone should by any chance think they were afraid.

" We were hoping to find out from you. You read the papers."

" What's in the papers—' battles in the bend of the Don '. That's all. Heavy battles. Voroshílovgrad has been abandoned."

" What about Rostóv?"

" Rostóv—no. There's no report about it yet."

" No report?"

The lieutenants hesitated. One of them asked casually, as though in passing:

" And what's it like there . . . at the front . . . they're really on the run?"

" Who's on the run?" Igor put on a surprised expression.

" Well, our chaps . . ."

" Nobody's on the run. There's fighting going on. Defensive battles."

The lieutenants stared incredulously at our ragged appearance and our cart with its wobbly wheels.

"What about you?"

"What about us?"

"Not on the run?"

"Why should we be? We're on our way to be re-formed . . ."

The lieutenants laughed and tipped golden Caucasian tobacco into our pouches.

"Take us with you, eh, lads?" said Igor suddenly, slapping his holster. "We've got guns, what else do you want . . .?"

The lieutenants exchanged glances.

"Honestly, chaps. We've had enough of this."

"Well, what can we do . . .?" the lieutenants hesitated again. "We're small fry. Go and see the chief of staff. maybe he'll take you. Or, maybe . . . Anyway, go and see him. Major Sazánsky. In that shack, where the cart with green wheels is standing."

We did ourselves up properly, tightened our belts and left our revolvers behind—just in case, so's he shouldn't take them away. Off we went.

"Mind you address him properly," the lieutenants cried after us. "He knows all the rules by heart. Don't be afraid to click your heels!"

The major was sitting in a tiny hut, eating borshch with sour cream straight from a mess-tin. By his side on the table was a pair of pince-nez.

"Well, what do you want?" he asked without raising his head and vigorously chewing what was evidently tough meat.

With our hands tightly at our sides we explained what we wanted. He finished chewing his meat, put his spoon down on the table and put on his pince-nez. Then he took a long look at us, while he picked his teeth with a bit off a matchbox.

"What am I to say to you, my friends?" he said in a low, rumbling bass. "I can't give any good news. Do you think you're the first ones to come to me? Goodness! There have been ten—here, what did I say, ten—fifteen, just like you, who have approached me. Where could I put them all? You wouldn't do as privates, and I've already got two officers to a platoon. And another ten in reserve. Now do you see?"

We said nothing.

"So there it is. I'd be only too glad, as they say, but . . ." He again picked up his spoon.

"All the same, comrade major . . ."

"What, all the same?" He raised his voice. "What does that mean—all the same? Are you in the army or not? I said no and there's an end to it. I have a regiment, not a labour exchange. See? About turn, quick march!" Then he added in a softer voice: "Make your way to Stalingrad. They say that all the top brass is now in Stalingrad. What army are you from?"

"The thirty-eighth, comrade major."

"The thirty-eighth . . . the thirty-eighth . . ." He rubbed the bridge of his nose with his little finger. "Somebody told me . . . I forget who it was . . . but somebody did say. Anyway, try to get to Kotélnikovo. It's on the way. It seems as though your army's there. Off you go." And again he drew the mess-tin towards him.

We saluted and departed.

In Kotélnikovo they told us that the staff was in Abganérovo. In Abganérovo it was not to be found. We were directed to Karpovka. Not there either. A captain said he'd heard our army might be in Kotlubán. We went to Kotlubán. Not a trace. At the commandant's they said that a major from the thirty-eighth had been there and gone to Dubóvka. At Log station we met three lieutenants from Dubóvka. The thirty-eighth was not there. Everyone was making for Klétsko-Pochtóvaya.

The trucks were making for Kalách. There, they said, was heavy fighting.

We were badly off for food. For some unknown reason one passing unit gave us bread and preserves. Valéga and Sedykh got hold of a sack of oats from somewhere.

Anyway . . . we were making for Stalingrad. Come what may!

X

We came into Stalingrad as the sun was coming out from behind the rooftops, casting long, cool shadows.

The cart rattled cheerfully along the cobbled roadway. Shabby old trams clattered along towards us. There were lines of snub-nosed Studebakers. On them were long boxes—shells for "Katyúsha". On the empty squares, crossed with trenches, there were anti-aircraft guns pointing upwards, and ready for action. In the market were great piles of tomatoes and cucumbers and huge bottles of amber-coloured baked milk. Here and there could be seen people in jackets, caps and even ties. It was a long time since I'd seen that. The women still wore lipstick.

Through a dusty window a barber in a white coat could be seen lathering someone's chin. *Anton Ivanovich Is Cross* was on at the cinema. Programmes at 12, 2, 4 and 6. Over the black mouth of a loud-speaker on a tramway post someone was telling with great feeling how Vanka Zhúkov, a ten-year-old boy, had written to his grandpa in the country on Christmas Eve.

Meanwhile, above all this was a blue sky. And dust and more dust . . . And acacias and little wooden houses with wooden ornaments and " Keep out—beware of the dogs ". Next to them were great stone buildings with statues of big-bosomed women supporting something along the façades. Offices of the Lower Volga Co-op Supplies, " Galoshes Repaired ", " Primuses Mended ", " Procurator of the Mólotov Borough ".

The street turned to the right and dropped towards the bridge. The bridge was wide, with lamp-posts. Beneath it was a non-existent stream, with the fine name of Tsaritsa— the Czarina. A little bit of the Volga could be seen—quays, barges and endless rafts. We turned again to the right and began to climb. We went to the sister of Igor's former company commander in a reserve regiment : " Not just a woman, but pure gold, you'll see for yourselves."

We stopped at a single-storeyed stone house with peeling plaster walls. The windows had strips of paper stuck in crosses on them. A white, big-eyed cat sat on the steps and studied us disapprovingly.

Igor disappeared into the doorway. A minute later he reappeared—happy, without his hat and in his vest.

" Come on in ! Sedykh, lead the way ! " Then, in my ear : " All's well. We're just in time for breakfast."

There was a small, cosy courtyard, and a glassed-in terrace with clothes-lines drawn across it. There was something green on the lines. A barrel stood under the rainwater pipe. Washing was hanging out to dry. A goose was tied to the rails by his leg. And another cat—this time a black one—was washing itself with its paw.

Before long we were seated on the veranda at a table covered with a cloth, and eating supernaturally tasty bean soup. There were four of us, but they kept filling our bowls over and over again. Maria Kuzmínichna's hands were rough and cracked from kitchen work, but her apron was white as snow, while the primus and the pan for jam-making that hung on the wall looked as if they were polished

44

every day. Maria Kuzmínichna had a little grey bun on the top of her head, and her glasses were bound with cotton-wool where they sat on her nose.

After the soup we drank tea and learned that Nikoláy Nikoláyevich, her husband, would be back for dinner—he worked at the transport depot—and that her brother was still in a reserve regiment . . . And if we wanted to have a really good wash after the journey, there was a shower in the yard, only the tank would have to be filled up with water. She was going to launder our underwear that very day, that would be no trouble at all.

We each drank three cups of tea, then filled the tank with water and for a long time and with much laughter splashed about in the little wooden shed. It is difficult to convey what pleasure it gave us.

Nikoláy Nikoláyevich came in to dinner—short, bald and wearing an ancient, linen jacket. He had an exceptionally lively face. He was constantly tapping the table with his fingers.

He was very interested in everything. He questioned us about the situation at the front, about our food, what was Churchill thinking about not opening a second front—" it's a disgrace, that's what it is "—and what did we think: would the Germans get to Stalingrad, and if they did would we have the troops to defend it? Everybody was going to work on the trenches now. He himself had been twice and some captain had told him that there were three lines of defences round Stalingrad, or, as he called them, three rings. This was apparently very good. The captain had given him the im-pression of being a very sound chap. The sort who wouldn't indulge in idle gossip, as they said.

After a cup of tea Nikoláy Nikoláyevich showed us his map on which he had marked the front with small flags. With a metal ruler he measured the distance from Kalách and Kotélnikovo to Stalingrad and sighed and shook his head. He didn't like the latest developments. He read the papers carefully—he was on the local committee and therefore re-ceived not only the Stalingrad but the Moscow *Pravda* as well. He had them all stacked in two piles on the cupboard, and if Maria Kuzmínichna needed to wrap up some salt fish she had to run to the neighbours—his papers were sacro-sanct.

Later we slept in the yard in the shade of an acacia tree, covered with towels to keep off the flies.

In the evening we prepared to go to see a musical show—
The Borgia Garter. We cleaned our boots in the yard and
didn't spare the spit.

In the porch opposite a girl was sitting and drinking milk
from a thick, cut-glass tumbler. Her name was Lusia and
she was a doctor. We already knew that much—Maria Kuzmínichna had told us. The girl had incredibly dark, sparkling
eyes, black eyebrows, and hair that was quite golden and cut
like a man's. Her arms and neck were tanned from the sun.
Igor turned so as to have her constantly in view.

" Not bad legs, eh, Yurka? And altogether . . ."

He spat violently on his brush.

The girl drank her milk and watched us clean our boots.
Then she put her glass down on the step, went into the room
and returned with some boot polish.

" This is a good polish—from Estonia. Better than spit,
I should think," and she handed us the tin.

We thanked her and took the polish. It certainly was better
than spit. The boots began to shine like new. Now we
wouldn't be ashamed to show ourselves in the theatre. So
we were off to the theatre? Yes, to the theatre, to see *The
Borgia Garter*. Perhaps she would keep us company? No, she
didn't like musical comedy; unfortunately there was no
opera in Stalingrad. Wasn't there really? No. She was fond
of opera? Yes, especially *Yevgeny Onegin, Traviata* and
The Queen of Spades. Igor was delighted. It appeared that
Lusia had studied at a college of music—that was before the
institute—and that she had a piano. We put off the musical
comedy till another day.

" Come in for a minute—mother will make some tea."

" With pleasure—it's ages since we've done such a thing."

Sitting in the drawing-room on velvet-covered divans with
curved legs, we were afraid that they would collapse under
us—so frail and elegant were they and so coarse and clumsy
did we feel. Beklin's " Isle of the Dead " was hanging on the
wall. On the piano was a bust of Beethoven. Lusia played
Liszt's *Campanella*.

Two stout candles melted slowly into the candlesticks.
The divan was soft and comfortable, with a sloping back.
I put a cushion embroidered with beads under my back and
stretched out my legs.

The hair on the back of Lusia's neck was cut short. Her
fingers skipped nimbly over the keyboard—she must always
have had good marks for technique at college. I listened to
the *Campanella* and studied the Beklin, the plaster Beethoven

46

and the line of elephants in semi-precious stone on the sideboard . . . But for some reason or other it all seemed strange and distant, as though seen dimly through a cloud.

How many times had I dreamt of such moments at the front—with silence all around and no shooting, and there you are, sitting on a divan, listening to music with a pretty girl beside you. And here I was in reality sitting on a divan, listening to music . . . And yet for some reason or other I wasn't enjoying it. Why? I didn't know. I only knew that from the moment we moved back from the Oskól, no—later, after the incident at the farm buildings—I had had all the time inside me a disagreeable feeling of resentment. The point was that I was not a deserter, nor a coward, nor a hypocrite, and yet I felt as though I was all of these things.

The most frightening thing in war is not the shells and not the bombs—you have to get used to all that. The most frightening things are inactivity, uncertainty and the absence of any immediate aim. It's far more frightening to sit in a trench in an open field under bombardment than it is to go into the attack. Even though in the trench the chances of being killed are much less than in attack. But in the attack there is a purpose and a task, whereas in the trench you only count the bombs and wonder if you'll get hit or not . . .

Lusia rose from the piano.

" Let's go and have a drink of tea. The samovar must be on the boil by now."

The table was laid with a crisp white tablecloth. There was thick, stoneless cherry jam in little crystal dishes. My favourite jam. We drank the tea from thin glasses. We just didn't know where to hide our hands, they were so coarsened and unwashable and full of cuts and scratches. We were afraid of dropping jam on the cloth.

Lusia's mother—a fine woman in tortoiseshell glasses and a high collar like a school-mistress—served us more jam and kept sighing all the time:

" Eat, eat. You don't get spoilt at the front. It's bad at the front, I know ; my husband fought in the last war and he told me all about it "—again she sighed. " Unfortunate generation, what an unfortunate generation."

We refused a third glass. For appearance's sake we sat for another five minutes and then took our leave.

" Just drop in any time, my dears. We shall always be glad to see you."

Then we lay in the yard beneath the dusty acacia and for a long time were unable to go to sleep. Sedykh was sleeping alongside. He smacked his lips in his sleep and let his hand fall on me. Igor was turning from side to side.

"You not asleep, Yurka?"

"No."

"What you thinking about?"

"Oh . . . nothing."

Igor started looking for his tobacco in the dark.

"Have you got a smoke?"

"Have a look in my boot, in the little bag."

Igor fumbled in the boot, found the bag and rolled himself a cigarette.

"I'm fed up with all this, Yurka."

"All what?"

"All this hanging about."

"Oh well, we'll stop hanging about to-morrow. We'll go along to the personnel officer. First thing, before lunch."

"That'll be a great pleasure, too—the personnel people. They'll push us off somewhere into the reserve to spend our time parading and saluting. Or into a reserve regiment—even better."

"I shan't go into a reserve regiment."

"You won't go? And you won't go for training either? To Alma-Ata or Frunze? They say they're sending all lieutenants and senior lieutenants for training now."

"Let 'em send 'em. I still won't go."

For a few minutes we were silent. Igor's cigarette flickered.

"And what shall we do with the men?"

"With which men? With Valéga and Sedykh?"

"They'll have to be sent to a transit camp."

"They are not going to any transit camp. You and I will hand over the horses and cart. But I won't hand over the men. Nine months I've been fighting with Valéga. And we're going to stick together till the end of the war, unless one of us gets killed."

Igor laughed.

"He's a funny one, your Valéga. He quarrelled with Sedykh yesterday about how to cook potatoes. Sedykh wanted to do them in their jackets, but Valéga wouldn't have it—the lieutenant, you see—that's you—doesn't like getting the skin off, he likes them clean. For about ten minutes they squabbled."

"Well, there you are, it means he's a real batman," I said, turning over to the other side. "Go to sleep. We've got to get up early to-morrow."

48

Igor gave a long-drawn-out yawn and stubbed out his cigarette on the ground.

Somewhere, very far away, there was anti-aircraft fire. Searchlights were sweeping the sky. Valéga sighed in his sleep. He lay a couple of yards from me, curled right up with his hand over his face. He always slept like that.

My little roundheaded Valéga! How much we had been through together in those last few months, how much *kasha*[1] we had eaten from the same tin, how many nights had we spent wrapped up in one ground-sheet! And how unwilling you were to become my batman! It took three days to persuade you! There he stood, his eyes cast down, muttering something unintelligible—I don't know how, you see, I'm not used to . . . You were ashamed to leave your chums. You had crawled along the front line with them, had known much sorrow with them and all of a sudden they wanted to make you an officer's orderly. A nice comfy little spot. Are you trying to say I don't know how to fight or that I'm worse than the others?

I'd got used to my flop-eared Valéga. No, not used. It wasn't habit, it was something else, much bigger. But I had never thought about it, there had just never been time.

The point was, I'd had friends before. Lots of friends. We had studied together, worked together, drunk vodka together and quarrelled about art and similar important matters . . . But had all that been enough? Drinking and quarrelling and those so-called common interests and common culture.

Védim Kastrítsky had been an intelligent, talented and sensitive fellow. It had always been interesting for me to be with him and I learnt a lot from him. But would *he* have dragged me, wounded, from the battle-field? This had never interested me before. But it interested me now. And Valéga *would* have rescued me—that I knew . . . Or Sergéy Valédnitsky. Would I have gone with him on a reconnaissance job? I wasn't sure. But with Valéga—to the ends of the earth if necessary.

It was only in a war that you got to know people properly. This was now clear to me. War was like litmus paper, like a sort of special photographic developer. Valéga could read only with difficulty, would make mistakes in simple division, didn't know what seven times eight was, and if you asked him what socialism or his country meant to him, he, honestly,

[1] Gruel made of oats.

couldn't give you an intelligible explanation: for him these
ideas were too difficult to put into words. But for that country
—for me, Igor, for his pals in the regiment, for his ramshackle cottage somewhere in the Urals, for Stalin, whom
he had never seen but who was for him the symbol of everything good and right—he would fight to the last bullet. And
when the bullets ran out, he'd fight with his fists and his
teeth . . . He was a real Russian. Sitting in the trenches he
would curse his superiors more than the Germans, but when
it came to business he would show what he was made of.
After all, you can always learn to divide and multiply and
read fluently, if you have the time and desire . . .

Valéga mumbled something in his sleep, rolled over on
to his other side and again curled himself up with his knees
right up to his chin.

Sleep, sleep, flop-eared Valéga. Soon there will be more
trenches, more sleepless nights: "Valéga, come here! Valéga
go there!" But when the war is over, if we're still alive,
we'll think up something together.

XI

Next morning at the personnel office we ran straight into
Kalúzhsky—clean and shaved and looking as if everything
was in order again.

"Hello, me boys . . . All alive and well? Where are you
off to?" He stuck out his warm, moist hand.

"The same place as you've come from."

"One minute. Don't rush. Got any tobacco?"

"Yes."

"Simply must have a smoke. And do a bit of thinking.
Here's a decent bench to sit on."

He dragged us to a bench in the dusty square.

"There's no need to rush headlong into this. Do you
understand? The situation here's quite straightforward. Either
the reserve or the front line. One, two, and you're done
for."

"Well?"

"Does that suit you?" His shaven brows rose in surprise.
"You know what's going on at the moment at the front line.
Officers are few and far between. I spoke to a wounded
lieutenant to-day. He left Kalách only yesterday. They send

50

you to the first place that turns up. There are the men, there's the line—hold it. Do you understand? Messerschmitts overhead all the time. In short . . ."

With his thick, short finger he described a cross in the air.

" As for the reserve?—Wheat *kasha*. Bread-like clay. And perhaps some salt herring. And training from morning to night—regulations, field training manual, Sten gun . . . Do you want a sunflower seed?"

Without waiting for an answer he tipped small over-dried seeds into our palms.

" Now there's something else "—he leaned slightly nearer and spoke in a mysterious half-whisper. " I came across a certain captain here—I'll introduce you to him. He's a good chap. He has worked as deputy head of intelligence in a divisional HQ. We got talking. It turned out we had mutual friends. To cut it short—in five or six days, ten at the most, Lt.-Col. Shuránsky will be here. Do you know him? A wonderful fellow. We are close friends. We've drunk a lot together . . . And he, this Shuránsky, will fix it. He's in Moscow at the moment on an official trip. Anyway, my advice is: turn back for the time being. You've got somewhere to live? I'll keep you in touch with events . . ."

He suddenly jumped up and stuffed the seeds into his pocket.

" Wait a minute . . . I just want to have a couple of words with that major over there . . ."

And, putting his hat straight, he disappeared round the corner.

We went into the house with the dirty windows. A colourless lieutenant in polished boots informed us that the engineering section was in Turkestanskaya street. That was where they were registering all sappers. All other special services—riflemen, mortarmen and gunners—in room five. From eleven till five.

We went to Turkestanskaya. Igor decided to call himself a sapper.

" To hell with anti-gas work! I'm fed up with it! You can teach me all the tricks of the trade in three days."

At Turkestanskaya there was another lieutenant—only dark this time and in canvas boots. From him to the major. Then five questionnaire and—" Come along to-morrow at ten."

Next day, at ten, we filled up some more cards and with a note saying, " For Major Zabávnikov, admit to the reserve ', we strode off to Uzbekskaya street, No. 16.

There we found about twenty sapper officers. They were drinking tea, sitting on the window-sills, smoking and cursing the reserve. The major wasn't there. Then he arrived—small, bad-tempered, with watery eyes. Again, who were we, what could we do and where had we come from? And the programme—from nine to one training, then dinner. From three to eight more training. For meals we were put on the roll of some sapper regiment. Then we went home.

In the evening I strolled with Lusia along the quayside. The sky was red and threatening. The clouds above the horizon were just like thick black smoke. The Volga was roughened up by the wind, without the slightest sparkle. And rafts, endless rafts. The tugs were decorated with green branches, like a church at Whitsun. On the other bank were little houses, a tiny church and tall draw-wells in every courtyard.

We walked hand in hand, stopping from time to time to lean on the parapet and gaze into the distance. Lusia said something, I think it was about Blok and Yesénin, and asked me something and I made some reply, but I was for some reason not myself and I had no desire to talk either about Blok or about Yesénin.

All these things had interested and excited me at one time, but now they had receded far, far away. Architecture, art, literature . . . For the period of the war I had not read a single book. And I didn't want to, it didn't attract me. There'd be time for all that later, later . . .

Meanwhile, to-morrow, the reserve again . . . To take a Degtyaryóv machine-gun apart and put it together again twenty times over. And the day after to-morrow, and the day after that. And that jaundiced, watery-eyed Major Zabávnikov would tell us again that when the orders come we shall be sent to the front, that there are people whose job it is to think about these things and so on and on and on.

We walked past the monument to Kholzúnov, a Hero of the Soviet Union. To my shame, I didn't know what he had done. A heavy figure of bronze in a leather greatcoat, he stood there confidently, firmly and calmly. We read the inscription and studied the bas-reliefs on the base.

We came out on the central square. A Heinkel that had been shot down lay there, grey, with neat little black crosses and a medieval lion on a heraldic shield. It looked like a fierce wounded bird that had fallen to earth and dug its claws into it. Children crawled over its broken wings, clambered into the cabin and fiddled with the instruments.

Grown-ups gazed with gloom and respect from behind the barrier at the wrecked engines and protruding machine-guns.

" The whole thing's armoured, damn it."

" Yes, they don't spare the metal."

" Just fancy coming up against that with a wooden one."

" How many guns has he got?"

" Two and two cannons."

" And bombs?"

" Two tons of bombs."

" Two tons?"

Lusia tugged me by the sleeve.

" Come on, I'm fed up with looking at it. Let's go along to Mamai Hill."

" Where!"

" To Mamai Hill. You can see the whole of Stalingrad from there as though on the palm of your hand. And the Volga. And you can see far, far beyond the Volga. It's lovely there, honestly!"

We went to Mamai Hill.

The top was flat and unbeautiful. Young trees had been planted in rows. Lusia said there had been plans to lay out a park. Maybe some day it would be beautiful there, but so far there was little that was attractive about it. A few water-towers, dried-up grass and an occasional prickly bush.

But the view was really remarkable.

The great sprawling city seemed to cling to the river, a cluster of new stone buildings, unwieldy, but appearing quite beautiful at a distance. They stood out like a small white island from a sea of wooden buildings. These tumbledown and windowless shacks straggled along the edge of the ravines, crept down to the river or clambered up the hillside, squeezing themselves in between the reinforced concrete blocks of buildings. The great smoky factories with the rumbling of cranes and the whistling of trains. " Red October " " Barricades ", and far away, way beyond the horizon, the big buildings of the Tractor Works . . . There they had their own housing estates—white, symmetrical blocks of buildings and little cottages with their corrugated tin roofs sparkling.

And behind all this the Volga, peaceful and unruffled, so wide and restful, and on the other bank the curly greenery with little houses peeping out, and the violet distances, in which a rocket sent up by some fool scattered a beautiful green-red rain . . .

We sat on the edge of the rugged, bare cliff and watched a train crawling along below. It was terribly long and on its trucks was something covered with canvas—probably tanks. The little engine with its short funnel looked just as though it was ready to burst and puffed with a heavy and dissatisfied air. It gave off clouds of smoke and drew its load slowly with all the persistence of a cart-horse used to heavy loads.

" What are you thinking about?" Lusia asked.

" About machine-guns. This is a good place for a machine-gun."

" Yurka . . . How *can* you?"

" A second one could be put over there. It would cover the far side of the ravine perfectly."

" Aren't you really tired of all that?"

" What do you mean by ' all that '?"

" War and machine-guns?"

" Tired to death."

" Then why on earth do you talk about them? If you have an opportunity of not talking about them, why do you . . .?"

" It's just a matter of habit. Nowadays I even look at the moon from the point of view of its advantages and usefulness. A woman dentist once told me that, whenever she was told about somebody, she would first of all recall his teeth, his cavities and fillings . . ."

" But look, when I am out of the hospital I try not to think about all those stumps, trepannings and similar horrors."

" You haven't long been working in a hospital, that's all."

" It's my second month already."

" And I'm in my second year. And a wartime year is worth a good three peacetime ones. Perhaps even five . . ."

Luisa laid a hand on my knee and looked me in the eyes. She had a little birthmark by her left eye and eyelashes like Sedykh's—long and curling slightly upwards.

" What were you like before the war, Yurka?"

What should I reply? The same as I am now, only a bit different. I liked to look at the moon, I liked chocolate and lilac and sitting in the third row of the stalls and having a drink with the chaps . . .

For some time we sat and gazed silently at the opposite bank.

" It's beautiful, isn't it?" asked Lusia.

" Beautiful," I replied.

" Do you like to sit like that and look at it?"

" I do."

" I suppose in Kiev too you used to sit with somebody on the banks of the Dnieper in the evening and stare?"

" Yes, I used to sit and stare."

"Have you got a wife in Kiev?"

"No, I'm not married."

"So who did you sit with?"

"I used to sit with Lusia."

"With Lusia? How funny—another Lusia."

"Another Lusia. And just like you she had her hair cut short. But it's true she didn't play the piano."

"Where is she now?"

"I don't know. She stayed there when the Germans came in. Lots of people stayed behind under the Germans. My parents are also under the Germans."

"Have you got a picture of her?"

"Yes."

"Can I have a look?"

I took the photograph out of my wallet. Lusia and I had been taken together. It was a wretched little amateur snapshot on daylight paper and almost completely faded. Lusia took it in her hands and leaned so low over it that her hair touched my face. It smelt of fresh perfumed soap.

"Your Lusia's face isn't symmetrical. Had you noticed?"

"No, I never noticed."

"Do you love her? Or is it just like that?"

"I rather think I do. Anyway I miss her."

"A lot?"

"Quite a lot, I suppose."

"Why 'I suppose'?"

"Oh, well just a lot, then."

Lusia dropped her eyes.

Then suddenly she blushed. Even her little ears, pierced for earrings, turned red.

Down below another train was crawling by, just as long and just as breathless. A tram clattered along somewhere, but it was out of sight. And stars, pale and timid, began to appear in the sky.

I looked at the stars, at the little pink ear with the little hole and at Lusia's slender hand . . . On her little finger was a ring with a green stone. She was a pleasant, likeable girl, Lusia, and I was enjoying being with her. But in a few days we would part and never see each other again. And I would meet other Lusias in the course of the war and would sit down, maybe, with them, and then they, too, would fade away somewhere, and I would forget their faces and their names, and they would all fuse together into a sort of single, big, vague, pleasant something, creating an illusion of the past, so far away and so enticing.

55

Just in case, I gave her the address of my friend in Moscow, where she could write to me if she felt like it after the war. She wrote the address down in a tiny notebook and said she was sure to write.

An hour later we moved on. Lusia was silent and held on to me firmly, with both hands, and I could feel how her heart was beating, how warm and soft were her hands and how very pleasant and touching she was altogether.

XII

They gave us something to do—me, Igor and a couple of other officers from the reserve. We were called a special purpose group. The officer in charge of us—a Major Goldshtab—was terribly intelligent, bald and short-sighted. The leader of the group was the sullen Captain Samóilenko, with a twitching nose, also from the reserve.

The work was not very difficult. The city's industrial plants were being prepared for possible destruction. We had to draw up a plan for the distribution of explosive charges, calculate the amount that would be needed, decide on the method of demolition and train the demolition groups specially set up in the factories. That was all.

It fell to my lot to deal with the meat plant, the refrigeration plant, flour-mill No. 4 and the machine bakery. Igor got the brewery, the second flour-mill and the "Metiz" factory.

We moved into a different flat—big, empty and uncomfortable, with a balcony giving on to Station Square. There was practically no furniture. A table, four chairs, three rickety beds and an electric cooker someone had left behind.

Igor and I grabbed two of the beds, by throwing our greatcoats on them. The third was taken by the senior lieutenant with an odd surname—Pengaunis—presumably a Latvian. The fourth—Shapiro—fixed himself up on some chairs. Valéga and Sedykh were in the next room, on the floor. The gloomy captain was in some private flat. Once a day he would come along, twitch his nose, ask what we had done, roll a cigarette and go away.

At the factories the managers made difficulties—waved their hands, saying that they had no men to spare for the demolition squads and that there were only women left. The workers eyed us suspiciously: why are these soldiers visiting us so often? I pretended to be an expert on fire precautions and inspected the fire extinguishers.

In the refrigeration plant they served us ice-cream on big plates. At the meat plant it was sausages and hamburgers.

The days were cloudless and hot, the nights stifling.

Maria Kuzmínichna complained that everything was getting dearer at the market. Nikoláy Nikoláyevich studied his map and sighed. The bulletins were not very reassuring. Máikop and Krasnodár had been given up.

There were a lot of wounded in the city, and every day brought more and more of them. They moved, pale and unshaven, in long lines towards the Volga, their bandages showing up against their dusty, blood-stained uniforms. The hospitals were being evacuated. Patrols were going round the city into every flat, checking documents. The roads to Kalách and Kotélnikovo were jammed with traffic. In every courtyard they were strenuously digging trenches and big, deep holes, which they said were for storing water in case of fire. Occasionally the Jerries would fly over, drop two or three bombs somewhere on the outskirts and fly off again. There were plenty of anti-aircraft guns in the city.

Churchill flew to Moscow. The communiqué was very vague.

Battles were going on somewhere, but we didn't know exactly where. The bulletins talked of " to the north-east of Kotélnikovo " and " in the bend of the Don " . . . They said Abganérovo was already in German hands . . . That was sixty-five kilometres from us. Maria Kuzmínichna had heard that our troops had abandoned Kalách and moved back to Karpóvka. Most of the wounded were from Kalách. They threw up their hands: " Tanks and aircraft . . . what can you do . . .?"

There was so far no order to evacuate, but Lusia's neighbours, a dentist with his wife and two children, had departed the day before for Léninsk . . . to visit a sister.

Meanwhile at the theatre—*Sylvia, Maritsa* and *Rose Marie*. But in the restaurant there was nothing except Volga water at five kopeks a bottle. And on the stage were top hats, stiff white shirts, seductive smiles and risky jokes.

In the zoo the elephant looked as melancholy as ever, the monkeys quarrelled and the fat, lazy boa-constrictor dozed in the corner of its cage on some old straw.

At the Red Army Club *Izvestia* and the Stalingrad *Pravda* were displayed regularly in showcases with wire mesh in front of them.

In the city library, with its balcony right over the Volga, a charming old lady in a hairstyle of the 1880's handed out Balzac and asked you not to fold the pages.

Little boys shot at sparrows with their catapults and fought each other at a game called " Jerries and our chaps ". The girls played hop-scotch, jumping on one leg.

And so a stifling, cloudless August crept by.

Once I came across Kalúzhsky, in a brand-new tunic and a cap with a dazzling cap-band. He had got himself fixed up as quartermaster in one of the evacuated hospitals. The hospital was at the time being evacuated to Astrakhan and he was up to the eyes in work—there were a million casualties and no transport, in short, honestly, it was better at the front . . . And incidentally if I was in need of sugar he could let me have about ten kilograms—they would never be able to cart it away anyway, so it would have to be sent to the front.

I knew that Valéga would be annoyed with me, but I said I had no time. That was the end of the conversation. With a bold wave of the hand he drove off somewhere in the direction of the Volga in a 5-cwt truck loaded high with sheeps' carcasses. I watched him as he drove away and then dropped into the post-office on the off-chance that there might be something waiting for me.

XIII

On Sunday I woke up earlier than usual. Fleas had appeared from somewhere and I just couldn't get to sleep. Igor and the others were still sleeping.

" There's a lot of ack-ack in the town," said Shapiro, getting some pancakes on the primus. Valéga was meddling with the loud-speaker—he had long had a passion for radio.

Through the window came the dazzling glare of light from the sunlit wall of the house opposite and a patch of pale blue sky that seemed as though it had faded from the heat.

I was not going to the factory that day—the plans had been drawn up, the quantity of explosives calculated, and the training kept being put off from day to day: the demolition groups had still not been formed.

I pulled Igor's greatcoat off him.

" Get up! Let's go and have a bathe."

He screwed his face up in displeasure, tried to pull the

greatcoat over his face, grumbled, but got up all the same. His sleepy eyes blinked.

Sedykh brought in pancakes sizzling in the frying-pan.

" They shot a Jerry down this morning." He set the frying-pan down on a brick. " I saw it myself. First it started smoking and let out a great long black tail, then it started to heel over—steeper and steeper until it went down somewhere outside the city. The engine must have been hit."

" There's a lot of ack-ack in the town," said Shapiro, getting off his chairs, " something like twenty-five batteries."

He was very fond of figures and all sorts of calculations.

" If they all open fire at once, they'll send up at least 750 shells in one minute."

" But how many aircraft have the Germans got?" asked Igor. He was always making fun of him, but Shapiro didn't care.

" At the beginning of the war there were about ten thousand. There's more now probably."

" Why?"

" Simple arithmetic. If you reckon that they've got a hundred aircraft factories and each one turns out an aircraft a day—I am taking an improbably low figure—then you get three thousand a month. They can't have losses on that scale. That means . . ."

" Are you coming down to the beach?" Igor interrupted him.

" No. I've got a boil, the sixth this month. And in the most inconvenient place—I have to sit on one half . . ."

There was no beach in Stalingrad. We dived straight off the rafts into the water, greasy with oil that reflected all the colours of the rainbow. It was as warm as though it had been heated up.

Afterwards we lay on the logs and screwed up our eyes to look at the Volga. It shone with a dazzling light. It was not like the Dnieper. Nothing like it. The last time I had seen it was a few days before the war. Then it had been more carefree and cheerful. There had been the huge sweep of the beach, covered with naked bodies, black from the sun, and the sunshades, kiosks and the smart drink-stands. And there was no end to the number of boats—canoes, dinghies, skiffs, narrow racing boats, punts and swift yachts with snow-white sails. All were scurrying about, flashing white and yellow and blue and trembling in the scorching midday sun.

But now there was nothing of that. Here it was more down to earth and serious. Here were rafts and barges, fussy, smoke-stained launches, and tugs that hooted hoarsely and splashed their ropes on the water. Before the war there were probably yachts and dinghies here too, but I had not been here before the war. And now this wide, brilliant expanse of water, covered with rafts and with its shores crowded with cranes and sheds, reminded me of a workship in some special factory unlike any other.

And yet this was the Volga. You could lie on your stomach and watch the rafts floating downstream, the oil film making bright patterns that ran one into the other, while an ancient steamer with flopping paddles puffed along against the stream. I lay and stared, while Igor said he was fed up with having nothing to do, with Shapiro and his boils, with Pengaunis and his daily laundering and drying of collars on the balcony, with the factory managers and all the useless paper-work.

I listened with one ear as I watched a little launch struggling to get alongside the other bank and tried not to think of the fact that maybe in a week or two the front-line and the Germans would be here, where we were lying now, while we would be over there, in the curly greenery of the other bank, with bombs spurting up white fountains of water, and blown-out bodies would be floating down this glistening surface somewhere towards Astrakhan and the Caspian.

Igor slapped me between the shoulders with all his might.

"Let's get in the water . . . There's a steamer coming."

With a running jump he plunged into the water from the slippery log. For a few seconds he could not be seen. Then his head appeared snorting noisily, far from the shore. With powerful short strokes—nearly the whole of his back out of the water—he swam across in front of the boat. He was a good swimmer. Lusia also swam like that, not so strongly and briskly, but also very well.

That style of swimming was called the crawl. So far I had not managed to do it. The breathing wouldn't come right and my legs got tired. They had to work all the time, quickly and evenly, like scissors.

The steamer went by—broad and deep in the water but with a tall funnel and a long tail of barges behind. Igor returned quite out of breath.

"My heart's letting me down. I'm getting old. Anyway it's not a river, it's more like an oil-tank. It's shining and overflowing with oil. Better go to the library."

At the library Igor found pleasure in reading *Apollo* for

1911. I enjoyed some short stories from Peru in *International Literature*. The wicker chairs were very comfortable. The room was quiet and cosy, with portraits of Turgénev, Tyútchev and someone else with a moustache and a big pin in his tie. The big wall clock struck each quarter of an hour tunefully. A couple of boys were killing themselves with laughter at Doret's illustration to Munchhausen. I once had a copy of the same book in a red and gold binding and similar drawings. I could look through it twenty times a day. I particularly liked the way the baron dragged himself out of the bog by his own hair. There was another picture I liked: a horse cut in two by some gates and standing, quite unconcerned, drinking water from the trough while a whole waterfall poured out behind.

We sat on until the woman in charge of the library pointed out that it closed at six:

" Come along to-morrow. We're always open from twelve to six. And there are more *Apollos*—for 1912 and 1917."

We took our leave and departed. Valéga was probably grumbling already—the dinner would be cold.

Near the entrance to the station a square black loud-speaker was wheezing hoarsely:

" Citizens, an air-raid warning has been sounded in the city. Attention, citizens, an air-raid warning . . ."

In the last few days air-raid warnings had been sounded three or four times a day. Nobody paid attention to them any longer. There would be some shooting—you couldn't see the aeroplane anyway—and then they'd give the all-clear.

Valéga met us with a sullen scowl.

" You know very well we've got no over. I've warmed it up twice already. The potatoes have gone all soft and the borshch is quite . . ." He waved his hand in a gesture of despair and uncovered the borshch which had been wrapped in a greatcoat. Somewhere on the other side of the station the anti-aircraft guns began to bang away.

The borshch was really good. It was made from meat and there was sour cream with it. And plates—rather pretty ones, with little pink flowers—had appeared from somewhere.

" Just like in a restaurant," Igor laughed. " It only wants knife-rests and triangular napkins in the glasses."

And suddenly the whole lot went flying—plates, spoons, glass and the loud-speaker on the wall.

What the devil . . .?

From behind the station the planes came in a steady stream, just as they do in a fly-past. I had never seen so many of them.

There were so many it was difficult to make out where they were flying. They flew in flocks, black, repulsive, unperturbed, at various levels. The whole sky was studded with puffs of anti-aircraft fire.

We stood on the balcony and gazed into the sky. Igor, Valéga, Sedykh and I. We couldn't drag ourselves away.

The Germans were flying straight at us. They flew in triangular formation, like migrating geese. They flew so low you could see the yellow tips of their wings, the white-edged crosses and the under-carriages reminding you of extended claws . . . Ten . . . twelve . . . fifteen . . . eighteen. They drew themselves up in a line right opposite us. The leading one turned upside down, with his wheels in the air and went into a dive. I could not take my eyes off him. He had red wheels and red cylinder heads. He switched on his siren. Little black spots began to fall from beneath the wings. One, two, three, four, ten, twelve . . . The last one was white and big. I shut my eyes and clutched instinctively at the rail. There was no earth in which to take cover. And you had to do something. Then it was no longer possible to distinguish anything at all.

The din dominated everything. Everything shook with a horrible tremor. I opened my eyes for a second. There was nothing to be seen. You couldn't tell whether it was smoke or dust. Everything was covered with a sort of dense cloud . . . Then there was the shriek of more bombs and more noise. I hung on to the rails. Somebody pinched my arm as if with pincers—above the elbow . . . Valéga's face—caught motionless as if by a flash of lightning . . . white, with big round eyes and open mouth . . . Then it vanished . . .

How long would it go on? An hour, or two hours, or fifteen minutes. There was neither time nor space. Only the cloud and the cold, rough rail. " Nothing else."

The rail disappeared. I lay on something soft, warm and uncomfortable. It moved under me. I clutched at it. It crawled away.

There was no time for thought. The brain was cut out of action. There remained only instinct—the animal desire to live, and expectation. Not even expectation, but something not to be explained in words . . . Get it over, get it over quick . . . Whatever it is—only get it over!

Then we were sitting on the bed and smoking. How that happened I didn't quite know. All around was dust—just like a fog. And the smell of TNT. In our teeth, in our ears and down the backs of our necks—there was sand everywhere.

On the floor were fragments of plates, pools of borshch, cabbage leaves and a piece of meat. In the middle of the room was a chunk of asphalt. Every single window was smashed. My neck ached as though somebody had struck it a blow with a stick.

We sat and smoked. I saw how Valéga's fingers were shaking. Mine were doing the same probably. Sedykh was wiping his leg. Igor was trying to smile. He had an enormous bruise on his forehead.

I went out on to the balcony. The station was burning. The little house to the right of the station was also on fire. That was where the editorial office or the political department had been—I couldn't remember. To the left, towards the grain elevator everything was aglow. The square was empty. There were a few craters with the asphalt torn up. Somebody was lying on the other side of the fountain. A ramshackle cart lay abandoned, and looked as though it had sat down on its hindquarters. The horse was still struggling. Its belly had been ripped open and its intestines were scattered in a pink jelly over the asphalt. The smoke was getting thicker and darker. It spread over the square in a solid cloud.

" Do you want to eat?" asked Valéga. His voice was quiet, not his own, rather shaky.

I didn't know whether I wanted to eat, but I said Yes. We ate the cold potato straight from the frying-pan. Igor sat opposite me. His face was grey from dust, like a statue. An evil-looking purple bruise had spread over his whole forehead.

" Oh, to hell with the beastly potato—it just won't go down my throat . . ." He went out on to the balcony.

Pengaunis and Shapiro arrived pale and covered with dust. The raid had caught them on the main square. They had sat it out in a trench. Bombs had fallen on the Red Army Club and the corner house opposite, where the hospital had been. The southern part of the city was on fire. An ammunition truck had been hit and the shells were still exploding. One woman had had her head knocked clean off as she came out of a cinema. About twenty people had lost their lives there. It had happened just as the programme ended.

I asked what the time was. Pengaunis looked at his watch. A quarter to nine. It had been about seven when we returned from the library. Which meant that the raid had lasted nearly two hours.

Igor came in from the balcony.

" Where does our captain live?"

63

Nobody knew. An idiotic situation. Maybe someone should go and see Goldshtab? But he knew our address and would get in touch if necessary. No, all the same it would be better to go down there. It was impossible to sit still. It was only about half an hour's walk.

On the street were people with bundles and with carts. They were running and stumbling along. Things were falling off the carts. The people would stop and rearrange them. Silently, without swearing and with staring, lifeless eyes. The pungent, throat-searing smoke rose above the houses and floated around the streets. Glass crunched under our feet. Bricks, bits of cement, tables and a cupboard upside down. Someone was being carried on a blanket. An old woman in a check headscarf was dragging a stool and a bundle of gigantic dimensions.

"O Lord God! Holy Mother of God!"

The bundle slipped down. The scarf came off her head and dragged along the ground.

At the corner of Gógol street was an enormous crater— big enough to take a whole house. Soldiers were clearing up the chunks of asphalt scattered in all directions. The air trembled from the penetrating, ear-splitting wail of the fire engines.

And people were running, running, running . . .

The smoke crept into every corner of the city and shut out the sky. Long yellow tongues of flame leapt out of the windows and licked the walls of the corner house. The firemen were unwinding their hoses.

They wouldn't let us enter the house. We tried for a long time to phone Goldshtab from a kiosk. But we couldn't get through. Something was interfering with the connection. It just wheezed and crackled. Goldshtab's voice came through from far away, as if from the other world:

"Go home . . . wait."

We went home. People were still running, running, running. From the bottom flat they were dragging out a huge sideboard with mirrors.

We tried to get some sleep. We turned from side to side. For some reason it was hard and uncomfortable. There was no light. The radio was silent. The fires raged throughout the night.

XIV

Our captain arrived at dawn. In five minutes, he said, there would be a half-ton truck and we would go to the tractor plant.

" To the tractor plant? What for?"

" I don't know. Orders."

" Who gave the orders?"

" Goldshtab. He is also setting off for the tractor plant."

" What are we going to do there?"

" I said I don't know. Get your group together, he said, and wait for transport."

" Nothing else?"

" Nothing. He came out of the commander's office for a moment, told me about the transport and went back in again."

" And what else did you hear?"

The captain shrugged his shoulders—what could anyone tell?

Sedykh called me to one side:

" The stores down at the station have been bombed. Better go down there, perhaps?"

" I'll—— you if you do."

" There's vodka, they say."

" You heard what I told you?"

" I heard."

" Go and pack up your belongings."

I picked up the rolls of blueprints and stuffed them into my grip. Shapiro pricked up his ears.

" They're coming again . . ."

Silence. Valéga was at my side, with a knife in one hand and a tin in the other. There was the low, but still distant, familiar rumbling of aircraft engines.

" We must go down to the cellar," said the captain, his nose twitching, and he made for the door. In the doorway he ran into a red, perspiring chap in a leather coat.

" Are you Samóilenko?" His voice was hoarse and breathless.

" I am."

" Where are your men? I've brought the truck. Be quick. The sirens are going."

Valéga looked questioningly at me—with a knife and a tin in his hands.

"Get in the truck. Do you hear?"

As we climbed into the truck the first bombs began to pour down: somewhere behind us on the railway-workers' housing estate. The planes flew overhead and turned away slowly to the right.

I removed my cap so that the wind shouldn't take it off. We drove out of the city. Then we could clearly see the planes diving on the station, the centre and the quayside. There was a solid cloud of dust above the town. From somewhere by the river there rose a high column of thick black smoke that spread out at the top like a mushroom. The oil tanks must be on fire.

The road was crammed with people. They were all making for somewhere, turning back from time to time to look at the town—some half-naked, some in fur coats and some black from the smoke . . .

Goldshtab was sitting in a cellar. You couldn't push your way in for people. Boxes, bundles, and greatcoats thrown down. Somebody was shouting over the telephone in a hoarse voice. Goldshtab was pale and unshaven. He looked at us with his eyes screwed up and didn't recognise us.

"Who do you want?"

"We have come to you. Sappers."

"Aha. Sappers. Fine. Put your greatcoats down here, on the box. You came in a truck? Good. Come over here." He spoke jerkily, hurriedly, rubbing his dry little hands, covered with black hair. "Time is short. The Germans are on the other side of the ravine "—he searched for something in his pockets but didn't find it—" five hundred metres, no more. They're bombarding the tractor plant with mortars. It's a commando raid, apparently, not a big one. Our regulars are not here yet. The workers are holding the position." He looked at his little, extremely elegant gold wrist-watch. "It's now quarter past six. At about 0800 hours the factory must be ready for demolition. Understand? There are sappers there, from an army battalion, but not many. Everything's there—charges, leads and detonators. You must help. Make contact with Lieutenant Bolshóv—you'll find him there, in a blue greatcoat and blue cap. Fix everything up with him. At 0800 hours I'll be there . . ."

He reflected for a moment, biting his lips.

"Oh, all right . . ."

He took out of his side pocket a tiny morocco notebook with a pencil attached. He made some notes.

"Kérzhentsev—the power station, Svidérsky—the foundry, Samóilenko—the assembly shop, etcetera." He put the notebook back in his pocket and buttoned it up. "I won't keep you any longer. Your greatcoats and things you can leave here for the time being."

We drove on.

We found Bolshóv quite quickly—by his blue greatcoat and cap. He was very thin, pale, with prominent, ironical, intelligent eyes. He had a cigarette end in the corner of his mouth. His hands were in his pockets.

"Helpers, eh?" He smiled with the corner of his mouth not occupied by the cigarette.

"That's right, helpers."

"Well, you've come at a good time. A couple of hours sooner would have been better. Now . . ."—he yawned and spat out the cigarette end—"the main job's done. You don't have an ohm-meter?"

"No. Why?"

"The capsules are not calibrated. In fact, if they tell us to do it to-day it probably won't work. What's that, are they bombing the town?"

"Yes, but why won't it work?"

"Why?" Bolshóv smiled lazily. "The explosive's useless. The TNT is no good. And the rest is ammonite. It's got damp and lumpy. And the capsules are not calibrated. There's nothing to test the circuit with. No ohm-meter."

"What about the detonating fuse?" asked Igor.

"They promise to produce some to-morrow. And ohm-meters to-morrow. Everything to-morrow. But we've got to blow it up to-day . . ."

"To-day?"

"That's what they say. If they don't push them back, it'll be to-day."

He took a carefully folded newspaper out of his pocket and tore off a neat square of it.

"Do you have any makhorka?"

We lit up. Groups of workers were going past along the tree-lined asphalt avenue. They were carrying machine-guns taken from tanks. Some of them had nothing at all, not even rifles. They marched tensely, silently.

I asked: "Where are the Germans?"

"Over there, behind the workshops. There's a ravine

there. They're spraying us from mortars. About ten tanks. Not even tanks, but sort of baby tanks. You can see it clearly from that hill."

"Where are our objectives?"

"What have you got to do?"

"The electric power station," I replied.

"The power station? It's only a few yards from here. Behind that block to the left. You'll find my sergeant there. Vedérnikov. He's probably asleep there somewhere in an office. He was working all night. I advise you to have a nap too."

The sergeant was indeed asleep, with his head buried in the corner of a divan and his legs spread out on the floor. He had obviously thrown himself on the divan and dropped off immediately.

"Hey, friend!"

The sergeant turned over and rubbed his eyes for a long time. They were small and deep-set and quite lost in his high-cheek-boned face. He just couldn't wake up.

"Did the lieutenant send you?"

"Yes. Bolshóv."

"Are you going to take over?"

"First of all let me know what you've done."

"All over again? One chap has already been and got the hang of it. Some Captain—Lvóvich, I think."

"And now me."

The sergeant stretched himself and stood up.

"Oh well, let's go . . ." He felt in his pocket for makhorka. "We carted sacks all night, blast them. I can't feel my shoulders any more. Paper sacks—the bloody things kept tearing."

"A lot of them?"

"About a hundred, if not more. Hundredweight apiece. There won't be much left of the power station after that."

"Is the circuit ready?"

"Yes. Only the electrical one. We dragged up a devil of a lot of accumulators, but there are no ohm-meters. An electrician here was helping me—he said they had something like it here but he just couldn't find it. But everythings ready. The detonators are loose. Just push them in and press down the switch."

"Where is the demolition point?"

The sergeant pointed towards the window.

"About three hundred metres from here is a trench. The whole outfit is there. And the captain's there, and the electrician too probably."

We went round the station. It was big and clean. There were eight generators with a charge under each—three or four sacks. Apart from that there were charges under the boilers, on the oil switches and on the transformers about three hundred metres from the station itself. The circuit was extremely long: some two kilometres. It had been done very neatly—the ends of the wires had been carefully bound with insulation tape with two capsules to each charge. A great deal had certainly been done in the course of the night.

Somewhere on the other side of the electricity station mortar shells could be heard exploding.

"They're firing on the outskirts," said the sergeant. "From company batteries. It's nothing. Are you going to the trench?"

"Where is the telephone?"

"In the trench. Everything's there. They've made a sort of command post there."

XV

The trench was crammed full of people. Igor, Sedykh, a tall, dark, curly-headed man in military uniform, with small side-burns, some workers in overalls, and an undersized, consumptive-looking character in a shiny jacket and a cap with a button on top. The soldier turned out to be Lvóvich, and the man in the buttoned cap was the electrical engineer from the power station. Everybody called him Geórgi Akímovich.

They were all sitting down and smoking in the light of a lamp. It was not a bad dug-out: its sides were boarded, it had a floor, hermetically sealed doors and wooden bunks. It was the sort you found in the engineering course—in the form of an H, with two entrances.

"What are we going to do without an ohm-meter?" I asked.

Geórgi Akímovich gave me a sidelong glance.

"We've got a Whitestone bridge."

"Why didn't you say so?"

"I'm telling you now. Only it's in the safe and Puchkóv, the chief engineer, has got the key. And since yesterday evening Puchkóv has been at HQ."

"So we'll have to send for him."

"We've sent already. You see, they set off for the 'Red October' plant. They rang up three hours ago to say they were on their way. And they're still on their way."

Geórgi Akímovich had a very mobile expressive face. When he talked, it was not only his mouth that moved, but his nose, his forehead and his sunken and feverishly flushed cheeks. One of his teeth was missing, a front one, and that gave him a lisp. His age was difficult to determine—probably about thirty-five.

"Two nights running I haven't slept, there's no sense in it . . ."

Nervously he stubbed out his cigarette.

"Supposing they phone now and tell us to act, what'll happen then?"

"We shall act, I suppose," I replied.

"What, throw the switch? Yes? Is that what you think?" His big, dark-lidded eyes bored fiercely into me.

"Yes, I think so."

"And what about the workers at the station? Send 'em to blazes along with the machinery? Who is going to warn them? Are *we*? We shall have our plates full up to here as it is," He quickly drew his hand across his throat. "There's no plan, no organisation, nothing . . ."

"Geórgi Akímovich," Lvóvich interrupted him. He was sitting apart on some spare accumulators, bending and unbending a piece of wire.

"Well, what about it? You've got to use your heads a bit. There are sixty-five men at work in the power station at the moment. Where are they to go if . . . er . . . if we do have to make the big bang? Just follow their noses? Scatter in all directions? Then again—is there any particular order for the various workshops? Not a damned thing. The foundry will blow up while we are only just getting ready, or the other way round. Altogether . . ." Nervously he pressed out his cigarette with his long, dry fingers. "See how the Germans are bashing away with their mortars now: If a bit of shrapnel hits a wire, that'll be the end. Our whole circuit is no bloody good. How many times have I said it was idiocy to keep the Whitestone in the safe! They were afraid of burglars. And now we can only sit and wait for things to happen."

He took a few quick, short drags on his cigarette, stubbed it against the wall and stood up.

"Maybe they've got there. But we'll never get through by telephone. The exchange is in a mess . . ."

Igor also stood up.

"Shall we go down to my place at the foundry? Eh? You can have a look at that."

We went to the foundry.

"How do you like that character?" Igor asked.

"How shall I put it? I don't envy his wife. He must have TB plus indigestion. On the other hand, everything he says is absolutely true."

"He gets on my nerves."

"You're getting to be a neurotic, honestly, everything annoys you. Shapiro annoys you, if the Latvian launders his collar-bands, that annoys you. What the hell do you want?"

"I don't like grousers. I can't help it."

"Oh well, we shall see. You know, we ought to train Sedykh and Valéga to do the capsules. So they'd fill 'em up like clockwork and not be scared."

Sedykh smiled:

"What is there to be scared of in it? I stunned carps as big as this with TNT when we were at Kupyánsk. Do you realise how many fish there were there? To-morrow, if we don't blow this place up, I'll get you more sturgeon than you can lift with two hands. I've already noticed a boat moored behind the fence . . ."

Near the entrance to the foundry a group of workers were standing round a healthy-looking lad with a bandaged arm. His sleeve was torn away from the shoulder and there were red stains on the bandage.

They've got as far as the institute, the bastards. They've got automatics, and we've only got rifles. We had only just got to the entrance when they started firing from the windows. It was a good thing a Voroshílov tank came up and banged straight into the building. So they poured out like cockroaches. Now they're on the other side of the Mechétka . . ."

His eyes were glistening. It pleased him to have an audience, to be wounded already and to have fired on the Germans, and he didn't want to bring his story to an end.

"The Voroshílov only fired one shot. It landed right in the second floor. Then the stones began to fly. And the Jerries got out by the back way, from tree to tree."

"Are there a lot of Jerries?" asked someone in the crowd.

"Enough to be going on with. A couple of divisions, and possibly more."

"Did you count 'em?"

"Count 'em . . ." The youth spat scornfully and stood up, holding his left arm with his right hand. "You go and count

71

'em. There's something else besides arithmetic to do over there . . . Where's the first-aid post, fellows? You talk too much."

On the way back we came across some more casualties—an old man and a boy. They were both lightly wounded—the one in the arm, the other in the head. The Germans were still on the other side of the ravine, they said. They were firing from mortars. But they weren't attacking. Nor were we. It was a pity there were no real commanders. It was said that some artillery units were due to move up. German tanks had twice driven up the ravine, fired a few shots and gone away. There was little firing on our part, either: there was probably no ammunition. On the whole it wasn't too bad, you could still get by. The chaps from the tractor plant would defend their factory. And, with an entirely youthful wink, the old man went off with the boy to find the first-aid post. A board nailed to a lamp-standard, with a hastily drawn cross, pointed in the direction of the Volga. When we went to the workshop it had not been there.

In the dug-out Geórgi Akímovich was already tinkering about with his " bridge ". It was big and handsome and highly polished, with a mass of meters and switches. Geórgi Akímovich was in a good mood. The circuit was in order.

" You see how wonderfully the needle jumps? It's a fantastic bridge. There's not another like it in Stalingrad. They even used to send for it from the central power station. It's as sensitive as the devil. Now we can recalibrate all our detonators. Are there any spares?"

" As many as you could wish for," replied Vedérnikov. " Two or three hundred."

Just as we were finishing the calibration the bombardment began. It lasted about an hour. Every two or three minutes a shell came over. Most of them landed around the station. Some fell in the machine room, and two right in the boiler-house. They were called mortars, but they were not mortars. Mortars have no power of penetration, while in the machine room there were already gaping holes in the roof.

The needle on the Whitestone rested helplessly on zero. The circuit was broken. Geórgi Akímovich was looking for his cap with the button.

" We'll have to dig the cable in ; we shall get no peace from the shrapnel."

And, without waiting for the end of the bombardment, he clambered out of the dug-out. It wasn't so easy to find the break. The circuit was connected in series and the slightest break put it completely out of action. With connections in parallel it's easier to find a break—the circuit is broken up into sections and each section can be checked separately.

We went along the whole of the wire, feeling it with our hands. Valéga came with us, carrying the " bridge ". Geórgi Akímovich shouted at him the whole time to be more careful —we'd never find another one like it. We quickly found two of the breaks, took a fairly long time about the third but found it in the end. Quickly and skifully Geórgi Akímovich bound the damaged place with insulating tape.

Right up to evening we were digging the cable in and switching the circuit over to parallel. Twice the Germans repeated their raid. Geórgi Akímovich did not take his eyes off the Whitestone. But everything went off all right—there were no breaks.

About eight o'clock Goldshtab arrived. He brought an ohm-meter. He took me and Lvóv off to one side, rubbing his hands.

" The first signal—'what is the time?'—means get ready. The operative one is ' send list number 5 '. Understand? Don't move an inch from the telephone."

" Very well."

" Remember that after the preliminary signal you won't have more than half an hour left. Inside half an hour everything must be finished and at the ready. You, Lvóvich, will be responsible for the evacuation of the workers, and you, Kerzhéntsev, for the demolition."

" That's clear. What about the sequence?"

" There's no sequence. The first and the second orders are to be passed on to all the workshops simultaneously. After the explosion you will gather at the landing-stage—Lvóvich, you know where the motorboat will be."

" Fine."

" Is everything clear?"

" Everything."

Goldshtab departed. Somewhere quite nearby, on the other side of the foundry, Verey lights were going up. There was the crackle of Sten guns and occasionally the more regular beat of machine-gun fire.

The switch was nailed straight on to the wall close to the door. It was just a small, ordinary switch with a black handle. Just the same as were fitted to meters in flats. I looked at it. There were two wires leading from it: one to the accumulators—there were eight boxes of them buried in a hole —and the other to the charges—three thousand pounds of

73

ammonite in sacks. One wire was disconnected and was sticking out. The handle of the switch was thrown back and tied with a bit of string, just in case. In an hour or two, or maybe sooner, they would get through on the telephone and I would connect the wire and undo the string, test the circuit once again and with two fingers carefully push the switch in . . . And then . . . There would be no generators, no boilers and no machine room with metal plates as snow-white as in an operating theatre . . . Nothing . . .

We sat and smoked. Valéga was darning his trousers at the knee. Sedykh was with the sergeant at the power station. The telephone gleamed in the corner. Every minute Geórgi Akímovich switched the " bridge " on. Igor lay on the wooden bunk and stared at the roof.

At twelve o'clock Goldshtab phoned. The order was to test the circuit and not to go to sleep.

It was so smoked up in the dug-out that you couldn't make out people's faces: as in a badly developed negative. There was another call at three o'clock. It was Bolshóv, wanting to know if there were a couple of dozen calibrated capsules to spare. There were. He would send the sergeant for them. Fine.

We had another smoke. We would go out into the courtyard, look at the stars and Verey lights and the four enormous chimneys of the power station. Then we'd go back in, and sit and smoke. We switched on and we switched off. We said nothing.

At five there was another call. Goldshtab. We could go to sleep.

Thank the Lord for that!

We lay down on the bare boards, moving our revolvers round on our stomachs.

It was a mistake to have left our greatcoats with Goldshtab.

XVI

The very same business was repeated on Tuesday, and on Wednesday and on Thursday. Bombardments, break in the wire, long periods of waiting for the telephone to ring. At five o'clock—you can sleep.

The atmosphere became less tense.

One day followed another, clear and blue, with autumn spiders' webs floating in the air.

Still no order.

There was nothing left of the town apparently. The Germans bombed it from morning to night. There was a dense cloud of smoke and dust hanging over it. The oil tanks were burning. Sometimes the smoke, black as soot, would screen the sun and then you could look at it without screwing up your eyes, as through a smoked glass during an eclipse. Fighting was going on in the southern part of the town, near the grain elevator, and in the northern part, on Mamai Hill.

Nothing changed on our ravine. One night two divisions came up. They were a long time passing through, without a break, the whole night through—battalion after battalion. With artillery and transport. A couple of times the Germans tried to get across the ravine and then there was the rattle of Sten gun fire—usually at night. And Goldshtab would phone —be at the ready—but in the morning everything would quieten down and we would lie down to sleep.

We started to make ourselves at home in our dug-out. We laid on electric light, did our cooking on a ring, covered the walls with excellent paper from the factory's technical department. Valéga and Sedykh even had a portrait of Stalin in their corner and two postcards—the Odessa operatic theatre and a reproduction of Répin's "Zaporózhye Cossack".

Sedykh brought Kruber's geography textbook from somewhere, as well as Chékhov's *Letters* and the *Niva* for 1912.

In the evenings, with much spitting on his fingers, he would read. His brow would wrinkle up and his lips move. Occasionally he would ask the meaning of "Royal salute" or "general-of-infantry", or how the Tsarevich Alexei came to have so many decorations when he was only seven years old. I liked Sedykh, I like his snub-nosed, boyish face, his slightly slanting, laughing eyes, and the youthfulness that burst out of him without restraint. Even his habit of picking at the palm of his hand when he was embarrassed pleased me.

He did everything with pleasure and relish. To watch him washing himself made you want to wash too, so violently did he snort and so loudly did he slap himself about the shoulders and stomach. If you told him to fetch a little firewood, he'd get nearly a cart-load. His young muscles were straining for action. He undid screws with his fingers. He had a fight with Igor one day and for two days afterwards Igor couldn't move his neck. And Igor considered himself an expert at French wrestling and knew all the fine points of *tour-de-bras* and *tour-de-tête*.

Sedykh's curiosity was almost laughable. He would squat down, wrap his arms round his knees and listen with his mouth slightly open, as children listen to a fairy story. His questions were unexpected and childishly naïve. Why couldn't the Germans guess the secret of the " Katyúsha ", and why did it always rain when there was a new moon, and why did the needle of a compass point to the north, and was it true that Roosevelt had lost the use of his legs? In the evening the conversation would sometimes turn to heroes and awards. Sedykh would listen with attention and concentration, his arms round his knees, in his favourite position.

" What do you have to do to get the Order of Lenin?" he asked.

Everyone laughed.

" All right, not the Lenin one, something else, a bit less?"

I said in explanation that it wasn't so easy. He listened in silence, staring away somewhere into a corner. A fag-end was stuck to his lip.

" Then that's all right," he said quietly.

" What's all right?"

" I shall get a medal." He spoke terribly simply and convincingly, as though about something that had already happened.

Then he stood up and went for some wood. I looked at his broad back, which somehow did not tally with the golden down on his cheeks, and I recalled how he had cleaned his gun with a rag—just before a German attack—every screw, every crack, and I believed what he said.

Valéga was jealous of my affection for Sedykh. That was apparent all round.

" Senior lieutenant Svidérsky hasn't got a batman—go to him," Valéga said grumpily as he took from Sedykh the jug from which he was pouring water over my hands.

Sedykh brought an armful of straw from somewhere. Valéga prodded it and frowned: " The lieutenant won't sleep on that sort of rubbish," and brought another armful, in no way different from the first.

But on the whole they got on well together. They cooked their meals together, with Valéga raising his voice a bit and criticising the underdone kasha. Sedykh would laugh happily, teasing Valéga and calling him, for some reason, a " schnaps ".

In the evenings Valéga and Sedykh would prepare charges —we had five boxes of TNT in reserve. In the mornings they would stun fish and return with sturgeon and sterlet wriggling in the buckets.

Sergeant Vedérnikov was transferred to another workshop and we saw no more of him. And we seldom came across Shapiro and Pengaunis. Bolshóv sometimes dropped in on us and then we would play *kozyol* or *vingt-et-un* on a thick copy of the *Niva*. Geórgi Akímovich couldn't bear that—he would grab Chékhov's *Letters* and retreat ostentatiously into his corner. He slept on a door laid across two bunks.

I was getting to like him, despite his peevish character and his everlasting discontent with something or other. He worked without a break and without sparing himself. He always tested and mended the circuit himself—and it broke three or four times a day. He grumbled, cursed, got very excited and accused everybody else of idleness. But he worshipped his power station, every machine and every screw in it, like a living thing. In fact he was a mixture of pessimism, ill-temper, incredible energy and liveliness.

" What's the use of us trying to fight the Germans?" he said, nervously tugging at his tie and wrinkling up his brow. " They have travelled right from Berlin to Stalingrad in motor transport, and here are we lying about in jackets and overalls with an 1890 model rifle."

Igor flared up. He was always quarrelling with Geórgi Akímovich.

" And what exactly do you mean by that?"

" That we don't know how to fight."

" What does it mean, ' to know how to ', Geórgi Akímovich?"

" Know how to? To go from Berlin to the Volga—that's knowing how to."

" To retreat from the frontier to the Volga also takes some doing."

Geórgi Akímovich laughed a little dry laugh.

Igor began to lose his temper.

" What are you laughing at? There's nothing funny about it. France fell to pieces to all intents and purposes in a couple of weeks. They put the pressure on and she collapsed, crumbled like sand. And this is already our second year of fighting quite on our own."

" Why do you compare us with France? Forty millions and two hundred millions. Six hundred kilometres and ten thousand kilometres. And who was in power there? People like Pétain and Laval who are now working happily with the Germans."

"That's just it . . ." Igor's temper was still rising. "Pétain Laval . . . It's precisely because of people like Pétain and Laval. We don't have any of them. We finished them off. That's the most important. Don't you understand that is the most important thing, that our people are of a slightly different sort? And that is why we fight, and why we are still fighting. Even here on the Volga, after losing the Ukraine and Belorussia, we are still fighting. What other country, tell me, what other country, what other people, would have withstood that?"

Geórgi Akímovich smiled at the corners of his mouth. "No other."

"Aha! No other? So you admit there's no other."

"I admit it. But does that make it any easier? Does the admission that other countries are less capable than we are to resist really make it any easier? That's known as lulling yourself to sleep. And we don't need that. You've got to look at everything soberly. Heroism alone is no use at all. Heroism's one thing, and tanks are another."

"Our tanks are no worse than the Germans". They're better than the Germans'. A man in the tanks told me . . ."

"All right, I don't dispute it. Maybe they are even better, I am no judge of these things. But with one good tank you won't knock out ten inferior ones. What do you think?"

"Now wait a minute. We shall also have a lot of tanks."

"By that time you and I'll be in the Urals."

Igor shot up as if he'd been stung.

"Who's going to be in the Urals? You and me and him? Not bloody likely. And you know it damn well. You keep on like that just out of stubbornness, out of some stupid desire to argue, you always have to argue. It's a revolting habit." Geórgi Akímovich's nose, eyebrows and cheeks twitched.

"Why do you get so cross? Sit down. Come on, sit down for a minute. Everything can be discussed calmly."

Igor sat down.

"Now you say that even retreating takes some doing. That's true. We also retreated before Napoleon right to Moscow. But on that occasion it was only territory we lost, and even that was a narrow strip. And Napoleon acquired nothing except snow and burned-out villages. But now? The Ukraine and the Kuban have gone, so there's no grain. The Donbas has gone, so there's no coal. Baku has been cut off.

Dneprostroi has been destroyed and thousands of factories are in German hands. What are the prospects? Everything now depends on economics. The army must be shod and clothed and fed and supplied with weapons. Not to speak about the civilian population. I don't mention the fact that we're short of a good fifty million people who are over there under the German jackboot. Have we still the strength to overcome all that? In your opinion, have we the strength?"

"We've got the strength . . . Last year it was even worse. The Germans got right to Moscow and still they were driven off."

"And that's just what I'm not sure about—that it was worse. The Donbas, Rostóv, the Kuban and Máikop were still ours. Now they're not. The Volga line of communication is now cut in effect. Do you realise what a journey Baku oil now has to make? You will say there's still the Kuzbas, Barnaúl, the Urals . . . It's true they are mighty industrial centres. But before the war started there were, apart from them, also Krivoi Rog, Níkopol, Zaporózhye, Mariúpol, Kerch, Khárkov. All that has been lost. We've evacuated some of the factories, but evacuating isn't putting them into production. Meanwhile, you see what's happening."

Just then a group of Junkers-88's passed over, their bombs gone, and turned slowly to make another sortie.

"They don't even have a fighter escort. They come over with complete impunity, the bastards."

For a time we stayed silent and followed the yellow-winged aircraft in the sky, so black and repulsive, so calm and sure of their own strength. Geórgi Akímovich smoked one cigarette after another. There were already a dozen cigarette butts around him. He stared at one point—in the direction in which the aircraft had disappeared.

Igor sat and threw stones at an empty tin lying nearby. The stones fell very close but just missed the tin. He seemed to be completely lost in this occupation.

All of a sudden he stood up.

"No. It can't be. They will go no further. I know they won't."

He walked off.

It can't be . . . That was all we could say for the moment.

After all, there had been 1917, damn it! And 1918 and 1919! That had been worse. Typhus, destruction and famine. The Maxim and the three-inch gun—that had been all. And still we had got out of it somehow. And later we'd built Dneprostroi, and Magnitogorsk, and this very factory here that I now had to blow up . . .

I knew that Geórgi Akímovich would only smile scornfully at this. When he talked about this he always spoke as though we were little children. He would smile and say something to the effect that that had been the fourth year of the war, that it had exhausted not only us but all the others as well, and that the French, British and German soldiers no longer wanted to fight. And more in the same strain.

He once said:

"We shall fight to the last man. Russians always fight like that. But our chances are slim all the same. Only a miracle can save us. Otherwise they will flatten us out. They'll flatten us with organisation and tanks."

A miracle?

Not long ago some soldiers had marched by. I was on duty at the telephone and went out to have a smoke. As they marched they sang, quietly, in low voices. I didn't even see them—I only heard their steps on the asphalt and the quiet, rather sad song about the Dnieper and the cranes. I went across to them. The men were resting along the roadside on the trampled down grass under the acacias. The half-concealed lights of the cigarettes twinkled. And a young, quiet voice reached me from somewhere under the trees:

"No, Vasya . . . don't say it. You'll never find any better than ours. Honestly, the soil's like butter, rich and good." He even smacked his lips in a special way. "The corn will come up, it'll be over your head . . ."

Meanwhile the town was burning, and the red reflection of the flames flickered over the walls of the factory, and somewhere quite in the distance machine-guns rattled—sometimes more and sometimes less frequently—and Verey lights went up, and ahead was uncertainty and death was almost inescapable.

I never saw who said that. Someone shouted: "Get ready to move!" There was a clatter of mess-tins and they were off. They went off slowly with the heavy gait of the soldier. They set off for that unknown place which their officers had probably marked with a red cross on the map.

I stood for a long time, listening to the sound of marching feet going into the distance and then fading away completely . . .

There are some little things that remain with you throughout your life. Small and seemingly insignificant, they somehow eat into you, grow into something big and significant and become a sort of symbol.

I remember one dead soldier. He lay on his back with his arms spread out. There was a cigarette-end stuck to his lip. A small, still smoking fag-end. And that was more frightful than anything I saw before or after during the war. More frightful than cities in ruins, than stomachs ripped open or arms and legs torn off. The arms spread out and the fag-end on the lip. A minute before there had been life, thoughts and desires. Now there was death . . .

And in that song and in those simple words about the soil as rich as butter, about the grain growing higher than your head, there was also *some*thing . . . I didn't even know what to call it. Tolstóy called it the inner warmth of patriotism. Maybe that was the most accurate definition. Maybe that was the miracle that Geórgi Akímovich was waiting for, a miracle more powerful than German efficiency and tanks with black crosses.

I looked at Geórgi Akímovich. Small and acrimonious in his shiny jacket, he sat curled up on the steps, with his knees tucked up, thin and knobbly. He had pale hands with blue veins and the same kind of veins at his temples. He looked as though his home was in terrible disorder, his children got on his nerves and he quarrelled with his wife. Even before the war he probably found fault with everything and got cross with everybody.

And yet, the previous evening, under my very eyes, a shell had exploded near him, about twenty paces away. He had been looking for a break in the wire. And he only ducked slightly and went right on taping up the damaged place and then checked the whole cable again where it lay near the explosion.

" You know," he said to me afterwards, " my whole life is tied up with this factory. I came here as an apprentice when people were still moving around here with a theodolite. The power station and all these workshops grew up under my very eyes. I didn't sleep for five nights when number six generator—the American one, second from the window— was put in. I know them all like the back of my hand. I know the character and habits of every one of them. Do you understand what this demolition means to me? No, you don't understand . . . You are soldiers, you are simply sorry to lose a factory, and that's all. But for me . . ."

He didn't finish what he had to say, and went back to his " bridge."

Six weeks previously Igor and I had sat on a twisted log by the roadside and watched our troops retreating. There was no front. There were roads along which transports were going somewhere. And there were men marching. Also going somewhere . . .

That was six weeks back—in July.

Now it was September. We had already been ten days in this factory. For the tenth day the Germans were bombing the town. If they were bombing, that meant our people were still there. That meant fighting was going on. That meant there *was* a front. That meant it was better now than it had been in June. . . .

A shell burst near the power station. That was the beginning of the dinner-time bombardment. From three to half-past, as regular as a chronometer. In half an hour we should have to go and mend the circuit. Valéga and Sedykh rushed off with the mess-tins for dinner.

XVII

A couple of days later, early in the morning, Goldshtab turned up in our dug-out. There were quite a dozen other officers with him.

We were sitting on the steps of the dug-out making celluloid cigarette cases. In the factory laboratory were tons of all kinds of celluloid and beautifully iridescent concentrated pear juice in those great jars you see in chemists' shops. There we were, busy with our cigarette cases. We sawed and cut and scraped and glued, and tore ourselves away only to restore the circuit or to eat.

"Well, we shall have to say good-bye," said Goldshtab, turning over in his hands Igor's miniature cigarette case with a lid that opened and shut. "Your replacements have arrived. Sappers of the two hundred and seventeenth engineering battalion."

"And what's going to happen to us?"

"Over to the other side. To front HQ, in the engineers' section."

Oh well, never mind. We handed over our responsibilities and in half an hour we were striding across the shaky planks of an emergency bridge thrown across the branch of the Volga to the island.

For some reason or other we embraced Geórgi Akímovich when we parted from him. He shook my hand tenaciously and, with his eyes blinking and his forehead wrinkled up, he said:

"I shall often recall the talks we had on these steps. I hope that all I tried to prove to you will never come about. We'll meet after the war and you'll say to me: "Well, who was right?" and I shall say: 'You were.'"

He accompanied us to the footpath that led along the red cliff edge right down to the Volga and for a long time he waved his cap with the button at us.

Another person had crossed our lives, had left the little mark by which he would be remembered and had disappeared. Probably for good.

Later we found ourselves sitting on the left bank, on an overturned, dried-up boat, looking at the smoking chimneys of the tractor plant—it never stopped working for a minute— and Shapiro was recounting how in July the factory had turned out thirty tanks a day and in August as many as fifty, that at the moment it was taken up exclusively with repairing damaged vehicles, and that some of the machinery had already been transferred to the Urals and that they were about to shift the rest if they could only manage to drive the Germans away from some place where there was either a bridge or a landing-stage.

We passed the night in a little cottage in a wood. The whole of the next day we spent searching for the forester's house— the reference point by which we could find the engineering section of the front.

There were so many headquarters and administrative offices —in every little wood and copse—that it was by no means easy to find the section we needed. Everywhere were sentries, barbed wire and signs saying "No Entry".

Nevertheless we found it towards evening. The section, that is, but not the little house. The little house had long ceased to exist. Only on the map was there a little black rectangle with a line jutting out from the side. The section consisted of four dug-outs. In one of them—it was so well camouflaged that we wandered around it for about ten minutes —sat a major with terribly thick glasses without frames and wearing a celluloid collar-band. He glanced quickly over the contents of the packet we had brought and at once brightened up: "Wonderful! Simply wonderful! I really didn't know what to do. Sit down, my friends. Or—no, we better go outside. There isn't room to turn round in here . . ."

It appeared that the captain from the engineering section of the sixty-second army had been just before us—" Didn't you meet him?" They were short of regimental engineers. The hundred and eighty-fourth division was to have made the crossing to-night, but in the morning, during the bombardment, the engineers and a company commander had been put out of action. And the divisions now in action were under establishment—with sergeants replacing regimental engineers. There was not a soul in the reserve. There had been so much trouble with the tractor plant that they had called for replacements on two occasions.

" In short—you're probably hungry? Go down to our mess—straight along this little path—get some supper there and come back here. I'll get the papers ready. You'll still have time to catch the division on this side."

After eating some rice pudding with jam we called on the major again. He was addressing envelopes in a fine, woman's handwriting, with elegantly curling tails to his g's.

" Which of you is Kérzhentsev?"

" I am."

" You'll be on your own. To the hundred and eighty-fourth. I advise you to join it here. At about eight o'clock they will be moving to the crossing from Burkóvsky. Otherwise to-morrow you will search the whole front and not find them." He held out an envelope for me, glued together out of a topographical map.

" Try to see the divisional engineer and then carry on to the regiment. Anyway, you'll know best . . ."

The rest received a general instruction to report to the engineering troops of the sixty-second army.

" It's on that side. Yesterday it was in the Bannoi ravine. It's moved somewhere else now. But somewhere in the same area. Just keep looking for it."

" But don't they need any more sappers in the hundred and eighty-fourth?" asked Igor. " You said the company commander had been put out of action."

The major looked at Igor through the thick lenses of his glasses, so that his eyes looked big and round, like a bird's.

" You are a senior lieutenant. We shall post you as an engineer. We are worst off of all for engineers now." And, scratching the bridge of his nose with his pencil, he added: " All of you, by the way, except the comrade who's posted to the hundred and eighty-fourth, would do well to wait here. Somebody is coming from the sixty-second to-night to fetch some spades and you could go with him. Meanwhile, make yourselves comfortable here under the trees."

We went out and sat under the aspen trees.

"Will you go on foot?" asked Igor.

"I'll go as far as a traffic control and look around."

"I'll see you on your way."

I took my leave of Shapiro, Pengaunis and Samóilenko. Sedykh gave my hand a long squeeze in his rough palm.

"We shall meet again, comrade lieutenant."

"We're bound to," I replied, with that extra cheerfulness that comes at such moments of parting. I would gladly have taken him into my company.

A few minutes later he caught up with us.

"Take my cigarette case, comrade lieutenant. You still didn't have time to finish yours. And mine's a good one— a double one."

He pressed into my hand a transparent yellow cigarette case of such dimensions that I wasn't even sure it would go into my pocket—it would take a good half pound of tobacco. Again he shook my hand. Then Valéga's and then mine again. I was sorry to be separated from him.

Without speaking we reached the traffic control.

"The hundred and eighty-fourth hasn't been through yet. Some sapper battalion went through just now, but apart from that there has been nothing but trucks," said the traffic controller, a man no longer young, with a thin, fair moustache, like a Tartar's, and big ears covered with dust.

We sat down on the body of a wrecked lorry and had a smoke. The sun had set but it was still light. In the west, over Stalingrad, the sky was quite red and it was difficult to say what caused it—the setting sun or the fires. Three black columns of smoke slowly weaved their way up into the air. Lower down they were slender, dense and black as soot. The higher they went the more they spread out, and at the top they ran together into one long unbroken cloud. It was flat and motionless and, although it was receiving ever fresh supplies of smoke, it got no wider and no denser. For more than a fortnight now it had been floating, quiet and motionless, over the town.

All around there were golden aspen trees on a black background—slender and delicate. Trucks were driving along the road. They would stop, ask how to get to the sixty-second crossing or the fisherman's hut, and carry on. The road was wide, much used and covered with little squares and triangles from tyre-treads. It was difficult to know where its edge was

85

and where it turned. There was a broken-down signpost that must have been standing once at the roadside. Now it was in the very middle and someone had already run over it. It had heeled over and the arm with the words " Stalingrad—6 km " was pointing straight into the sky.

" The road to paradise," said Valéga gloomily.

It appeared that he was not entirely without a sense of humour. I hadn't realised that.

The traffic controller came up to us. " Look at the cranes flying," he pointed with a dirty, crooked finger at the sky. " No war for them. Are you well off for tobacco, comrade commander?"

We gave him something to smoke and for a long time we followed the southward-flying triangle that looked just as if it had been embroidered in the sky. You could even hear the croaking of the cranes.

" Just like Junkers," said the man on traffic duty and spat; " it's unpleasant."

The same association had evidently struck all of us and we laughed.

" Are you going over there or coming back?" asked the traffic man, holding my hand to get a light.

" We're going."

He shook his head and drew a few times on his cigarette.

" Yeah . . . It's not much fun there, whatever you say." And he walked away.

There were wounded passing by. In ones and twos. Grey and covered with dust and with indifferent, tired faces. One sat down near us and asked whether we had anything to drink. Valéga passed him a flask of milk. He drank long and slowly. He was wounded in the chest. Through his torn tunic could be seen the dirty, bloodstained bandages over a chest that was bony and covered with black hairs.

" Well, what's it like there, at the front?"

" Lousy," he replied without emotion, with difficulty wiping his dried-up lips with a dirty, bloody hand. In his eyes, as grey as the rest of him, there was nothing but a terrible, deadly fatigue.

" Are they attacking hard?"

" They certainly are! Once you're there you can't lift your head."

He tried to get up, but started to cough—a pink foam appeared at his lips. He sat down again, breathing heavily. There was something croaking in his throat or his chest.

" There's nobody there. That's what's so rotten . . ."

"Who's in the town? They or we?"

"Who can tell where the town is! Everything's on fire. They bomb from morning till night . . . Let me have another sip, sonny."

Limply, even reluctantly, he pressed his lips to the neck of the flask and from the corners of his mouth ran a thin stream of milk made pink by blood. Then he stood up and walked away, dragging his feet with difficulty and leaning on a bent, knotted stick.

Three horsemen rode up to the man on duty.

I sent Valéga to find out whether they were from the division we wanted. He went and asked something, with his hand on the reins. He returned.

"They say that the eighty-fourth has gone straight to the crossing. They are not from there, but they have seen the troops."

The horsemen galloped off, raising a cloud of dust.

"Oh well, I'll go," said Igor.

"Well, off you go," I replied and stretched out my hand.

It seemed as though there were something else to be said, but nothing came.

"I am not going to say good-bye," said Igor.

"Neither am I."

We shook each other's hands.

"Cheerio, Valéga. Take good care of the lieutenant."

"Don't worry . . ."

"Well, I'm off."

"All the best, Igoreka."

"Oh . . . I think I've still got your penknife."

"Really?"

"I borrowed it from you yesterday when we were cutting bread." He rummaged in his pockets. "Here it is, got stuck in the lining."

Igor stretched his hand out with the knife—Valéga's loot, an expensive Solingen steel knife with two blades, a corkscrew, a file, a screwdriver and a whole bunch of other curious instruments.

"Well now, that's the lot. Cheerio."

"Cheerio."

And he went off with his usual easy, casual stride, his cap pushed to the back of his head and his hands stuffed in his pockets.

Was it really possible that I might never see him again?

XVIII

At the crossing it was, as usual, difficult to make out what
was going on. Horses, carts, guns with their fore-carriages,
and lorries reversing in the dark. And people. There were
more people than anything else—swearing, bumping into
each other, taking things from each other. Somebody had
driven into someone. Some boxes had been forgotten. They
were looking for somebody called Stétsenko. Others were
waiting for a launch and cursing it. It should have been there
long ago and it still didn't come . . .

Two divisions were being embarked at once—the one-
eighty-fourth and another one, the twenty-ninth, it seemed.

And in the midst of all this confusion I had to find some
div. engineer, or a divisional commander or the chief of
staff—hand over the envelope and await further instructions.
But there would not, in all probability, be any instructions.
Everybody was already so confused—they had to load the
guns and the supplies and the horses and they mustn't lose
the men, and what the devil do you want to get in the way for
when you can see what's going on!

I found an engineer, but not the right one; I found a
regimental commander, but also the wrong one—from the
twenty-ninth.

Somebody tugged at my sleeve.

"Listen friend, you don't have a lamp?"

"Yes I have."

"Show a light then, chum. I'm quite lost. They gave
me a map, but you can't see anything in pitch darkness . . ."

I could distinguish only a massive figure in a padded jacket,
with an automatic swinging at his chest.

"Let's get underneath the boat . . . Just for a couple of
minutes, that's all, honestly."

It was very cramped under the boat and it smelt of rotten
wood. I switched on my torch. It gave out a dim light—the
battery was coming to an end. The man turned out to have
a big, heavy face, with wide-set eyes and thick lips. He had
captain's tabs on his collar. With some difficulty he extracted
a map from a case which was bursting with papers and held
together by a rubber band.

"Just try and sort it out," he pointed with a dirty nail to a red, irregular triangle on the map. "They call this a map! A white square stands for a factory. What can you make out?" He swore long and colourfully.

"They were supposed to change the division. They said there would be a representative at the crossing. Like hell there was! Not a soul. Now try and find that triangle in the town. That's theirs—the division's HQ. No co-ordinates, not a damn thing."

I asked from what division he was. He turned out to be a battalion commander in the 1147 regiment, 184 division.

"Wasn't it your engineer who was killed to-day?"

"Yes, ours. Tsygéikin. What about it?"

"I've been sent to replace him."

"Well!" The heavy-faced captain seemed to brighten up. "That's very good. You can come with us. I've been left quite on my own. The commissar is in the field hospital and the chief of staff can't see a thing at night . . ."

We crept out from under the boat.

"Wait a minute. I'll just check the horses. You know what these NCO's are . . ."

He vanished, and it seemed as though he had dissolved in the crowd and the shouting. I looked for Valéga. He had found himself a spot alongside some boxes and was sleeping peacefully, with his legs drawn up so as not to be stepped on. His capacity to sleep in any circumstances was amazing. I sat down near him. A faint, relaxing freshness came up from the river. It smelt of fish and oil. Horses were stamping nearby, their harness clanking. Somewhere, now quite far away, people were still looking for Stétsenko.

The town was burning. Not just the town, but the whole shore, as far as the eye could see. It was something bigger than a fire you could ever see in town. This was probably the way the taiga burnt—for weeks and months, over tens and hundreds of kilometres. A crimson, swirling sky. The black outline of the burning city, looking as though it had been cut out by a fret-saw. Black and red. Nothing else. The black city and the red sky. And the Volga was red. "Like blood," the thought flashed through my mind.

There were practically no flames to be seen. Only in one place, lower down the stream, were some short, leaping tongues of fire. And opposite us were the oil tanks looking like paper cylinders, collapsed and distorted. And the flames from them were mighty protuberances leaping upwards and losing themselves in the heavy, slowly swirling clouds of leaded-red smoke.

In childhood I loved to look through an old English magazine of the time of the 1914 war. The beginning and the end were missing, but it had wonderful large pictures, covering a whole page: British Tommies in the trenches, attacks, sea battles—waves foaming and destroyers ramming each other; and Blériot, Marman and Taube soaring in the air in those funny-looking aeroplanes looking like hen-coops. It was hard to tear myself away.

But the most terrifying of all was an enormous picture, spread over the two centre pages, so depressing as to make me shudder, of Louvain burning after the German raids. In it were flames and columns of smoke like cotton wool, and people running and houses in ruins and searchlights in an ominous sky . . . It was so terrifying and fascinating that I just hadn't the strength to turn the page. Times without number I copied that picture, coloured it with coloured pencils, paints and small crayons and then hung the drawings around the walls. It seemed there could be nothing more terrifying or more majestic.

The picture hadn't been badly drawn. I could still recall every detail in it, every curl of swirling smoke—and it would suddenly become clear to me how powerless art was in certain circumstances. No columns of smoke, no tongues of flame and no ominous shades of light would suffice to convey the feeling I was experiencing at that very moment as I sat on the shore opposite burning Stalingrad.

There was a battle going on on the other bank. Bursts of tracer bullets from machine-guns and Sten guns sprayed along the very edge of the river. Surely the Germans hadn't got right to the waters? A few long bursts sailed across the Volga and lost themselves on this side.

Somewhere in the rear a " Katyúsha " was firing. The red-hot rockets sailed along, not hurrying, overtaking one another in air that trembled from the glow, and landing on the opposite bank. The bursts could not be seen. Only the flash was visible. And after that came the explosion.

Somebody next to me spat with evident pleasure and gave a little contented cough. It was only then that I noticed that there were troops lying stretched out nearby.

" Did you have time to shoe the gelding?" someone asked.

" Yes. What about you?"

" I managed to do Lyútik, but only the two forelegs of the black one. He's got a wound of some sort. Just won't let you touch him."

The battalion commander came up. He was breathing heavily.

" Honestly, these crossings could drive you silly. They put five years on your life." He blew his nose noisily. " The general was there. He was quite definite: we go first and then the twenty-ninth. I only went away for a minute and they had already piled their boxes on. They sent the artillery over but left their ammunition on this side. And what the devil made them do it? Now I always take the shells along with each gun. Oh Lord, there's that blighter again!"

The battalion commander disappeared once more. He could be heard swearing at someone. Then he returned.

" Oh well, all right . . . none of that matters. We'll get ourselves over to the other side somehow or other. What matters is how things are there . . ."

It turned out that the regiment had received orders to complete the crossing by 0200 hours and by 0400 to have replaced the practically non-existent division in the area of Metiz-Mamai Hill. It was then already one o'clock and not a single battalion had yet got across. On the other side there were only the sappers, the scouts and the operations group of the HQ. The regimental commander and the chief of staff were also there apparently. And most important, all the artillery—the forty-fives and seventy-sixes attached to the battalion—had to be drawn up to the front line to point-blank range by dawn.

" All right," I said, " you give me two companies and some anti-tank troops, while you take care of the artillery with one company. How many men have you got to a company?"

" About a hundred."

" Ample. That's agreed, then. Only give me the exact destination."

" Well, it's that blasted triangle on the map. Frankly speaking, I reckon there's nobody there by now. There were about a hundred men in that division, not more. They've been fighting on that bank for a fortnight already . . ."

And, with a noisy spit, he dashed off again to swear at somebody. He had the sort of voice that could probably be heard on the other side.

A launch came up. It was small and low, just as if it were hiding itself in the water so as not to be seen. On the end of the tow-line was a sprawling, clumsy barge with a long projecting rudder bar.

It took a long time for the launch to come alongside— it backed down, snorted and churned up the water with its propeller. Finally the gangways were put ashore. The wounded came off in a long, hesitant line. There were a lot of them. First the "walking", then those on stretchers. They were led off somewhere into the bushes. Lorries could be heard hooting their horns nearby.

Then the boxes were loaded. The guns were drawn up. Horses' hoofs clattered on the gangplanks. One of them fell off and was hauled out of the water and was again led on. Contrary to expectations, everything went quietly and efficiently.

By the time we cast off it was beginning to get light. A solid, indistinct mass of something behind us turned into the delicate lacework of an aspen. We stood jammed up close to one another. Someone was breathing garlic straight into my face. The smothered thumping of the engine could be heard under our feet. Someone was chewing sunflower seeds and noisily spitting out the husks. Valéga, his elbows leaning on his greatcoat thrown across the side, stared at the burning city.

"It's certainly pretty big," said somebody behind my back, "like Moscow."

"Not big, but long," somebody's boyish voice corrected him. "Fifty kilometres long. I was there before the war."

"Fifty?"

"Not a yard less, from Sarpéta to the tractor plant."

"Oho!"

"What does that mean?"

"Need a lot of troops to hold that. Ten or even fifteen divisions."

"Do you reckon there's less than that here? They're sending them over every night."

The launch skirted round a sharp projecting point, practically invisible in the darkness. A mortar shell sailed over us with a whistle. It landed behind in the water.

"Jerry doesn't like us coming over, wants to shove us in the water."

The boyish voice laughed:

"What else could he want? Of course he'd shove us in . . . Russky—plop, plop! . . ." Again everyone laughed.

"Jerry wants an awful lot," commented a third person, rather older, to judge by the voice. "But we just can't go any further. We've gone back to the limit, to the very edge of the country . . . How could we go any further

Somebody could be heard patting somebody else on the greatcoat.

"That's right, pa. That's the way we think in the navy. We just can't make up our minds to go swimming. The water's too damned cold . . . That right?"

And everyone laughed.

I tried to turn my head. It was very difficult—I was squashed in from both sides. Squinting sideways I could see only white patches that were faces and someone's ear. We were approaching the shore.

XIX

The launch just couldn't get close alongside the landing-stage. We jumped out straight into the muddy, cold water.

On the shore some boxes were being carted about. The whole shore was piled up with them. Chains and ropes were all mixed up under our feet. On the boxes and on the ground were the wounded, silent and sullen, huddling close to each other.

Near the water the shore was flat and sandy. Further on there was a high, practically vertical cliff. And above it all was the sky, red and full of smoke. There was shooting quite close, behind our backs it seemed. It started to get cold. I put my greatcoat on.

The battalion commander—his name turned out to be Klishéntsev—was shouting at someone who had not turned a gun properly.

"Now what the devil did you stick the gun-carriage out in front for? Don't you have any brains, you calf's head?"

The men splashed about in the water with their machine-guns and mortars and shells swinging about on their chests and backs. They were gathering in groups on the shore. Of course, they were having a smoke. Klishéntsev ran up to me. He was already quite hoarse.

"Take the fourth and fifth and get moving! I'll unload the guns. Then I'll come straight after you. Only send a runner, so as not to hang about doing nothing. I've got a chap called Sídorko—he'll find everything. Ask Farber, commander of the fifth company, for him," and, drawing me closer, he whispered in my ear: "They say there was nothing left of that division. Try and find our scouts. They're somewhere over there . . . And don't get mixed up in a fight without me . . ." He pressed a flask into my hand. "There you are —take a shot for the road."

The vodka caused a pleasant burning sensation in my throat, and ran down inside me in a hot stream.

The officers were gathering the men together. One was a lanky, stooping figure in glasses and a short greatcoat reaching to his knees. His name was Farber. He was obviously a man of some education: "Don't you see", "actually", "I am inclined to think", The other, Petróv, was thin, diminutive, quite a boy. This didn't give me much pleasure.

We went along the shore towards the town. Our feet sank into the sand. We crouched down when mortar shells whistled over. The men walked in silence, moving their feet with difficulty, breathing heavily and holding on to their swinging mortar shells. That day they had covered about forty-kilometres.

Coming towards us were lines of wounded—in twos and threes and singly. They were leaning on their rifles. They asked me where the crossing was.

Bullets whistled over our very heads and plopped into the water. Tracers shot high up and expended themselves in the air.

"Where are the Jerries?" the men asked the men coming towards them.

The latter pointed vaguely in the direction in which we were going:

"Not so far away . . . Nearer than home."

We passed some white structure. It must have been a pumping house: there were pipes coming out of it. Then the path led upwards. A gun was being carried down it by hand.

"Where are you going?" I asked.

"Who are you? Can't you see what we're doing? Should we leave it for the Germans?"

I took my revolver out.

"Turn back."

"Where?"

Someone in an unbuttoned great coat with his cap on the back of his head pushed me in the chest.

"What do you know! A hero! Don't take any notice, Katsúra. Carry on!"

I suddenly felt short of air and something gripped my throat.

Bullets were striking now right along the river bank.

Up above the path—from where we were could be seen only a level-crossing bar sticking up in the air, a tilted pole and rolls of broken-down wire—there appeared several figures.

Bracing themselves against the pole they fired and then rushed downwards.

Someone caught me with his shoulder and swore.

I turned and lashed out with all my might at a white face bounding in front of me.

"Go back!" I shouted at the top of my voice, so that my ears sang, and I ran up along the path.

The Germans, it appeared, were alongside us on the other side of the railway. The tracks went almost along the edge of the high bank. The columns of tank wagons halted there stood out against a background of something burning. From somewhere to the right, from under the wheels, our machine-gun was in action.

I scrambled beneath a truck. My greatcoat caught in something and split. It was a terrible nuisance, tangling with my legs and getting in my way. With my face pressed against the rail—which was pleasantly refreshing—I tried to see where the Germans were. At right angles to the railway was a street. It was cobbled and as straight as an arrow. To the left were oil tanks. Oil was streaming out of one of them. In a broken-down wall there were three great shell-holes with torn, twisted edges. Just like wounds.

To the right were burnt-out barns surrounded by barbed wire.

The Germans were apparently holding positions among the tanks—red, white and green flashes were coming out of there. The shots clattered against the tank wagons.

My brain worked incredibly clearly. They apparently had two machine-guns and, it seemed to me, hand ones. They had no mortars. That was fine. Farber ought to strike from the left, straight at the tanks. I should go along the road, around the tanks and approach from the right. The machine-guns were firing point-blank. We'd have to dash across the road and then along the stone wall.

Farber crawled away. He crawled awkwardly, on his side, leaning to the right.

A few bullets cracked against the tank just above our heads. A thin, curving stream of kerosene struck the rail in front of me and I felt a fine spray on my face. A rocket went up. It lit up the tanks, the barn and the stone wall. The shadows danced around, lengthening and shortening in an unnatural way. The rocket fell somewhere behind us. You could hear it hissing . . .

The moment had come . . . I stuck my fingers into my mouth —I had lost my whistle as far back as Kupyánsk. For some

95

reason it seemed to me that it was somebody else nearby who whistled.

I ran straight for the tank with the three holes. There was shouting from the right and the left. Sten guns rattled. Someone with the streaming ribbons of a sailor's cap ran ahead of me. I couldn't keep up with him. The tanks disappeared somewhere and I saw only ribbons. They were terribly long, probably down to the waist.

I also shouted something. Just "aaaaah", I think. For some reason it was easy and fun to be running. And there was a slight trembling in the stomach from the Sten gun. The joints of my index finger ached from pressing the trigger.

Again the tanks appeared, but different, smaller ones, with pipes twisting about like snakes. There were lots of pipes and you had to jump over them.

Behind the tanks were the Germans. They were running at us and also shouting. The black ribbons disappeared. In their place was a grey greatcoat and an open mouth. It also disappeared. A thumping started in my temples. My jaws ached for some reason.

The Germans were no more to be seen.

Ahead were some white gates with an iron grille. I decided to run as far as them, sit down and then go further . . . But I couldn't stop. The gates were already behind and ahead was an asphalt roadway and some buildings.

Then I lay on my stomach and found it impossible to push a fresh magazine into the gun. My hands were shaking. Something was jammed in the slot.

"Your gun's bust. Take this one."

It was Valéga, it seemed, but I had no time to turn round.

Through the netting—I was lying near a low stone wall with fine netting, as in a hen-house, drawn across it—Germans could again be seen running. There were a lot of them. They were running across the factory yard and firing from their black automatics, holding them to their stomachs, and it was like some frantic firework. Even in the daytime the Germans fired tracer bullets.

I let off a whole magazine, and then another. The fireworks vanished. It suddenly became quiet. I drank water from someone's flask and couldn't stop.

"Been eating salt herrings, comrade lieutenant?" asked the person holding the flask, who had a tuft of hair, and wore a striped vest and a sailor's cap.

I drank the water to the end. Never, it seemed, had I drunk water so tasty and so cold. I looked for Valéga. He was right there, filling the magazine. Bullets were lying on one side in a little golden heap. Next to him was a young fellow hastily puffing away at a home-made cigarette to finish it. He spat on it and trampled it into the ground.

In front was the smooth asphalted factory yard. Beyond it was a heap of iron, a locomotive with wrecked trucks and some kind of white structure that looked like a railway hut with a little balcony. Behind was another yard—big and empty.

It was a lousy place: nowhere to dig in, nowhere to hide —nothing but the wretched low wall with the netting.

We should have to take the little hut and the iron, that was clear. We couldn't hang on there. I passed the order to Farber and Petróv. They were also under the wall, to the right and the left of me. The fellow in the striped vest was stuffing capsules into the round grenades.

" That's right . . ." he winked a black, twinkling eye. " I know that little hut . . . It's a wonderful hut. And just the little cellar you need! "

" You've been in it?"

" Spent a whole night in it. Until the Jerries chucked us out. We got there of an evening. Recce. Looking for an HQ."

He stuffed one grenade in his pocket and another in his belt.

Farber made a sign that everything was ready on his side. A bit later Petróv did the same. From somewhere to the left the Germans started to fire machine-guns. That meant they had already dug in, the bastards. We'd have to hurry, before the others got to work.

The lad in the striped vest, crouching down as if for a race—one leg out behind and the other bent under him— watched me out of the corner of a tense, unblinking eye. On his left arm, just below the elbow, there was something tattooed—it looked like a name.

I gave the signal.

Something flashed—dark and sudden, causing a wind. The plaster started to fall from the wall. The netting shook as though it had been struck hard. The lad in the striped vest ran straight for the hut, waving his automatic. It was about sixty metres to the hut and the yard was absolutely flat.

And suddenly it was completely full of people, running, shouting, green, black and striped. The lad in the vest was already at the hut. He vanished into the doorway. The Germans were firing wildly. Then they stopped. You could see them running. It was easy to tell them by their full, unbelted greatcoats.

All this happened so quickly that I had no time to think. There was nothing at all around us. Valéga and I. And someone's cap on the grey asphalt.

We crept through the netting. I ran, doubled up, to the hut. In the middle of the yard were three or four dead. All face downwards. There were no faces to be seen.

Near the hut was a long trench which disappeared somewhere amidst the iron. We leapt into it. Someone was fishing in the pockets of a dead German.

"What do you think you're doing?"

Without standing up the soldier turned his head. Two little grey eyes in a pimply face loked at me with astonishment.

"What do you mean? I'm searching the Jerry."

He stuffed something into his pocket, hastily, getting mixed up with a chain. Obviously a watch.

"Quick march out of here! Don't let me catch . . ."

Someone tapped me on the shoulder.

"Listen, that's my scout, lieutenant. Take it a bit quieter . . ."

I spun round. It was a young man in a striped vest, with a cigarette in his mouth. His eyes were narrow and evil-looking. They shone out from under a fringe of hair.

"And who are you?"

"Me?" His eyes got even narrower, and the muscles twitched on his rough, sun-burnt cheeks.

"Commander of infantry reconnaissance. Chumák."

With an imperceptible movement of the lips he flicked the cigarette to the other corner of his mouth.

"Stop this business right away . . . Understand?"

I spoke slowly and unnaturally calmly.

"Get your men together and station sentries. Come and report in fifteen minutes. Is that clear?"

"And who are you, giving all the orders?"

"You heard what I said? I am a lieutenant and you are an NCO. That's all . . . And let there be no looting until I give permission."

He made no reply. He just stared. His face was narrow, his lips thin and tightly pressed together. A slanting fringe of hair fell right over his eyes. He stood, with his legs apart, his hands deep in his pockets, swaying gently to and fro.

We stood like that and looked at each other. Unless he turned at once and went off I would draw a revolver.

Tsik-tsik . . . Two bullets struck the wall of the trench

98

just between me and him. I dropped on my heels. One of the bullets spun round at my feet having hit something hard. Chumák didn't flicker an eyelid. His thin lips quivered and a mocking light came into his eyes.

" You didn't like that, lieutenant, did you?"

And, tipping his tiny cap right over his eyes with a lazy, habitual gesture, he turned and went, slowly and unhurriedly, swaying slightly from side to side. The seat of his pants was stretched tight and rather prominent.

Two soldiers were dragging a machine-gun along the trench. The trench was narrow and the gun just couldn't get through.

" Why the devil are you trying to get it through here! You're blocking the way!" I shouted at them, and it annoyed me that they said nothing and only blinked their eyes.

They stood up and pressed themselves against the wall to let me pass.

" Well, what are you standing there for? Drag it on."

They both immediately seized hold of a side-plate and tried to force the gun through further. I clambered over it and went along the trench.

" He's just like a dog let off the leash," I heard one of them say.

I turned to the right. Petróv was fussing about, shouting at the men, just couldn't get the machine-gun set up: for some reason it kept slipping down.

Petróv was still very young. He was obviously not long out of college. He had a very slender neck and very wide boots that were loose on his feet.

" Well, what do you think, is that all right, comrade lieutenant?" he asked, when he had pushed a box under the gun.

He looked at me with his questioning, intense blue eyes.

" All right, it'll do."

" My second one is over there beyond that corner. Do you want to have a look? The whole embankment can be seen from there."

We went across. There really was a good view: the Germans were behind the embankment. Helmets flashed from time to time.

I squatted down and wrote a report. The fourth and fifth companies and a platoon of scouts had taken up defensive positions on the western fringe of the " Metiz " factory. There were so many men and so much ammunition. I understated the latter figure somewhat, although it was in any case pretty unlikely that any ammunition would be sent up to-day.

Sídorko—the man Klishéntsev had recommended to me—
quick and slant-eyed like a little Chinese—had only just
managed to stuff the report into his cap when the Germans
started to attack.

Tanks appeared from somewhere. Six of them. They
crawled across from the right, from behind the embankment.
There appeared to be a bridge there which could not be seen
from our positions. But we had only four anti-tank guns and
a couple of dozen grenades. What had happened to the big
gun? I had quite forgotten about it. Surely they hadn't run
away again? All our hope now lay in the scrap-iron. Perhaps the tanks wouldn't be able to get over it?

Next to me was a sunburnt lad from an anti-tank unit,
with a ginger, curled-up moustache. He was obviously very
hot. One after the other he threw off all his clothes—padded
jacket, tunic and shirt. He finished up naked, showing an
unbelievably white and smooth back.

It was cramped and awkward in the trench. All the time
people were clambering over each other, jabbing their knees
and swearing.

The tanks came straight at us.

The worst of it was there was no telephone. It was
difficult to find out what was going on and where.

The tanks stopped near the iron and opened fire. The
shells landed behind us. They were probably blanks—no
bursts to be heard. From somewhere to the right could be
heard Chamák's voice, sharp and guttural. He was shouting
at someone called Ványushka to give him some anti-tank
grenades.

"In the cellar . . . In the corner . . . Where the kettle
is . . ."

One tank at any rate had got across the iron . . . its
tracks clattered. Rolling from side to side, it crept straight
towards us. The repulsive black cross could be clearly seen.
The half-naked anti-tank man took aim with his feet wide
apart and his rear braced against the wall of the trench. His
cap had fallen off, revealing on his head a white circle
untouched by the sun.

Would he put it out of action or not?

The cross came nearer and nearer . . .

Somebody was shouting right into my ear. I couldn't make
out a damned thing.

"What's that?"

100

"The Germans are outflanking us on the left. Their infantry has gone round to the left of the locomotive . . ."

"Why are the machine-guns silent? There are two over there, after all."

I ran along the trench. Petróv and someone else was at the machine-gun. It had stuck. The belt wouldn't go through.

"Why is the other machine-gun silent?"

The blue child-like eyes were near to tears.

"Honestly, I don't know. Five minutes ago . . ."

"Grenades! Let's have some grenades, then!"

Bullets were whistling straight over our heads.

I threw the grenades, one after the other. They were German, with long handles. I pulled the pins and hurled them through the breastworks. The Germans were already right up to the trenches. They shouted . . .

Why was the machine-gun not working?

"A-a-a-a-a-a!"

Something fell on me. I jumped aside and hurled a grenade with all my might. I had nothing else left in my hands. Something heavy slumped into the bottom of the trench. I threw four more grenades. That was the lot—there were no more. Where the devil could I find a Sten gun?

I tried to draw my revolver out of its holster, but the strap had got caught. It just wouldn't come out. Blast!

Then suddenly . . . quiet!

At my feet there was somebody in a grey greatcoat. His face was buried in a corner of the trench. In front of the trenches there was no one. Had we really beaten them off?

I ran back along the trench. The men were clearing their bolts. Petróv was at the machine-gun.

"It's all right now, comrade lieutenant. It's working!"

The blue eyes were now smiling happily, like a child's.

"Did you see how they cut them off? They scuttled off pretty quickly . . ."

He turned back to the gun and gave a burst. His neck shook. How slender it was. And the deep hollow behind it and the loose collar . . .

That was how he had probably looked not very long ago, standing at the blackboard, not knowing the answers, his blue eyes blinking.

"But why doesn't this one work? It seems to me this is also your business."

The blue eyes dropped in embarrassment.

"I'll look into it right away, comrade lieutenant . . ."

101

Leaning on the barrel of the gun he lifted himself up. His hands were so slender, a child's hands with freckles.

"It seems to me . . ."

His eyes suddenly froze, as though he had seen something unusually interesting and he sank slowly sideways to the ground.

We hadn't even heard the shot. The bullet had hit him right in the forehead, between the eyes.

They dragged him away. His feet—so small in the big, loose boots—dragged helplessly along the ground. Someone else was already at the machine-gun. His neck was thick and red. I put the political officer in command of the company and went off to the white hut.

The Germans were silent, apparently getting ready for the next attack.

There were lots of dead in the trench. They were now getting in the way of the survivors. They were moved into a side trench. Two men, bent over, were carrying someone. I stood aside. The smooth white arms with hands so sunburnt that they looked like gloves dragged along the ground. The face was not visible. He was covered in blood. The head hung loose. On the back of his head was a white circle from his cap. I recognised the anti-tank man with the moustache. They laid him in the trench too, on top of someone in blood-stained trousers with an aluminium spoon sticking out of his puttees.

I didn't have time to get to the white hut. The Germans attacked again. We beat them off . . . Then later . . . again they came.

So it went on until lunch time. Twenty or thirty minutes' peace—time to have a smoke, load the guns, stuff a bit of bread into your mouth—and again the grey figures, the shouting, the crackle of guns, the confusion . . .

On one occasion some Heinkels bombed us from high in the skies—we didn't even notice them. But the bombs fell on the Germans. The men laughed.

Sídorko was still not back. Nor were the other two sent later. Maybe they had got caught in a raid. The drone of engines in the air never stopped for a minute. From a high point you could see a white cloud spreading out along the bank.

After our midday meal our artillery began to fire from somewhere. It was aiming at the embankment. A few stray shells fell in our own trenches. The Germans did not withdraw. But the tanks did not get through. The one with

102

the cross remained stuck on the iron, out of action. The mortars dominated the situation. We had a lot of dead and wounded. The "lightlys" we sent off to the shore. The "badlys" we carried into the cellar of the hut which was quite roomy and had a reinforced concrete roof.

Towards nine o'clock the Germans seemed to get tired. By ten everything was quiet. Only now and again a machine-gun would splutter.

XX

The cellar was unbearably full of smoke. It floated in layers. A wick smoked in a saucer. The wounded—the whole cellar was crammed with them—were begging for water. There was no water. It had to be fetched from the Volga and on the way back it got drunk up.

Valéga gave me a piece of bread and lard. I ate it without the slightest relish.

Chumák came in with his vest torn and quite dishevelled. On his muscular and sunburnt chest was tattooed a blue eagle with a woman in its claws. Beneath his left nipple was a heart pierced by a dagger, and on his shoulder a skull and crossbones. Below his elbow was a small hole right through his arm with practically no bleeding. The bone was apparently untouched and he could use his hand. His wound was being dressed by Marúsya, the nurse—whose cheeks were so very red and broad and who had two yellow plaits tied back behind.

That day the scouts had knocked out two tanks. One had been accounted for by Chumák, the other by that same pimply scout over whom we had quarrelled.

I asked him why he had made no report about anything.

"What is there to report about?"

"About to-day. About the losses. That's the way things are done in the army—always report after a battle."

Chumák turned slowly round. I could not see his face. His back, with a deep hollow down the backbone, glistened with sweat.

"The day—as you saw yourself—was sunny, and as for losses—well, what losses? I lost my cap, that's all. Will there be any further questions?"

"There will be, only not here. Let's go outside for a minute."

103

"There are bullets there. Might get killed."

I swallowed this pill and went towards the exit. So did he. Leaning his shoulder against the door-post he chewed on a cigarette.

"Do you know what comrade lieutenant? Let's take it easy. Don't interfere with the scouts. It'll be much better, honestly."

"Better or worse, that's another question. How many men have you got?"

"Twenty-four. We've still got as many as we ever had. But I advise you to leave the scouts . . ."

"Who knocked out the tank?"

"Whoever knocked it out—isn't it all the same?"

"Did you do it?"

"Well, I did . . . It wasn't you, anyway . . ."

"Tell me how you put it out of action."

"Honestly, I want to sleep. We'll talk about tanks after the war . . ."

"I advise you to keep in mind that I am now acting for the battalion commander."

"How do I know that?"

"I'm telling you now."

"The div. commander in Klishéntsev. Apart from that I take orders only from the regimental commander and the chief of intelligence."

"They are not here now, and for that reason you have to take orders from me. I am deputy-regimental commander on the engineering side."

Chumák glanced sidelong at me with a keen eye.

"In place of Tsygéikin, do you mean?"

"Yes, in place of Tsygéikin."

A pause. He spat between his teeth.

"Well, we are usually on the very best of terms with the sappers."

"I hope that's the way it'll be in future."

"I hope so."

"What's the name of the other one who knocked out a tank?"

"Korf."

"Private?"

"Private."

"Was that his first tank?"

"No, his fourth. First three at Kastórnaya."

"Decorated?"

"No."

"Why?"

"Goodness knows why. We made a report . . ."

"You'll let me have a fresh report in an hour. About him and about the others as well. Understand?"

With that the conversation came to an end. It was conducted in the most restrained tones.

"May I go, comrade deputy-regimental commander on the engineering side?"

I made no reply and went below again. My whole body ached. My eyes were burning. Probably from the smoke—it was certainly terribly smoky.

I drew up a report. Nearby, with his head on his arm, Farber was asleep. He had dropped in for a minute for some tobacco and to report on casualties. And he fell asleep on the spot, over his opened cigarette case with an unfinished cigarette in his mouth. In the corner someone was talking quietly, puffing on a cigarette. Only odd sentences reached me:

"Just at that moment mine got stuck . . . Had to bash it out with my heel. I asked Pavlénko for ammunition . . . But he was lying with his face to the ground and a kind of grey stuff running from his head."

Then suddenly Igor appeared. He stood in front of me and laughed. His moustache was no longer thin but like an anti-tank man's—dashingly curled up at the corners of his mouth. I asked him how he had got to us. He made no reply but only laughed. On his chest too was a blue eagle with a woman in its claws. Right on his tunic. The eagle's eyes were screwed up and it was also laughing. It had to stop laughing. I must rip it off the tunic. I reached out with my hand but someone held me by the shoulders. Held me and shook me.

"Lieutenant . . . Hey, lieutenant . . ."

I opened my eyes.

An unshaven face. Grey, cold eyes. A straight, bony nose. Hair brushed back under the cap. The most ordinary tired face. The eyes too cold.

"Wake up, lieutenant, you'll burn your hair."

The plate with a wick next to my head was smoking unbearably.

"What do you want?"

The man with the grey eyes took off his cap and put it down on the table.

"My name is Abrósimov. I am regimental chief of staff."

I stood up.

" Sit down." He became less official. " You are lieutenant Kérzhentsev? The new engineer—in place of Tsygéikin, as I gathered from your report."

" Yes."

He ran his hand over his face and eyes and stared for some time without blinking at the smoking wick. You could tell that, just like us, he was deadly tired.

I reported on the situation. He listened attentively, without interrupting, scratching the board of the table with his nail.

" Petróv, you say, was killed, then?"

" Yes. Must have been a sniper. Right in the forehead."

" So . . ." He bit his upper lip with his bottom teeth.

" Losses on the whole are pretty considerable. Twenty-five dead. Around fifty wounded. One machine-gun's out of action. Shrapnel hit the barrel."

" Who've you got alongside?"

" On the left the second battalion of our regiment. And on the right . . ."

I stopped to think. Farber had told me, but it had gone out of my mind.

" The forty-fifth are on the right, comrade captain," Chumák interjected. He was standing near with his hands stuffed into his pockets. " A representative of theirs came over. We are in touch with them."

" The forty-fifth . . ." said Abrósimov thoughtfully, and stood up, buttoning up his tunic.

" All right, then, Kérzhentsev . . . We'll go along the defences and then . . . then you'll have to take over the battalion."

He stared at me, as though weighing me up. He did up his buttons. They were big and wouldn't go through the button-holes.

" Klishéntsev, the battalion commander, has been killed. By a bomb. A direct hit. You'll have to command the battalion for the time being. Nothing else for it."

Then—turning towards Chumák:

" The anti-gas officer had a leg blown off. He's been taken over the other side. Well, come on, engineer. Battalion commander, rather . . ."

It was only as we went outside that I noticed that there were signallers busy in the corners—two of them, with little gold stars, cut out of tins, in their caps. We climbed out of the hut. There was a sentry at the entrance. I knew him already.

His name was Kalábin. He had a big birthmark on his cheek. He was a good marksman. I had seen him kill four before my very eyes. He was from Kostromá and at home his wife was expecting a baby.

It was cold outside. I filled my lungs with the fresh night air. The sky was clear and starry. The Great Bear was above Mamai Hill. Somewhere overhead was the monotonous drone of a " corn-cob ", like a motorcycle. It seemed to stay in one place. If you looked hard you could distinguish its outline. It was flying in the direction of Mamai Hill. To the right, probably over the " Red October " factory, there were rockets in the sky—about a dozen. They spilt a golden rain of sparks. There was no shooting. It was absolutely quiet.

We went along the trench. Figures huddled in greatcoats. Rifles on the breastworks. The " corn-cob " was already dropping its bombs somewhere beyond Mamai Hill, you could see the flashes. German searchlights were peering into the sky. The wrecked tanks—we had set fire to three of them in one day—were still burning, and an offensive, pungent smoke was drifting over our trenches. The wind was blowing our way.

I took leave of the captain on our left flank by a hole in the wall. Beyond that was the second battalion.

" Well, watch out, comrade, don't let us down! It'll be real hell again to-morrow . . . We'll send some ammunition. And by morning there'll be some big guns. It's a bit more fun with them, after all."

He went off with his orderly in the direction of the half-ruined factory building. That, it seemed, was our neighbour's HQ.

For some time they could be seen hopping over the bits of iron. Then they were hidden.

Leaning against the breastworks I looked in the direction of the Germans. It was quiet and dark. Only in one place was there something resembling a light. It flared up and went out. Some careless scout. Smoking. Or maybe it was something smouldering . . .

To-morrow, hell would break loose again. Planes and shouting and gunfire.

At any rate we had held out to-day. Only in one place had the Germans pushed us back a bit—near Farber, on our extreme right flank. About forty metres. I should have to transfer over there that hook-nosed lieutenant with his

107

platoon. Rámov, was that his name? He seemed to be a real fighter. I was pleased with him to-day. At about three o'clock we would counter-attack.

I went down to the cellar.

There was a different sentry at the cabin—a small chap with a ground-sheet dragging on the ground. I didn't know him.

The signallers were swearing into the telephone:

"Hello, Marble! This is Granite. How do you hear me? Marble, Marble! The bastard, gone to have another smoke. Hello! Marble. Marble."

There was yellow straw in the corner. Valéga had been busy, of course. I would flop down right away. Two hours— for two whole hours I would sleep . . . Like a dead man.

"Wake me at two, Valéga. At quarter past two . . ."

I heard no reply. Huddled up against someone's soft sweaty stomach, I was already asleep.

PART TWO

I

I could not remember having experienced such an autumn. September passed, with warm days and clear blue skies, enchanting mornings and dreamy, violet sunsets. In the mornings the fish would rise in the Volga and great circles would spread out over the mirror-like surface of the river. High in the sky some belated cranes would fly past croaking. The left bank, green at first, would turn to yellow and then to reddish-gold. At dawn, before our guns fired their first salvoes, the bank would be softly tinted, like a water-colour.

Slowly and reluctantly the mist would disperse. It would remain suspended for a while, a white shroud just above the river, and then it would vanish, dissolving into the translucent morning air.

And long before the early rays of the sun appeared the first heavy guns would open fire. The echo would be carried backwards and forwards across the awakening Volga. Then would follow the second and the third and the fourth salvoes, until finally they would all run together into the single majestic roar of the morning bombardment.

That was how the day began. At the same time . . .

Exactly at seven o'clock, so terribly high that you couldn't spot it at once with the naked eye, appeared the " crate ". With the slanting rays of the morning sun flashing on the windows of its cockpit as it turned, it would circle above us long and persistently. It would drone away insistently with the peculiar intermittent sound of its engine and then, slowly, just like some fantastic double-tailed fish, fly away towards the west.

That was the introduction.

After him would come the " songsters ". The " songsters " or " musicians " as we called them, " Stukas " in German, were rednosed and web-footed, looking like birds about to seize something. They would fly over somehow sideways in a slanting line, among the cotton-wool puffs of anti-aircraft shells.

With our eyes hardly open and coughing from the morning cigarette, we would scramble out of our dug-outs and screw up our eyes to follow the course of the first ten. They determined the course of the whole day. According to them we would know which square was on the Germans' list to-day, where the ground was going to tremble, whether the sun would be visible for smoke and dust, and on which section we should spend the whole night digging out and again interring the dead, repairing damaged machine-guns and digging fresh trenches and dug-outs.

When the formation flew right over our heads we breathed more freely, took off our shirts and poured water over each other's hands out of mess-tins.

But when, before it reached us, the first one dropped over on its right wing, we would take cover in a trench, curse and look at our watches—Good Lord, still another fourteen whole hours till evening!—and, squinting our eyes, we would count the bombs whistling over our heads. We knew already that each of the " songsters " carried under its belly from eleven to eighteen of them, that they wouldn't drop them all at once, but would make another two or three runs, carefully judging the psychological effect of the dose, and that on the final run their sirens would scream in a specially terrifying way, but that only one would drop bombs . . . And maybe he wouldn't even drop any, but would simply wave his fist menacingly.

So it would continue the whole day long until the sun went down behind Mamai Hill. If they weren't bombing, they would be coming in to attack . . . And if they weren't attacking, they were bombing.

From time to time the heavy Junkers and Heinkels flew over. You could distinguish them by their wings and engines. The Heinkels had rounded wings, while the Junkers were short and the engines and fuselage were in one line.

They flew very high, in V formation. And they dropped their bombs, shiny and heavy, lazily, irregularly, without going into a dive. That was why we didn't like them, those Junkers: you never knew where they'd drop their bombs. And they always flew in from the direction of the sun, so as to dazzle you.

All day long Messerschmitts would buzz in the air, roving along the shore in pairs, and firing their cannons. Sometimes they would each drop four nice little bombs—two from under each wing—or long, cigar-shaped boxes with their " rattles " —anti-infantry grenades. The grenades would be scattered around, but the boxes would tumble over and over in the sky for a long time. We used to do our washing in them afterwards. The two halves were just like troughs.

In the mornings, with the first rays of the sun, our " Ilyushin "—dive-bombers—would pass over with a furious scream—and would return almost immediately, full of holes, without their tails and practically touching us with their wheels. Half of them, and sometimes less, would return. The Messerschmitts would go on circling over the Volga for a long time, while somewhere far away, beyond Akhtuba, would rise the sad black mushroom of a burning aeroplane.

Straining our heads back against our backbones until it hurt we followed the course of the air battles. I could never make out which were our chaps and which the Germans: small and black they twisted and turned like mad things high in the sky . . . Valéga was the only one who never made a mistake—he had the keen eye of the hunter—he could tell a MIG from a Messerschmitt at any height.

Meanwhile each day was more beautiful than the last—blue, cloudless, the most summery days you could imagine. If only a cloud had appeared, if only there had been a shower of rain! We hated those clear sunny days, with the air motionless and blue. We longed for mud and clouds and rain and the dull skies of autumn. But throughout September and October we only once saw a cloud. It produced a lot of talk: with a moistened finger in the air we guessed in which direction it was going, but the damned thing passed us by and the next day was just as clear and sunny and full of aeroplanes as before.

Only once—at the beginning of October—did the Germans give us a break—two days: they must have been cleaning up their equipment. Apart from the Messerschmitts there were no aeroplanes. In those two days we bathed the troops in the troughs and changed underwear. Then it started all over again.

The Germans were straining to get to the Volga. Drunken, wild, with their caps on one side and their sleeves rolled up. It was said that facing us we had SS troops—the " Viking " or the " Skull " or something even more terrible. They shouted like men possessed, sprayed us with showers of automatic fire, withdrew and then came in again.

Twice they nearly drove us out of the " Metiz ", but their tanks got mixed up in the scrap-iron scattered around the factory, and that saved us . . .

So it went on . . . the devil knows how long . . . five, six, seven, maybe even eight days.

Then, suddenly, stop. Quiet. They had switched over to the right—to the " Red October " plant. They battered it from the air and from the ground. Meanwhile we watched, poking our heads out from the trenches. There was nothing but splinters flying. But the splinters were ten-ton iron beams, girders, benches, machines, boilers. For three days the cloud of dust over the plant didn't move. When a wind blew from the north the cloud descended on us, and then we chased all the men out of the dug-outs, because the German front line was not visible and they, the bastards, might strike on the sly.

But on the whole it was quiet, except for the mortars at work and our artillery firing from the other bank. And we sat in our dug-outs, smoking, cursing the Germans, aeroplanes and the people who invented them. " I'd stick those inventors, the Wrights, in the next trench to us—it'd be interesting to see what they'd do." Then we would guess when the last chimney at the "Red October" would fall. Two days previously there had been six, the day before three, to-day only one remained—full of holes and with the top knocked off. It just went on standing and did not fall, as if to spite everybody.

Thus September passed and it was October.

II

I was summoned on the telephone from "Marble" to the "thirty-first"—the commander of the regiment, Major Borodín. I had not yet met him. He was down on the shore, where the HQ was. During the landing he had had his foot crushed by a gun and he'd not yet been up to the front line.

I knew only that he had a rich, deep voice and that for some reason he called the Germans, Turks. "Hold on, Kérzhentsev, hold on," he would boom into the telephone. "Don't let the Turks get the factory, do your utmost, but don't give it up." And I exerted every possible effort and just kept holding on. At times I myself didn't understand why I still held on—with each passing day the number of men got less and less.

But that was now behind me. For the third day we were resting. We even took our boots off at night . . . But was it for long?

Not that there was much point in guessing. I got hold of Valéga and set off for the shore.

The major was living in a tiny dug-out like a hen-house, half destroyed by the wind. He was no longer young; he was grey at the temples and had a kindly, fatherly appearance. On one foot he wore a boot, on the other a galosh. He was drinking tea and eating bread and garlic. He kept quietly clearing his throat. The sort of man who likes children. And the sort that children like. And children get in their way and pester them and make them rock them on their knees.

The major listened to me attentively, noisily sipping his tea from a big coloured mug. With his good foot he pushed away a chair standing nearby. He extended a soft hand. "So that's what you look like. For some reason I thought of you as big and broad." His voice was by no means as booming and heavy as on the telephone. "Want some tea?"

I accepted—it was a long time since I'd drunk real tea.

His orderly brought in a teapot and a cup, just as big and brightly coloured as the major's. With a pocket knife he cut a slice of lemon. My mouth began to water. The major winked with a small, deeply set eye.

"You see how we live. Not like you at the front line. We can even offer you a bit of lemon."

For some time we drank tea in silence, crunching the sugar. Then the major turned his mug upside down, put a tiny lump of sugar on it, moved it to one side and carefully brushed the crumbs from the table.

"Well, how are you getting on there? Eh, commander?"

"Oh, not so bad, comrade major, we've hung on so far . . ."

"So far?"

"So far."

"And how far do you think 'so far' will stretch?" His voice now had a somewhat different intonation, not entirely fatherly.

"So long as there are men and ammunition, I think we shall hold on."

"'Think' and 'so far' . . . These are unpleasant words. Not military . . . Do you know about the bird that thought a lot?"

"A turkey, wasn't it?"

"Precisely, a turkey." He laughed with the corners of his eyes. "Do you smoke? Have one. They're good. 'Guards' I think they're called."

He drew a packet lying on the table towards him and studied the design. Beneath a red, slanting inscription were red

113

soldiers in helmets running, with red tanks behind them and red aeroplanes above their heads.

"That's the way you go into the attack, eh?"

"We do more beating off than going into attacks, comrade major."

The major smiled. Then his face became suddenly serious and his soft, slightly flabby lips turned hard and thin.

"How many bayonets have you got?"

"Thirty-six."

"The men are fit?"

"Yes, they are fit. Apart from that there are signallers, runners, a pioneer platoon on the shore and six men on the other bank with the horses. That makes altogether about fifty. Well, then there's the mortar men. There'll be about seventy men altogether."

"Thirty-six and seventy. It works out neatly. Half and half . . . It's not good."

"I agree, it's not good. I've already tried to attach those six to myself and hand the horses over to the field hospital, but your assistant wouldn't allow it—they had to go for hay, he said."

The major bit the mouthpiece of his pipe. His pipe was big, twisted and much chewed on.

"You're an engineer by education, aren't you?"

"An architect."

"An architect . . . All sorts of palaces and museums and theatres, I suppose. Is that it?"

"Yes."

"All right, you can build me a palace. Our sapper is Lisagór . . . You don't know him yet? I'll introduce you . . . He had almost finished building one palace when Chúikov,[1] the commander-in-chief, took it over. So I live in this hole and after every bomb I hook the dirt out of the back of my collar." The major smiled again, the wrinkles gathering round his eyes. "Well, and you understand mines and similar barbed-wire entanglements and so forth, of course?"

"I do."

"That's what you are going to be dealing with now. When the battalion commanders come we'll talk about it. Meanwhile have a smoke." He flicked a packet across to me. "I've already asked for a battalion commander in your place, but they haven't sent anybody. And being without an engineer is like being without hands. Lisagór's a good lad,

[1] Chúikov, Vasili Ivanovich, now Marshal of the Soviet Union; then Commander of 62nd Army.

114

but he doesn't understand anything about sketches and diagrams. There are some like that . . ."

Bombs were exploding somewhere. The sound could scarcely be heard, but there was an unpleasant pressure in the ears and the flame in the lamp flickered alarmingly.

Then the battalion and other commanders arrived.

The conference didn't last long—twenty minutes, not more. Borodín spoke. We listened and studied the map.

It appeared that our division's sector was the widest—a kilometre and a half deep. To the left of us was a narrow strip right along the shore—the thirtieth guards, Rodímtsev's. It stretched along almost to the town, as far as the wharves— a narrow, twisting ribbon of land not more than two hundred metres wide. To the right, at the " Red October ", were the thirty-ninth guards and the forty-fifth. That meant it was they who were now getting it. The red line of the front went right through the white patch that marked the factory on the map. To the right there were another two or three divisions. And that was the end. That was the lot. All that was left on this bank was five or six kilometres by one and a half, and the one and a half was only in the very widest place. In the centre of the town were Germans. The tractor plant wasn't shown on the map, but they said that one of our divisions was still clinging on there somewhere. The Gorókhov division, apparently.

The ninety-second brigade was due to cross that night. They had already fought at Stalingrad. Now they were returning after a ten-day re-formation. Their place was between us and Rodímtsev. We should have to squeeze up a little towards the right and compress ourselves a bit. That wasn't a bad thing.

But I was going to have to say good-bye to the " Metiz " factory. The third battalion was going to be there. I was given the sector between " Metiz " and the eastern end of the winding cliff at Mamai. The lousiest sector of all. It was flat and practically without trenches. All the approaches were under fire. In the daytime there could be no talk whatever of contact with the shore. On my old sector the approaches were also under fire, but there had been lots of trenches and all sorts of storage tanks and buildings. That certainly made contact easier.

Yes, Kandídi, the commander of the first battalion, was in luck. He was taking over prepared positions. But I . . . The devil only knew where to choose a place even for a

115

command point. There was nothing like our nice white hut with its cellar.

The major spoke slowly, unexcitedly, even a little peevishly. He never let his pipe out of his mouth. He drew his thumb across the map.

"The task is simple—dig yourselves in, surround yourselves with wire and mines and hold on. One month, two, three— until you're told what to do next. Is that clear? We don't have the strength to occupy Mamai Hill completely. But what we hold now we mustn't give up."

The major turned away from the map and directed his small, deep-sunken eyes at me.

"You've got the most difficult of all, Kérzhentsev. The foundation of the salient is in your hands. The other side is with the forty-fifth regiment. The Germans will press hard in both these spots, to try and cut off the first battalion and at the same time two battalions of the forty-fifth. They are also on Mamai. Meanwhile, there'll be no more men. Count on what there are now. Any reinforcement will be only patchwork. In any case the reinforcements will be boys."

He took his pipe out of his mouth, spat on the ground and put his foot on it.

"How many experienced men have you got left, Kerzhént-sev?"

"About fifteen, not more. About ten of them are sailors."

"That's not bad. Sinítsyn and Kandídi haven't even that. That's our skeleton. Take care. Don't get them killed for nothing. Have you got spades?"

We were in a bad way for spades. When it set off after being formed, the division didn't have time to draw its engineering equipment. And the tools it had picked up in the villages on the way were rusty and rotten—they broke up in the first couple of days. There were no pickaxes at all. We were waiting every day for the arrival of a mobile engineering stores, but it had got stuck somewhere on the other bank, and we dug away with old things we found among the ruins.

"They promise to deliver some mines to-day, comrade major." An unshaven lieutenant, with his padded jacket unbuttoned, got up from the corner. "I spoke yesterday to the head of the army stores. They'll let us have about a thousand anti-personnel mines. But there won't be any anti-tank mines in less than a week."

The major dismissed this with a gesture: I know, he seemed to say, sit down.

"Concentrate on the trenches for the moment. So long as there are no sappers' spades, try to manage with infantry ones. You, Sinítsyn, have got more than the others—and as I recall, your sector's easier. Give half to Kérzhentsev. And you, Lisagór," a lieutenant in a padded jacket drew himself up, "will submit a plan of defence works by this evening—Kérzentsev will help." Then to me: "In a few days I shall be after you."

The major stood up and indicated by so doing that there was nothing further for us to hang around for: and they had smoked so much you could hardly breathe.

III

On the shore Lisagór came up to me.

"Allow me to introduce myself—Lieutenant Lisagór, commander of the sapper platoon of the 1,147 rifle regiment of the hundred and eighty-fourth rifle division."

His voice was ringing, accustomed to making reports. He saluted in accordance with all the rules—fingers together, forearm and palm in a straight line, and a violent movement downwards. His face was a little rough and unshaven. His eyes were intelligent with some cunning in them. He was thickset and strong. From his appearance he was about thirty.

"Are you interested in my construction work? It's a real bit of Metro building. This is the fifth day we've been hacking away."

He took me by the arm.

About twenty yards from the major's dug-out the sappers were digging a tunnel into the steep Volga cliff—a long one, of about ten metres. In the shape of a letter T.

"On the right for the major, on the left for the chief of staff," Lasagór explained. "Three by four—can you imagine? And there, to the left, will be another one—for the operations group and the commissar. But we've only eighteen men. Including the sergeants. And it's got to be ready the day after to-morrow. What do you think of that?"

Soldiers were hacking at the earth which was as hard as stone. Two would dig away while two others carted the earth away in buckets and two more fixed the timbers. A lamp stood on the ground. There was a smell of smoke and damp earth.

117

Lisagór squatted down and leant back against a wooden buttress. He lit up a cigarette.

"We had already dug one like this. We finished it off with boards. And we put a stove in the corner. That chap over there with the moustache, my assistant platoon commander, made it all with his own hands: the stove and the pipes. He's a jack of all trades. They got hold of a two-litre lamp with a green shade. The major had already indicated where he wanted his bed put. But Chúikov came along, sat on a chair and inquired how much earth there was above—there's about twelve metres of it—and the major had to say good-bye to his quarters and the sappers had to start all over again. That's the way it is in a war, comrade lieutenant. Meanwhile, we're terribly short of men."

"And I was also going to beg of you—perhaps five men."

Lisagór was at once on his guard.

"What for?"

"You heard what the major said just now about mines?"

"Let the divisional people deal with that. That's what they're there for. Our business is command posts and observation posts. There's a hundred of them and only eighteen of us. As it is, the men don't sleep for days on end. And you know very well when those mines will arrive."

"You said yourself that they'd offered a thousand."

"All right, so I did . . . One says lots of things. That's what the quartermaster is for—to tell lies. Surely you know that?"

"All right. Let's not argue. Fix me up with five men by to-morrow night—your own or someone else's—I'm not interested in anything else."

Lisagór breathed hard and jabbed at the ground between his feet with his knife.

"It's always like this—fix this, do that, by to-morrow morning, by this evening. But how and with what men nobody asks. I can't give birth to a battalion in the night. You can see how the men are sweating."

I stood up.

"Oh well, I shall have to report to the major that the sappers are working on the dug-outs and there's nobody to strengthen the defences."

Lisagór also stood up.

"You *are* a stubborn one . . . All right, don't go. I'll send the men. But they'll have nothing to do there. You've still got another couple of weeks to dig trenches."

" Trenches are trenches and mines are mines. To-morrow evening I'll send the men along."

" What for? The mines?"

" What else?"

Lisagór did not reply. Bending down, he scrambled out of the tunnel.

" Let's get some air while there are no Jerries about."

The sun dazzled us. On the shore it was just like an ant-heap. Everybody was hauling or digging or building something. Smoke was coming from field kitchens built against the cliff, washing was hung out to dry. Copper mountains of shells with red, blue and yellow heads shone in the sun. There were ammunition boxes. Sacks. More boxes. A twisted gun without its barrel. A wrecked " Katyúsha ". The swollen carcase of a horse smothered with flies. The hind legs had already been cut off.

To the left was a half-submerged barge. Only the bulwarks were sticking out. On these, like roasting hens, four soldiers were washing their shirts. They were laughing noisily and happily, splashing each other, their backs gleaming.

The sky was blue, dazzlingly blue, without a single cloud. And a tiny little snow-white church with a green, sharply-pointed dome peeped out from the gold of the aspen wood on the other bank. There were a lot of people over there too. They were fussing about on a beach that was white from the sun. From time to time luxuriant bouquets would spread out silently from exploding mines. Later the sound would reach us. People would scatter. Then, after waiting a few minutes, they would again creep out and again get busy.

A small boat, just like a water bug, was floundering about near the shore. There was a strong current that carried it to the right. The oars flashed terribly quickly.

" Now they'll start to shoot at it," said Lisagór, taking an old tooth-powder box from his pocket. He rolled himself a cigarette.

In a couple of minutes a white fountain shot up not far from the boat.

" What mugs they are—trying to get straight across," said Lisagór, carefully licking his cigarette and tipping the tobacco into it from his palm. " They're only tiring themselves out and making the Germans' job easier. They should go with the stream, then the Germans would have to adjust their aim all the time."

" To go with the stream would mean fetching up with the Jerries," said someone behind my back.

The sappers leant on their spades and also watched the boat.

There were more and more fountains. The boat flapped its oars furiously.

"He's a bad mortar-man," a skinny, narrow-chested soldier standing nearby said with authority. "Yesterday they blew it to splinters at third go."

"Yes, but yesterday the boat was five times as big," replied somebody else in a hoarse, slow bass, "and it was carrying a mountain of stuff—it could hardly move."

A mine exploded right at the side of the boat. The boat only danced on the waves and for a few second the waving of the oars stopped.

"Now the machine-gun will start," Lisagór said calmly, drawing on his cigarette and blowing a ring. "As sure as death he'll open fire."

And almost at once there appeared around the boat a whole series of little spurts of water that sometimes ran together.

Everybody around kept quiet. The boat stopped waving its oars.

"Look, the bastards . . ." somebody burst out behind my back, "they'll finish him off now."

On the shore and around us practically everybody was following the course of the boat. The oars again began to move. But not four, only two. One person had apparently been wounded or killed.

The little boat had now reached the middle of the river and was just opposite us. Again the mortar started up.

"Fifty metres more and then he'll be out of sight of the Jerries."

"Go on, lads press on!"

The density of the fire reached its peak. It was quite incomprehensible how the boat remained whole. True, it was being carried along swiftly and the spurts were always lagging behind.

Somebody right on the water's edge shouted at the top of his voice:

"Go on, get on!"

And suddenly, as though by order, the spurts of water vanished. Two or three mines still flopped in the water, but the boat was already far away from them. The soldiers moved away, pleased and swearing cheerfully.

Lisagór flicked his cigarette end away.

"So that's the way they bring us food and ammunition.

Did you see it? And you there on the front line—demanding more and more bullets."

It appeared that there was only one ferry, working for the whole of the right bank. It was the sixty-second—two launches with barges—the rest had been lost. Meanwhile there was no getting through from the north—it was mined. In the course of a night the launches could manage to make a maximum of six crossings, seven at a stretch, and for eight or nine divisions that was a drop in the ocean. We had to fetch the stuff with our own resources.

" There's a whole flotilla in our regiment," said Lisagór, " five small boats, three punts and a pontoon. There were fifteen vessels, but they've gone out of action bit by bit. They are old. They leak. And the shrapnel rips them apart. the pontoon's just like netting. Three of my men are constantly caulking them." He gave me a sidelong glance. " And you tell us to get mines. And to-night I've also got to send men to the forty-fifth. Yesterday we had two boats pinched. Ach! I'm fed up with all of it . . . Let's go to my place . . ."

On our hands and knees we scrambled into Lisagór's dug-out, as big as a dog's kennel.

" You see how we live? A cobbler without boots. I dug it myself . . ."

A slanting ray of sunlight fell like an arrow across the greatcoat, lit up the sooty mess-tins, boxes and, nailed to the wall, the photograph of a plump young woman in a beret.

From somewhere underneath a table attached to the wall—something like those in trains—appeared a small bottle of vodka.

We clinked our glasses against the bottle.

" In the front line we were only once issued with vodka," I said.

Lisagór grinned and rubbed his unshaven chin with the palm of his hand.

" It's a kilometre and a half to the front line, but I've got a store right nearby. Moreover, there are five of my men who don't drink." He winked. " Anyway, you settle up as quick as you can with your battalion and take to engineering. You'll see how we shall live. With me you won't go far wrong. I know our major like the back of my hand. Half a word and I understand him. He's a wonderful old chap. A bit quick-tempered at times, it's true, but he forgets it all in half an hour. Only he's very fond of good dug-outs—

that's his big fault. You practically have to provide him with carpets. Otherwise, life is possible. Have another?"

He brought out another bottle.

"As soon as I get these two tunnels finished I'll start to make my own. It's not right. The men are sleeping out on the shore, and in a month it'll be winter. You'll see what a mansion there'll be by the time you arrive. You'll be delighted."

I looked at the clock, with a lock instead of a weight, hanging on the wall.

"Is that right?"

"It's right. But don't hurry, comrade lieutenant. You've plenty of time to enjoy the front line." He slapped me on the knee. "You're not offended that I address you so familiarly? It's a front-line habit. I even do the same with Abrósimov, and he's a captain. By the way," Lisagór lowered his voice, leant over and breathed straight in my face, "he's a dangerous chap. He doesn't care about people. He loks very calm, but in reality, he's very excitable. Completely loses his head. Boils over and hits out. But don't give in to him. Learn how to get along with him."

He leant right back and stretched out his legs. He cracked his fingers. I asked him a few technical questions. He replied without any hesitation. He laughed. Two of his front teeth were chipped.

"You're checking up on me, are you? Well, I know that business inside out. After all, I'm a regular. Khalkhingol, Finland . . . Oh, lieutenant, you don't know me yet. Honestly, move as quickly as you can to the shore. Then you'll see how well we'll get on. D'you want an orange? I've got a whole boxful. And some biscuits . . . There's everything you could want."

I interrupted him:

"How many men did you say you have in your platoon?"

"Me? Eighteen. I'm the nineteenth. All good chaps. Carpenters, joiners, and plumbers. Even a tailor and a barber. A cobbler—you won't find one like him in Moscow. You see the boots I'm wearing—what do you think of them? Heels, soles, instep . . . a sight for sore eyes. And there's a watchmaker. The sergeant over there with the moustache. And a cabinet-maker . . ."

"And what are they like when it comes to mines?"

"They know about that too, of course. But in general that's not our business. Observation and command posts—they are ours, but as for mines, let the battalion lay them. But

122

it's a wonderful platoon. I can't complain. When you've worked with them a bit you'll see. I picked them myself when we were forming up. You won't find another like it in the army. Word of honour!"

I stood up.

"So I shall be expecting your men to-morrow."

Lisagór also stood up, swaying slightly.

"Well, you are a stubborn one, lieutenant. Those minefields have really got under your skin. It only means our own chaps will be blowing them up . . . Oh well, all right, I'll send 'em."

"It wouldn't be a bad thing if you looked in yourself."

"That I won't promise. I won't promise. You see for yourself how much work there is. Tunnels, boats . . . And now there are mines to get to-day. I'll send the assistant platoon commander—Garkúsha. A wonderful chap. He'll stick in mines with his eyes shut."

"I don't need anybody, but the first and third battalions are completely without sappers . . ."

Holding the table with his hand Lisagór looked at me for a few seconds with slightly glazed eyes.

"D'you know what I'd like to tell you, comrade lieutenant . . .? Battalion commanders have heads . . . let 'em use 'em. My job is simple—to carry out orders. If they take up a defence, it's: sapper, lay mines! If they attack, it's: sapper, clear the mines! On reconnaissance, it's: sapper, forward, find the mines . . . Oh, to hell with them!"

"As you wish. You're the engineer for the time being. You decide what's best. So long."

"Cheerio. Have a few more vitamins for the road!"

He stuffed into the pocket of my jacket two cold, rough and dazzlingly bright oranges.

"So I'm expecting you in a few days," he called after me; "I'll introduce you to Klava." And he laughed a little dry laugh.

IV

At night we changed positions. I hurried to try and get
everything finished by midnight, before the moon came up.
But the Germans set fire to two barns and the whole of my
sector was as bright as day. That held up the transfer for
almost the whole night. A machine-gun was firing from underneath the bridge practically without a break. I felt there was
going to be a lot of trouble with that machine-gun—it was
cutting off all my routes. Towards the morning a big gun
appeared there too. But I had nothing to reply with—there
were barely enough bullets for one day. So I got across under
cover of regimental mortars. The eight-two millimetre guns
had no mortars. I asked for support from our regimental
artillery. But they were short of ammunition—they fired
only three times throughout the night.

It was a horrible sector. It was divided by a high railway
embankment which wound along the foot of the hill. It was
full of wagons. From the left flank the right could hardly be
seen—only the upper part of the ravine. There were no
trenches of any kind. The troops of the first battalion
making room for us were huddling together in some holes
and craters, taking cover behind any old scrap-iron. Along
the ravine, on the other side of the embankment there was
something at any rate resembling trenches, though without, it
is true, the slightest signs of communicating paths.

Yes, it wasn't much like the " Metiz ". There you could
go from one end to the other practically without bending
down.

In itself the sector was not large for a normal battalion—
some sixty metres—but I had altogether thirty-six men. There
had been four hundred, but now there were thirty-six.

I tried to find myself a command point, if only a temporary
one, so as to fix up a telephone. There was nothing but ruins,
burnt-out barns and no cellars. Valéga solved the prob-
lem. Beneath the embankment he found a well-camouflaged
reinforced concrete pipe. But there were some artillery
men in it.

A lanky lieutenant with a little beard sticking out in all
directions gave us a cold reception:

" I won't let you in, and that's that . . . There are five of us crammed in here already, and you'll bring a whole staff."

But I wasn't in the mood for diplomatic negotiations. I ordered the telephone to be fixed and the senior adjutant to make out a report. The artillery men cursed, didn't want to move their boxes and said they'd complain to Pozhársky, the head of the artillery. I didn't know Pozhársky.

"Move in, boys, and that's that . . . Don't move until I tell you."

That was all the signallers wanted. They led the line in, set themselves up right on the stone floor and at once began calling up their "Forget-me-nots" and "Tulips".

Kharlámov, the senior adjutant, short-sighted and forever losing everything, lost, of course, his most important file of papers and got in everybody's way, searching under their feet.

"I must have left it behind, in the old command post," he muttered to himself, looking round bewilderedly. It was an amazing faculty that man had, always and everywhere to lose something. During our acquaintance he managed to lose his greatcoat, three helmets and his own notebook. Not to mention pencils and pens.

Towards five o'clock the company commanders arrived.

"Well, how's it going?" I asked.

Karnaúkhov—commander of the fourth company, replacing the dead Petróv—shrugged his enormously wide shoulders.

"I've fixed things up for the time being. The machine-guns aren't bad, and the men . . . We shall have to sit it out for a day somehow—it's already getting light—and then get hold of the spades at night . . . You can't hold out long in trenches like these."

Karnaúkhov had a low, somewhat muffled voice. He spoke with a slight stutter. Maybe he was simply choosing his words. On the whole I liked him.

He had come to us ten days previously. Big and rather clumsy, with thick eyebrows meeting in the middle and grey eyes, and with a pack on his back. He had difficulty in squeezing through the narrow low doorway.

We were just having our dinner. Soup made of dried potatoes and dried bread. He turned it down and asked for water. He drank a huge jugful with relish, wiped his lips and smiled.

"I must have swigged your whole supply."

Then he asked where his company was.

"You just sit down and recover first."

Again he smiled apologetically and wiped his wet brow,

with its red stripe from his cap, with the palm of his hand.

"I've been recovering for a whole month in hospital. I put on three kilos. But I didn't get any tobacco for the journey, and you know yourself what it's like without tobacco . . ."

I offered him a smoke. He twisted himself a cigarette of quite unbelievable dimensions.

I asked him some of the usual questions at a first meeting. He replied calmly, in few words, sitting in a corner on his pack. Then he stood up and looked around for somewhere to throw his cigarette end and, not finding an ashtray, threw it out of the door.

"Well? Who's going to show me the way?"

That evening I received from him a neatly written report along with fire plans for each machine-gun and a diagram of the disposition of the enemy's weapons.

The next day he drove the Germans out of a sector of trenches that we had lost the day before, and lost only one man in doing it. I managed that evening to get along to him in his dug-out which was clean and tidy in a very un-front-line way, with a little mirror, shaving tackle and a tooth-brush on a little shelf. He was sitting and writing something in a note-book placed on his knees.

"A letter home, eh?"

"No . . . It's . . . Just rubbish . . ." He was embarrassed and tried to stand up, with his head bent down and his shoulders pressed against the roof. He hastily stuffed the notebook into his pocket.

"Poetry, no doubt," I thought and asked no more questions.

The same night his company stole a machine-gun and six boxes of ammunition from the Germans. The men said that he had gone himself for the gun, but when I asked him he only smiled and, without looking me in the eyes, said that that was all made up, that he would never permit himself such a thing and that in general a company commander did not go after machine-guns.

There he was standing in front of me, bending down a little and unshaven. I knew that, like me, what he wanted to do most was sleep. But he would still, with the tip of his tongue sticking out, draw a plan of his defences or run to see whether the supper had been served.

Farber, commander of the fifth company, sat on the end of a box, tired and, as always, vague and indifferent. He was staring at one point, and the thick lenses of his glasses caught the light. His eyes were swollen from lack of sleep. His normally thin cheeks had sunk even more.

I could still not understand him properly. He gave the impression that nothing in the world interested him. Lanky and stooping—his right shoulder was higher than his left—he was sickly pale, like most red-headed people, and terribly short-sighted, and he talked to practically no one. Before the war he had been a post-graduate student in the mathematics faculty of Moscow University. I knew that from his questionnaire—he never said so himself. In general he never talked about anything.

Curiosity, as well as fear, was atrophied in him. Once, back at the " Metiz ", I came across him in one of the trenches. He stood, leaning against the breastworks in his short, knee-length soldier's greatcoat, with his back to the enemy, and absent-mindedly hacking away with the toe of his boot at the crumbling wall of the trench. Two or three bullets clattered down somewhere not far off. Then a mortar shell exploded. He went on hacking at the ground.

" What are you doing here, Farber?"

Slowly, as though reluctantly, he turned and his eyes, with their colourless lashes and heavy, slightly swollen lids looked at me questioningly.

" Just . . . Simply . . . Nothing . . ."

" But the Jerries could knock you off in a couple of ticks."

" I suppose so," he agreed calmly and squatted down.

It was difficult to call him untidy—he was always shaved and his collar was always clean, but that was apparently rather a matter of habit or education—he attached no importance to his outward appearance. His greatcoat was two sizes too small—the belt underneath his armpits, he wore ragged puttees, his cap flattened out at the top and no tabs.

I once said to him:

" You ought to sew your tabs on, Farber."

As always, he looked at me in astonishment:

" For greater authority, what?"

" Simply because it's laid down in the army to wear badges of rank."

He rose silently and went out. Next day I noticed on the collar of his greatcoat two cloth tabs, sewn across in all directions with white thread.

" You've got a rotten batman, Farber—he certainly didn't make a good job of the tabs."

" I haven't got a batman. I sewed them on myself."

"Why don't you have a batman?"

"There are eighteen men in the company, not a hundred and fifty."

"All right, but let one of them double up and be your batman."

"An unnecessary luxury, I would say."

"It's not unnecessary and it's not a luxury. You are a company commander."

He made no retort, as in general he never retorted and never got indignant, but I don't think he ever acquired a batman.

He was a strange chap. I always felt strained in his company, and for that reason I never detained him. He got the order and that was that—carry it out. Silently, absently, staring somewhere to one side, he would nod his head or mutter "I'll do my best" and depart.

Now he was sitting, apathetic, hunched up, with his pale, bony hands sticking out of his short sleeves, drumming his fingers on the table.

"Remember, Farber," I told him, "the sector you've got is not all that good. Don't count too much on the artillery. Everything depends on the machine-guns. Don't waste your time on frontal fire. Apart from the noise it makes, it's no use at all."

He nodded his head in silence. His long fingers drummed on the table continuously and monotonously.

Outside—I could see through a crack—it was already quite light.

I released the company commanders. I phoned HQ to say that the redisposition had been completed and that I was sending the handing-over papers by runners.

The artillery men reconciled themselves to our presence. At the other end of the pipe they would shout out their various co-ordinates over the telephone. It looked as though our own guns would soon begin to talk.

V

Throughout the morning we were expecting an attack—the Germans could scarcely have failed to notice our night activity. But, surprisingly, the day turned out to be so quiet that we even managed to fetch the midday meal up from the shore in daytime.

After round-the-clock excitement, interminable attacks, bombings and artillery raids it was very difficult to put any faith in that quietness. We were expecting some trick all the time.

But for the time being it was peaceful. The usual exchange of shells, pretty feeble and infrequent. At seven, as always, the " crate ". Lines of " songsters " over the " Red October ".

Valéga hauled two buckets of water up from the Volga, heated it up on the primus, and then we scrubbed each other's backs with some bast. After me the water was black as ink, though I myself was red and my whole body tingled. Valéga laughed.

" I will now give you some captured underwear. Silk. No chance of getting lice in it. It slips—doesn't grip."

I put on the delicate, sky-blue pants and shirt, shaved and went along to Karnaúkhov. Sitting on his haunches and squinting into a tiny fragment of mirror fixed on a half-ruined wall, he was scraping his chin.

" Well, how's life?"

Karnaúkhov smiled through the lather and stood up.

" I could live like this till the end of the war. Seems as though Jerry has gone on strike . . ."

I sat down next to him.

All around there was nothing but chimneys. There were no houses. Here and there were a few beams, blackened and still smoking—and chimneys, chimneys, chimneys—sinister black chimneys against the transparent sky of almost Crimean clarity. For some reason the chimneys were always saved. It was as though somebody left them deliberately, to remind people that here was once a house or a village or a town . . .

I was sitting on a post. It had apparently once been a gateway. The lamp with the number of the house still survived. It was a triangular, blue lamp, with the inscription, " Second Skew Lane, No. 24. This house belongs to I. N. Agárkova ".

On a piece of wall, still standing for some unknown reason, was a notice all askew: "Auerbuch. Ladies' and Gents' Tailor. Orders Taken." A red-cheeked character in well-pressed trousers and a bowler hat stared at me from the notice with a mixture of indifference and concentration, as if he were out to hypnotise me. They always have that look, those advertisement beauties.

"Everything's quiet with you," I said.

"That's only for the moment. And anyway, it's not very. I only hopped out to shave myself—it's so dark in the dug-out you can't see—cut yourself all over."

Screwing his face up as though in pain Karnaúkhov finished shaving his upper lip. I cleaned the back of his neck up for him and, grabbing hold of the shaving kit, we crept into the hole. In the hole there was a stove, a table with cut-off legs and two chairs. In the corner was a signaller with a telephone mouthpiece attached to his head. There were two more soldiers. A lamp made out of an old shell case was smoking. On the wall was a calendar with days underlined, a list of call signs, a portrait of Stalin cut out of a newspaper, and one of someone else, young, curly and with an agreeable open face.

"Who's that?"

Karnaúkhov caught the direction of my glance and was embarrassed.

"Jack London."

"Jack London?"

Karnaúkhov was standing against the light and I couldn't see his face, but by his ears through which the light shone I could tell that he was blushing.

"Why Jack London all of a sudden?"

"Oh, just . . . I have great regard for him . . . Have some milk?"

"Milk? Here? Where from?"

"It's condensed . . . American. The lads got it."

I took pleasure in licking up a spoonful of thick, sickly-sweet milk, similar to lime-blossom honey.

"But where *did* you get that portrait from, all the same?"

"Where from?" Karnaúkhov laughed. "From hospital, of course. I read through the whole library there. But I didn't manage to read *Martin Eden*. Well, so . . . I borrowed it for a bit."

"Do you like Jack London?"

"Yes . . . I've read his books several times over."

"I like him too."

130

" Everybody likes him. You can't *not* like him."

" Why?"

" He is so real . . . Even Lenin liked him. Krupskáya used to read Jack London to him."

" Will you let me have it afterwards to read?"

" All right."

" And what other writers do you like?"

He again turned shy.

" I have read very little. Our teacher had only London—I don't know where she got it from—you know, the edition in the brown binding that used to come out as a supplement . . . And then there was Mélnikov-Pechérsky, and someone else, I can't remember—a foreigner."

" Well, that was in school. What about afterwards?"

" Afterwards there was no time. I worked in a mine. In Suchan. Do you know it? Near Vladivostok."

" I know it."

" When I was a little brat I had quite made up my mind to run away to America—to look for gold in the Klondyke. I pinched a double-barrelled gun from my father, and gathered some food together. I even planned to get on to a Norwegian schooner. We lived in Vladivostok then. My father worked as a stevedore in the port."

" Well?"

Karnaúkhov smiled, glanced at the nails on his hand.

" They dragged me home by the scruff of my neck. Like a puppy. I had to stay in bed for five days. My father gave me a good beating. He was so strong he could bend a silver rouble in his hand."

And again he laughed.

Then from somewhere or other there appeared a gramophone, old and rattling, and it was more a case of guessing than of enjoying the performances by Davydova, Kozlóvsky and the duet from " The Zaporózhets from beyond the Danube". There was only one needle which we took it in turns to sharpen on a broken plate.

" Well, that's all I've got," said Karnaúkhov, scratching the back of his neck. " Unless I also show you the front line. Only you can't get right through to the trenches themselves at the moment. We have to look from here, out of the ruins."

We took up positions by a low stone wall. We stood in what must once have been a living-room. An iron bedstead, twisted by fire, a sewing machine, a meat mincer . . .

In front was the ravine. It began just to the left of us and

131

stretched in a long curve upwards to the very top. Opposite us was a wrecked gun. The barrel had been split open and the end of it had curled back making it look like some fantastic flower. This lent the gun a surprised, puzzled look. Alongside it was the fore-carriage, blown to bits.

On the opposite side of the ravine were the German trenches. So close you felt you could touch them.

" Ours are out of sight," whispered Karnaúkhov ; " the slope gets in the way. It's about seventy metres from the Jerries in a straight line. Do you see them, the bastards—they're digging even in daylight."

In one place you really could see something brown flying up out of the ground and the occasional flash of a spade.

" Oh dear, we've no shells . . . I'd teach 'em to dig right under our very noses! When I tried to do some digging this morning they turned their mortars on us at once . . . And where do they get so much ammunition from?"

We lay for a long time, observing the Germans. We tried to determine the exact position of their fire-points. They were well camouflaged and we couldn't find them at once. Two or three machine-guns were set up somewhere on the little mound, just opposite us, that looked like a camel's hump. Another was clinging on somewhere higher up in the ravine which it was covering downwards with its fire. But there was one we just couldn't find, although bullets from it were clattering close around us.

Yes . . . This was not quite the way I had imagined a front line before the war. Barbed wire zigzagging in two or three rows, an unending network of trenches, camouflage netting and proper embrasures to fire from. Whereas here, under our very noses, was just roughly dug earth. A wrecked gun. Something like old petrol cans, shot through with bullets.

I once had the book, *Heroes of Malákhov Hill*. With illustrations, of course. The fourth bastion, redoubts, lunettes, approaches . . . Mountains of sandbags, gabions of basket-work, funny-looking guns with long fuses on green wooden platforms and the bombs, which were bright round balls with fine trails of smoke.

Nearly ninety years had passed since then. Tanks and aeroplanes had been invented in that time. But there were we sitting in some sort of hole and calling it a defensive position.

That night I was going to start laying mines. I would put about three hundred around the place at first. There was no need of anti-tank mines here—a tank couldn't get through,

132

but over there where Farber was, on the other side of the embankment . . .

Karnaúkhov lay frowning, his black, grown-together brows looking as if they had got by accident on to his kindly grey-eyed face.

"Say what you like, they've got a jolly good fire system, blast them! Just look at it. From that camel's hump they cover the whole third battalion. From under the bridge they've got us in the back. And from the top of the ravine they look down the whole front line . . ."

And, as though to illustrate his words, as if by agreement, all three machine-guns opened fire.

"Oh, we'd shake the Jerries a bit if we took that hump! But what can you do with eighteen men . . ."

Karnaúkhov was right. If that hillock were in our hands we would make life much easier for the third battalion, paralyse the bridge, and have fire-points flanking the first battalion.

But how could we do it?

VI

In the evening I sent off everyone who wasn't busy at the front line for the mines. It was a good thing I had a cart. At least it made it possible in the dark to bring the mines almost right up to the embankment. And from there it wasn't too difficult to carry them.

By about ten o'clock I already had about three hundred. They were piled up alongside the pipe. About the same time the sappers also arrived—four men and a sergeant—the same one, with the moustache—Garkúsha.

They sat in a corner, chewing sunflower seeds and occasionally exchanging a word or two. They looked tired.

"All day long we hack away in the tunnel and then back we come in the morning—more digging. You can't tell whether you've got a back or any hands left."

Garkúsha stretched out his hard, rough hand, covered with one big callus as if it were lined with horn.

When the fourth company let us know that about a hundred mines had been brought up, Garkúsha stood up and brushed the husks from his knees.

"Well, what about it? Let's go while there's no moon. Who's going to show us the way?"

Clutching on to the bushes and the spiky, dry grass, we let ourselves down to the front line itself. The trenches—separate slit trenches each of two to three metres—stretched just along the middle of the slope.

What fool could have thought this up? Why not put them twenty metres farther back and higher? The field of fire would be better, the communications easier and it would be more difficult for the Germans to get to them. But the men were digging. They couldn't be seen in the darkness, but the clanking of the spades could be heard.

"What the devil are you digging here for, Karnaúkhov? Listen, being here is like being on the palm of their hand."

I couldn't help losing my temper. That's always the way when you feel that not only other people but you yourself are at fault. I even forgot that we could talk there only in a whisper.

Karnaúkhov did not reply. Only later did I find out that Sendétsky, the platoon commander, had started the digging on his own initiative. "The men had got cold, so I ordered them to dig to warm themselves up."

I ordered the men to be moved higher at once. Let them dig themselves in up there. In any case these slit trenches were not worth a bean. I'd leave two or three men to guard them.

The troops, groaning and cursing under their breath, scrambled upwards, dragging their spades, sacks and greatcoats along.

"Officers, they call themselves . . ."

This was aimed at me. I pretended not to hear. It was lucky there was no moon. Had there been a moon, a good half of them would have been missing . . .

We made our way farther down. It was a steep drop, and the clay, already beginning to freeze up, kept crumbling away underneath our feet. The sappers were carrying twenty mines each in sacks. From time to time there would be a burst of fire from the duty machine-gun—the one at the top of the ravine. But the bursts went high, crackling over our heads. They were explosive dum-dum bullets.

We got into some mud. It was evidently a stream: there had not been any rain for a long time. It squelched under our feet. A rocket went up. We flopped down, face, hands and belly, straight into the clinging, cold slush. Peering from under my arm, I watched the dazzling star quiver and float by slowly in the dark sky.

"Well, where shall we put 'em?"

Leaning his shoulder on me, the sergeant breathed right into my ear. After the bright light it was pitch black all round. I couldn't even see his face—only feel his warm breath that smelt of sunflower seeds.

"When a rocket flares up, look across to the left . . ." My voice shook slightly from the strain. "You'll see a metal canister . . . Start from that . . . And go to the right about fifty metres . . . In three rows. Chequered. As we said."

The words were squeezed out with difficulty.

Garkúsha made no reply. He crept off to one side. I could only hear him, and not see him. A minute later I again felt his breath on my face.

"Comrade lieutenant."

"What?"

"I'll make it a little bit higher. Otherwise the water'll freeze and then . . ."

Another rocket. Garkúsha flopped down right on top of me.

I pressed my face into the ground and tried not to breathe. My mouth, nose and ears were full of water and mud. The rocket died out. I lifted my face and said:

"All right."

I was no longer worried about the minefield.

I wiped my face with my sleeve.

Sappers certainly had a lousy job. Pitch darkness, mud and the Germans thirty yards away and your own chaps up there somewhere . . . And every mine had to have a hole dug for it, the detonator inserted—a sort of little tube with a spring, a little tube as sharp as a nail and a capsule—the mine checked, put in the hole, covered with earth and camouflaged . . . And all the time you have to listen carefully whether the Germans are creeping up, to plunge into the mud and not to budge whenever there's a rocket . . .

You could hear the men carefully tipping the mines out of the sacks.

I reckoned they'd finish the job in an hour.

Meanwhile I had to set about writing out lists and record cards for the minefields right away, while they were fresh in my mind. I would have this writing to do every night. In three copies and a diagram with co-ordinates and explanatory notes as well. Moreover, there were no forms—I'd have to do it all myself, by hand.

I clambered up to the top . . . Two or three times I nearly slid down again. You couldn't see a damned thing, no matter how you strained your eyes. I scratched my hands to pieces on some thorn bush . . .

The men dug in silence. You could only hear the spades striking the ground. Somebody quite close to me—you could see nothing for the darkness—swore at the hard, stony earth hoarsely under his breath as if coaxing a stubborn horse.

"They might at least issue a few picks to each battalion! As for these things they call spades . . . Good for cutting butter."

Picks . . . The devil alone knew where to get those. What wouldn't I have given for twenty picks! It seemed as though I had never yearned for anything in my life as I now yearned for them. And how many of them were there lying at the station in Morózovskaya. Heaps! And no one had even bothered to look at them. Everyone had been looking for vodka and for butter.

But at this rate we wouldn't dig ourselves in in a month.

Just after midnight the moon appeared. Tilted and orange-coloured it crept out from somewhere behind the Volga. It peered into the ravine. In half an hour it would be impossible to work there. There were only four of them—and a hundred mines . . .

The moon crept up, turning yellow and then white. It didn't give a damn for anything. It seemed to me that it rose even quicker than usual that day, as though it was in a hurry to get somewhere or had been late in rising. And, as luck would have it, the German side was in shadow, while ours got brighter and brighter every minute . . . The last remains of shadow slid slowly down, as if unwillingly, abandoning the bushes one after the other.

Somebody was looking for me. A young breathless voice, almost a child's—it sounded like Karnaúkhov's runner.

"Have you seen the lieutenant—the battalion commander—anywhere?"

"Which one's that? The one that goes around with field-glasses?" came somebody's voice in reply, somewhere down below, probably out of a trench.

"No! Not with field-glasses. The battalion commander. With a blue cap . . ."

"Aha—a blue cap . . . You should have said he wore a cap. So that's the battalion commander . . . How can you remember all these officers in a day . . ."

"Well, where is he then?"

"But I haven't seen him," answered the voice cheerfully.

"He hasn't been here. Honest, I haven't seen him . . ."

"You clot!"

"Maybe Fésenko has seen him . . . Fésenko, hey, Fésenko!"

I set off in the direction of the conversation. From another trench Fésenko replied just as cheerfully and unhurriedly that "one of the officers had been here and had shouted at the platoon commander that we weren't digging right, but where he went to the devil only knew . . ."

"Who's looking for me?"

"Is that you, comrade lieutenant?" A small, thin shape rose up in front of me?"

"It's me . . . And don't stand up, lie down!"

The shape squatted down.

"Well, what's the matter?"

"They called from your command post, for you to go there urgently."

"Me? Urgently? Who phoned?"

"I don't know . . . Some colonel."

What colonel? Where had he come from? I couldn't make it out.

"Urgently, they said, to be there in three minutes . . ."

Before I got to Karnaúkhov's cellar I ran into Valéga. He was running like mad and quite out of breath.

"There's a colonel waiting for you. Divisional commander or something. Wears a decoration . . . And some others with him . . . Kharlámov, the junior lieutenant, is getting mixed up over there. And they're cursing . . ."

Always Kharlámov, blast him! A real pain in the neck. Supposed to be the senior adjutant—the chief of staff. He ought to be working in the kitchen, not on the staff.

The Germans suddenly opened fire and we lay with our noses stuck in the ground for a good fifteen minutes.

VII

The colonel was quite small and puny, like a boy, with cheeks so sunken they looked as though they were being deliberately drawn in, and strained, vertical wrinkles between his brows. He was sitting, resting his hand on the table. His greatcoat with its gold buttons was undone. Next to him was our major. He had a stick between his knees. There were a couple of others as well.

Kharlámov stood at attention, buttoned up and looking quite smart. It was the first time I had seen him like that. He was blinking.

I raised my hand to the salute. I made my report: the battalion was digging in and laying mines. Two big black eyes stared unblinkingly at me from the thin, tubercular face. The dry, slender fingers tapped lightly on the table.

Everybody was silent.

I lowered my hand.

The pause seemed to drag out rather. I could hear Valéga breathing fast behind my back.

The black eyes suddenly became smaller and narrower and the thin, bloodless lips seemed to smile.

"What have you been up to? In a fight with someone? Eh?"

I said nothing.

"Give him a mirror. Let him admire himself."

Somebody produced a thick, peeling fragment of mirror. I had a job to recognise myself. Apart from the eyes and teeth I could distinguish nothing. Hands, jacket and boots were all thick with mud.

"All right," the colonel laughed, and his laugh was unexpectedly gay and young. "These things happen . . . I once appeared before the commander of a military district in my pants and got away with it. Ten days was all I got—saluting without a cap on . . ."

The smile vanished, as though someone had wiped it off his face. The big black eyes again turned on me. They were intelligent, rather tired and with three-cornered bags under them.

"All right then, battalion commander, shoot a line about what you've done in the twenty-four hours. If it's the same at the front line as it is on paper, I don't envy you."

"Very little has been done, comrade colonel."

"Very little? Why?" The eyes didn't blink.

"We're a bit thin on the ground with men and badly off for tools."

"How many men have you got?"

"Thirty-six able-bodied."

"And idlers, runners and suchlike?"

"Altogether around seventy."

"And do you know how many there are in the forty-third regiment? Fifteen to twenty men each, and still they keep fighting."

"I am also fighting, comrade colonel."

"He was holding the 'Metíz', comrade colonel," the major interjected. "Last night we moved him across to the right."

"Don't you defend him, Borodín. He's not holding the 'Metíz' now, and it's not from the 'Metíz' that the Germans are going to drive him . . ." Then again to me: "Are there trenches?"

"They are being dug, comrade colonel."

"All right, show me . . ."

I had no time to reply. He was already standing in the doorway and was doing up his buttons with quick, nervous movements.

I tried to say that there was heavy firing and that I would think it not worth his . . .

"Don't you try and teach me. I know."

Borodín also rose, leaning heavily on his stick.

"There's no point in you coming with us. You'll lose your last leg. Then what shall I do? Come on, battalion commander."

We—I, Valéga and the divisional commander's adjutant, a young fellow with an incredibly round, smooth face—could hardly keep up with him. With a short, quite unmilitary step, slightly swaying, he walked quickly and assuredly, as though he had been there many times before.

I stopped at Karnaúkhov's cellar. The colonel turned round impatiently:

"What's happened?"

"The company command point is here."

"All right, let it be here . . . Where are the trenches?"

"Farther on. Beyond those pipes there."

"Lead on!"

The trenches were now clearly visible—both ours and the Germans'. The moon was at its brightest.

"Lie down."

We lay down. The colonel lay beside me, supporting his head with his hands. I explained where the trenches were before and where I was digging them now. He said nothing. He asked where the machine-guns were. I showed him. Where were the mortars? I showed him. He was silent, apart from coughing occasionally in a restrained way as if he were trying not to.

"And where are you putting the mines?"

"Over there to the left, in the ravine."

"Stop it. Bring the men back."

I couldn't understand.

139

"Did you hear what I said? Bring the men back . . ."

I sent Valéga down. Let them mark the right flank with a peg and return. Valéga crept down silently on his stomach.

We remained silent. You could hear the men breathing heavily as they dug. Somewhere beyond the hill was the revolting noise of an " ishak "[1]—a six-barrelled mortar. Six red long-tailed mortars, just like comets, sailed slowly above us and exploded with a deafening noise somewhere behind in the region of the Meat Combine. We even felt the blast. The colonel didn't even raise his head. He coughed.

"You see his machine-guns? On the hillock?"

"Yes."

"Do you like 'em?"

"No."

"Nor do I."

A pause. I didn't understand what he was getting at.

"I don't like them at all, battalion commander. Not one little bit."

I made no reply. I didn't like them either. But I had no artillery. What could I suppress them with?

"So look . . . To-morrow you'd better be there."

"There? Where?"

"There where those machine-guns are. Is that clear?"

"Perfectly," I replied, but it was quite unclear to me how I could get there.

The colonel jumped up like a boy, leaning his hand on the ground.

"Let's go."

He went back through the ruins just as lightly and quickly, without tripping or stumbling over anything. At the command post he lit a thick, sweet-smelling cigarette, " Our Brand " I think, and flicked through the *Martin Eden* lying on the table. He glanced at the end. He frowned with displeasure.

"A fool . . . Really, a fool."

And, raising his eyes to me:

"Yours?"

"It belongs to the commander of the fourth company."

"Have you read it?"

"I've had no time, comrade colonel."

"You read it and then let me have it. I read it once but I've forgotten it. I remember only that he was a stubborn

[1] " Ishak: German mortar that made a noise like the braying of a donkey.—*isbak*.

140

chap. Only I don't like the end. It's a poor ending. Eh, Borodín?"

Borodín smiled shyly with his thick, heavy lips.

"I don't remember . . . It's a long time since I read it, comrade colonel.'

"You're lying. You've never read it at all. You'll have it after me." He was pondering something, the wrinkles gathering between his eyes.

"We shall not give you any artillery preparation. As soon as it gets dark send out the scouts. You seem to have some decent lads." He turned his head slightly in the direction of the major.

The major silently nodded his big head and sucked at his wheezy, gurgling pipe. The colonel tapped on the table with his knuckles. He looked at his watch—disproportionately big on his thin, dry hand. It showed a quarter past two. He stood up in a short, sharp movement.

"Well, battalion commander . . ." and he stretched out his hand. "Kérzhentsev I believe your name is?"

"Kérzhentsev."

His hand was warm and dry.

In the doorway he turned around.

"And that one . . . what's-it's-name . . . where he gets drowned at the end . . . *Martin Eden*—don't let anyone have it . . . If you don't bring it to me I'll come up the hill and get it from you myself."

The major went out behind him. He tapped me lightly on the shoulder.

"He's pretty strict, our div. commander. But he's a clever old son of a gun . . ." And he smiled at his not altogether appropriate expression. "Drop in on me in the morning—we'll give you a hand."

The sappers returned. They dragged something heavy and awkward inside. Garkúsha wiped his brow and breathed heavily.

"Boyádzhiev's been wounded." He sank down heavily on the bed. "Blew his jaw off."

Silently and breathing heavily the men sat the wounded man down on the other bed opposite. He flopped down on it, as though lifeless, limp, with his hands resting helplessly on his knees and his head hanging back. It was wrapped round in something red. His tunic was covered in blood.

"We were on our way back. They saw us. Started up the mortars. Koltsóv was killed . . . not a trace of him left. And with him it's the jaw."

141

The wounded man groaned. He shook his head. There was already a small round puddle of blood at his feet. Marúsya took off his bandage. Through the rapid movements of her fingers could be seen a nose, eyes, cheeks and a forehead with a clotted lock of black hair. But below was nothing but black and red. His hands clutched helplessly at her knees and skirt. He groaned and groaned and groaned . . .

"He was the best fighter," said Garkúsha wearily. His cap had fallen off his head and lay there on the ground. "He put down fifty mines to-day. And never said a word."

He was silent for a while, then:

"So it was a waste of time laying them all?"

I made no reply.

They took the wounded man away.

The sappers, when they had smoked a cigarette, also went off.

It was a long time before I could get to sleep.

VIII

In the morning everything annoyed me for some reason. I must have got out of bed on the wrong side. There was a flea in my foot-cloth and I just couldn't get it out. Kharlámov again lost the morning report—he stood before me, blinking his black, Armenian-looking eyes and gesturing helplessly: "I put it in the box and now it isn't there." Then I was fed up with the rotten millet porridge—every day, morning and night. And the tobacco was moist and wouldn't draw. And there hadn't been any Moscow papers for three days. And they sent up only eight cripples from the shore —the lame and the blind!

Everything was wrong . . .

Farber had two men killed by a direct hit on a dug-out. I told him to cover the dug-outs over with rails—there was a whole pile of them lying at the "Metíz"—but he simply put it off until he lost some men. I even shouted at him and, when he turned silently on his heel and went away, I made him come back and repeat the order.

In general I was fed up . . .

I sent Kharlámox off to the shore for some forms of which I had no need at all. Just so that he didn't hang about where I could see him.

I collapsed on the bed. I had a splitting headache. The signaller in the corner was reading a thick, tattered book.

"Now then, come here! No time for reading now . . ."

I took the book from him. *The Ordeal of Sevastópol*, volume III. Without the beginning or the end. Must have gone on cigarettes. I opened it at random.

"The number of casualties in the regiments was great, and the reinforcements, such as they were, were negligible, so that the very terms—regiment, battalion, company—lost their original meaning.

"In a fighting regiment such as the Volynsky, for example, instead of four thousand men there were by now not more than a thousand left . . ."

Not more than a thousand. What about us? If I had eighty men in my battalion and there were three battalions in the regiment, that made two hundred and forty. Gunners, anti-gas troops, signallers and scouts accounted for about another hundred. Three hundred and fifty altogether. Well, four hundred . . . Say five hundred . . . And the div. commander said there were even less in the other regiments. And how many of them were actually fighting? Not more than a third. What if the Germans got tired of pounding at the "Red October"? Or if they came at us again? Or threw tanks in against Farber? It was true the embankment was in the way. But they could easily come under the bridge, where they'd got a machine-gun and a "heavy" . . . What should I do then? There were fifteen men sitting in the holes. No mines at all. Borodín said we'd have them in three days, they were being unloaded somewhere . . . Even supposing they didn't let us down, it would still take another two or even three nights to lay them . . . Meanwhile we could only wait and pray . . .

I turned over some more pages.

" . . . Busiest of all were the restaurant owners, who had set up their roomy tents in a row. These tents were now being visited, after the attack, by officers who had come from the town and the bastion in search of amusement . . . In the hospitable tents which contained a buffet with a big selection of wines, spirits and sandwiches, and a dozen tables for customers, and even a kitchen hidden behind the buffet, they drank and ate, exchanged witticisms and laughed gaily . . ."

A kitchen hidden behind the buffet . . . A dozen tables for the customers . . .

I put the book on one side, pulled my greatcoat over my ears and tried to sleep.

The signaller was fussing and grunting away in the corner. The clock—Valéga had already got one from somewhere—very small, with hands hand-made from a tin, ticked away irregularly.

I could have eaten a good pork chop fried in breadcrumbs, with thin, crisp chips . . . I think the last time I ate pork . . . Goodness knows, I couldn't even remember. In Kiev, was it? Or somewhere later in the army . . . But no, that wasn't pork, just grilled meat . . .

I turned over on the other side. My eyes were burning from the smoking lamp.

At half-past ten the " corn-cob " would arrive. At eleven I would have to open the attack. Soon after twelve the moon would appear. Which meant that I would have about an hour and a quarter at my disposal. In that hour and a quarter I had to get down into the ravine, climb up the opposite slope, drive the Germans out of the trenches and consolidate the position. What if the " corn-cob " was late? Or were there to be not just one, but two or three? The div. commander—I remembered clearly—said " corn-cobs " and not " corn-cob ". What a fool I was not to have asked exactly how many there would be. The first would drop its bombs, I would go forward and then a second one would arrive. For I should have to attack immediately after it had gone, before the Germans realised what was happening . . . I would have to ask the major by phone to find out for sure from the div. commander.

How very black and penetrating were the div. commander's eyes. It was difficult to look into them for long.

They said that in the summer somewhere near Kastórnaya he had led a division out of encirclement with just a rifle in his hands.

Must have a nerve, the old devil!

And the way he walked about the front line . . . Neither bullets nor mines—nothing seems to exist for him. Is it just for show, to teach the young men? They say that Napoleon also had no fear of anything. The bridge of Arcole, the plague hospitals . . . When he was buried they found scars on his body which nobody had ever known about. I think I read that in Tarle.[1]

What was bravery, after all? I didn't believe those people who said they weren't afraid of bombing. They were afraid, only they knew how to conceal it. But others didn't. I

[1] Russian historian of French Revolution. Died 1955.

144

remember Maxímov once said: "Nobody is completely without fear. Everybody experiences fear. Only, some people lose their heads when they are frightened, while others, on the contrary, bring all their forces to bear at such times and their brains work especially clearly and precisely. Those are the brave ones."

That's exactly the sort of person Maxímov was. Was . . . He was probably dead by now. In his company there was nothing terrifying about the most terrifying moments. He would only turn slightly paler, compress his lips and speak more slowly as though weighing every word.

Even during bombing—and it was before Khárkov, during our unsuccessful May offensive, that we learnt for the first time the meaning of that word—he managed to keep up among his staff a sort of equable, even lighthearted, atmosphere. He joked, and laughed, and made up some kind of poetry and told funny stories. He was a good fellow. And now he wasn't there any more. Nor were a lot of others.

Where was Igor? Shiryáev? Sedykh? Maybe they too were no longer with us . . .

They had lived and studied and yearned for something and—trrrp!—everything had vanished—home, family, college, the history of architecture and all the Parthenons.

The Parthenon . . . As far as I could remember: 454-438 B.C. An enclosed colonnade—a peripter. Eight columns in the front, seventeen at the sides. While the Thesenon had six and thirteen . . . Doric, Ionic and Corinthian styles. I preferred the Doric. It was more severe, more laconic.

Who built St Peter's Church in Rome? The first was Bramante. Then, I think, Sangallo . . . or Raphael. Then somebody else, somebody else and then Michelangelo. He did the dome . . . But the colonnade? Possibly Bernini.

Oh, to hell with it . . . What rubbish it was that found its way into your head! What use was it? I had to seize a hill and there I was thinking about a dome. A one-ton bomb and the dome wouldn't be there . . .

What was to be done with Farber if I did finally take the hill? It would leave a gap. The fourth company in front and the fifth in echelon behind. It would probably be ordered to take the bridge. But maybe the third battalion? They would cut off the bridge and join up with us on the hill. That would be fine!

But it was funny . . . Not long ago I had been sitting on this hill with Lusia and looking at the Volga and the goods

145

train below. And we had talked about a machine-gun.
Maybe from that very place a machine-gun was firing at us
now . . .

Lusia asked then whether I liked Blok. She was a funny
girl . . . She should have asked whether I *had* liked Blok—
in the past tense. Yes, I had liked him. But now . . .

Somebody tugged at my greatcoat.

" Comrade lieutenant! Comrade lieutenant! They've come
from the political section—they're asking for you."

I peeped out cautiously. Two men in padded jackets, with
map-cases full of papers. Inspectors, probably, or representatives to observe the night attack.

I must get up.

The clock showed two o'clock. Still nine hours to go . . .

IX

The scouts arrived before it was light. Vests, jackets and
caps—all in order. On their backs they carried German
automatics with projecting magazines.

Chumák saluted—all present and at our service. His eyes
sparkled beneath his forelock. He smelt of vodka. We had
not met since the day of our quarrel—he had been summoned
to the shore.

Our conversation was strictly business—the object of the
operation, the time it would take and the point of departure.
He knew it all without me telling him and we spoke about
it only because we had to. Actually there was nothing else
for us to talk about. He made no effort at all to conceal that
fact. His tone was cold, dry and indifferent. His eyes, when
they met mine, were bored and slightly mocking. Three of his
lads—with their hair hanging over their foreheads, tunics
undone and hands in pockets—stood near. There were
half-smoked cigarettes stuck to their lips.

" Will you take camouflage capes?"

" No."

" Why not? I've got just four of them."

" Don't need 'em."

" Shall I give you some vodka?"

" We'll drink our own. Don't like other people's."

" Well, suit yourself."

" You'll be able to drink our health."

" Thanks."

146

" Don't mention it."

And he went off to Karnaúkhov. When I arrived there they had already gone.

It was very crowded in the cellar—no room to turn round. Two representatives from the political section. One from Div. HQ. The officer in charge of communications from the regiment. They were all observers. I understood the need for their presence, but they annoyed me. Everyone smoked almost continuously. It was always like that before an important operation. The representative from Div. HQ—a captain—was writing something in a notebook and spitting on his pencil.

" Have you thought out the course of the operation?" he asked, raising his grey, lifeless eyes. He had long projecting teeth that came over his lower lip.

" Yes, I've thought it out."

" The Command attaches great importance to it. You know that?"

" I know."

" What about your flanks?"

" Which flanks?"

" When you move forward, what will you cover your flanks with?"

" Nothing. I shall be supported by the neighbouring battalions. I am short of men. We're taking a chance."

" That's bad."

" Of course it's bad."

He wrote something down in his notebook.

" And what resources have you at your disposal?"

" I don't dispose of resources, but of a handful of men. Fourteen men will mount the attack."

" Fourteen?"

" Yes, fourteen. And fourteen will stay put. Twenty-eight altogether."

" In your place I wouldn't do it that way . . ."

He glanced at his notebook.

I did not remove my eyes from his teeth. As a matter of interest, were they ever covered up or did they always stick out like that? I was practically certain that he had been a book-keeper or a clerk before the war.

I took my cigarette case slowly out of my pocket.

" When you are in my place, then you'll do as you please. Until then allow me to act as I see fit."

He remained silent. The men from the political section dropped their heads and were writing something very earnestly

147

on their map-cases. They were good lads and understood that questions were out of place at the moment and minded their own business in silence.

Time crept by with painful slowness. Every minute there was a call from the HQ: had the scouts returned? The captain switched over to Karnaúkhov. Calmly, with an occasional smile and a glance thrown in my direction, he gave detailed replies to everything: what the men were armed with, how many grenades they had, and how many bullets each had. He had the patience of the devil! The captain wrote it all down.

Then I thought I would ask them all to leave. They could just as well sit at the battalion command post. After all, there was absolutely nothing for them to do here. They had found out what they needed, checked everything, and they could follow the course of the battle from the other place.

My watch showed a quarter past nine. I started to get agitated. The scouts could have been back by now. A soldier who came back from the front line for water said they had crept off a long time ago but that there was still nothing to be heard. The Germans were still sending up rockets and shooting. It didn't look as though the scouts had been caught or noticed.

I went outside.

The night was as black as pitch. Somewhere far away, beyond the " Red October ", something was burning. The thin, black silhouettes of twisted girders stood out sharply as though drawn with Indian ink. On the other bank a lone gun was thumping away—a shot and then silence, a shot and then silence. Just as though it were listening. Machine-guns fired from time to time. German rockets went up. For some reason they were yellow that night. They had probably run out of white ones. There was a smell of burnt wood and paraffin. A few yards from us was a whole train of fuel tanks—by daylight we could see it clearly. For days on end the paraffin had trickled in fine streams from the bullet holes in the tank. The men used to run over there at night to fill up the lamps.

From an old childhood habit I sought out familiar constellations. Orion—four bright stars and a belt of three smaller ones. And one other—quite small, hardly to be seen . . . One of them was called Betelgeuse—I couldn't remember which. Aldebaran should be somewhere, but I had already forgotten where it was to be found.

Someone put his hand on my shoulder. I started.

"What are you thinking about, battalion commander?"

With difficulty I made out in the darkness the massive figure of Karnaúkhov.

"Oh . . . nothing . . . just looking at the stars."

He did not reply. We stood and watched the stars twinkling. From some remote part of the brain there emerged thoughts of infinity, of the cosmos, of other worlds living and dead but still sending us light from the dark boundless realms of space. Stars fade out or flare up . . . But we know nothing. And nobody will ever know that a star which had lived for millions of years had died on that dark October night, or that a new one, also to be discovered in millions of years, had been born.

"By now there's snow in Siberia," said Karnaúkhov.

"Must be," I replied.

"And frost."

"And they're selling milk in frozen blocks."

"But in Vladivostok they're still bathing."

"They say the sea's cold there."

"It's cold, but they bathe all the same."

From somewhere very far away, beyond the Volga, scarcely audible, came the sound of a "corn-cob". Could it be ours? But the scouts were still not back. We listened carefully to the sound approaching from the right. It was not ours. Muffled explosions—far away, at the tractor plant. Germans searchlights nervously swept the sky. They got wider and then narrower, died out and then lit up again.

And we stood and stared at the searchlights, at the red-yellow-green flashes of the anti-aircraft guns in the sky, and at the rockets burning out slowly in the ravine. We had got so used to this spectacle that, if it had suddenly come to an end, we would have felt strange, as though something were missing.

"Well, what about it, shall we take the hill, battalion commander?" asked Karnaúkhov, very quietly almost into my very ear.

"We'll take it," I replied.

"I think so too." He squeezed my shoulder slightly.

"What's your Christian name?" I asked.

"Nikoláy."

"Mine is Yury."

"Yury. I've got a brother called Yury, a sailor."

"Alive?"

"I don't know. He was at Sevastópol. In a submarine."

149

"He's probably alive," I said, for some reason.

"Probably," Karnaúkhov replied after a slight delay, and we spoke no more.

A shooting star flared high in the sky. A soul had crossed over into the other world, they used to say in olden days . . . We made our way down. In the clouds of tobacco smoke it was difficult to make out faces. The men from the political sector were squatting down, eating something from a tin. The signals officer was sleeping, leaning against the wall, with his head hanging to one side. The captain had settled down by the lamp and was reading a newspaper.

He caught sight of us as he raised his head.

"It's a quarter to ten."

"A quarter to ten . . ."

"No scouts?"

"No."

"That's bad."

"Maybe."

I raised the wick with a safety-pin. The lamp gave practically no light—there wasn't enough air.

"I would ask everybody who is not taking a direct part in the operation to move over to battalion command post."

The captain's eyes became round. He put his newspaper to one side.

"Why?"

"Because . . ."

"I would ask you not to forget that you are speaking to a senior officer."

"I am forgetting nothing, but I'm asking you to leave here. That's all."

"Am I in your way?"

"Yes, you are."

"In what way?"

"By your presence. By the smoke. You see what's going on here? Can't even breathe."

I felt I was beginning to talk nonsense.

"My place is at the battalion observation post. I have to watch your work."

"You mean you intend to be on top of me the whole time?"

"Yes, that's my intention."

"And you'll attack the hill along with me?"

For a few seconds he stared at me without blinking. Then he stood up in a very deliberate manner, carefully folded his paper, stuffed it into his map-case and, turning towards me, slowly and carefully enunciating every word, declared:

"Very well. We'll talk about this in another place."

And he made his way out into the trench. On the way he got his case caught round a nail and took a long time to get it unhitched. The men from political section laughed. I had nothing against them. But I couldn't possibly turn out the captain alone. They laughed in understanding, wished me success and also left.

It became easier in the cellar at once. You could at least stretch your legs out and didn't have to squat down all the time.

I did not know why I had told the captain I was going to the hill. I had not intended to take part in the attack myself. I had had a talk with the major on this point already in the morning. He had shown me a leading article in *Red Star*[1]— "An Officer's Place in Battle". It criticised officers who personally led their units into attack. An officer should see everything and direct everything. In the front ranks he would see nothing. This was probably true.

And now, in conversation with the captain, that phrase about the hill had shot out of me somehow of its own accord. Come to think of it, how the devil could you at night direct a battle at a distance? Not a damned thing could be seen. Communications might break down any minute. Then you'd sit like a mole in the ground, without eyes and without ears . . .

The hands of the clock met near the figure ten.

Again they phoned from HQ: had the scouts returned? It was the assistant commander for the rear services, Korobkóv, acting as operational duty officer, who inquired. When he was on duty there was never any peace: "Report on the situation, have you enough sunflower seeds, do you need any gherkins?" Seeds were bullets (black were rifle bullets and white—Sten gun), gherkins were mines . . .

Just as I handed the telephone back to the signaller, Chumák's head appeared in the trench. After Chumák came the rest. Dirty, out of breath and their faces running with sweat. They immediately filled the place up.

I put no questions, but just waited.

Chumák staggered silently up to the table and sat on a box. In great gulps he drank water out of a mess-tin. Without hurrying he wiped his lips, his brow and his neck. Out of

1 Official newspaper of Soviet Ministry of Defence.

his pocket he took several green packets of German cigarettes. He threw them on to the table.

"Have a smoke."

He put a cigarette with a golden tip into his transparent cigarette holder.

"You can go ahead. The lights are green." And he nodded to his scouts. "Knock off. I shan't bother you till morning."

I asked:

"Are there mines?"

"Only in one place. Opposite the gun with its barrel upside down. Just a bit about it."

"A lot?"

"Didn't count 'em. We cleared about five of them. With whiskers. Anti-personnel—you know, the shrapnel type."

He held in his hand the polished copper detonator from a German mine, with three wires sticking upwards. The sappers called them whiskers. The body of the mine was buried in the ground and only the whiskers remained above the surface. If you stepped on them, the hammer struck the capsule, the capsule set light to the powder, the powder ignited the ejector charge, and the mine would shoot up above the ground and explode in the air, scattering splinters of shrapnel on all sides. A lousy mine.

"So don't go to the left of the gun. But to the right we've felt it all over for two hundred metres—there's nothing there."

"Are there many Jerries?"

"Godness knows . . . Not very many, it seemed. They're sitting in their dug-outs. Playing the gramophone. Mostly 'Katyúsha'."

Chumák felt in his pockets.

"Don't you write poetry?"

A dark eye with a golden rim looked mockingly at me from under his forelock.

"No. Why?"

"I wanted to make you a present of a fountain pen. It's a good pen. With special ink, in a little flask."

"No, I don't write poetry."

"Pity. I thought you did. You've got that sort of poetic look."

He turned a very fine pen over in his hands and then stuffed it in his pocket.

"We knocked off a Jerry over there—he was sitting in an outpost."

I phoned to HQ and informed them that the scouts had

returned. Valéga offered me some vodka. I wasn't very keen on having it, but I drank a couple of hundred grammes just the same. Chumák smiled ironically.

" To make it jollier for the men?"

I did not reply. I was looking for my automatic. Karnaúkhov was also getting ready. Chumák chewed on his cigarette holder.

" Is it far?"

" No. Not very."

" If you're thinking of the hill, I don't advise it. More comfortable here."

I woke up the officer in charge of communications. He had also stayed behind. His uncomprehending eyes blinked, still heavy with sleep.

" You take over command here in my place. I'm off."

" Where?"

" Over there."

I can see from his eyes that he doesn't understand a thing.

" Arrange things with the chief of staff Kharlámov. If you see things are going badly, open fire."

He stood up and hastily rubbed his eyes with his fist.

" All right . . ."

I scarcely knew him—I'd only seen him once at a conference with Borodín. They said he was a sensible lad. Senior lieutenant. He had taken some courses at the Academy.

Valéga wanted to go along as well. But it didn't seem wise. He had twisted his ankle and had been limping for two or three days.

" But—but how can you——?" He looked at me bewildered, his dissatisfied eyes peering out from beneath that round prominent brow.

I pushed the magazine into the gun.

" Maybe you'll take a bite for the journey? There's some tinned meat. After all, you didn't eat a proper dinner. I'll open a tin."

No. I didn't want to eat. I'd have something when I got back. All the same he stuffed into my pocket a crust of bread and a chunk of fat wrapped in paper. When I was still at school my mother also used to push my lunch at me as I was on my way. Only then it was French bread or a roll, cut in two and buttered.

X

The "corn-cob" was late. About ten minutes, which seemed to me like eternity. We couldn't smoke in the trench. There was nothing to do. It was cramped. Legs went to sleep because of the awkward position. I just couldn't get myself into a comfortable posture. Next to me was a soldier, a middle-aged Siberian. He was chewing a dry crust. They had again issued dried bread that day instead of fresh. By the light of the rockets I could see the muscles moving on his sunken, unshaven cheeks.

Karnaúkhov was on the right flank. In command here was company commander Sendétsky, not very intelligent, but a brave lad. At the "Metiz" he had been pretty good at holding the Germans off. He had even been wounded—lightly, it's true, but he didn't go into hospital.

My neighbour stopped crunching.

"Do you hear that?"

"What?"

"Isn't that the 'corn-cob'?"

We held our breath. The noise came steadily nearer from the direction of the Volga. Yes, that was ours. He was flying straight towards us. So long as he didn't tip his bombs out over us . . . Between us and the Germans were some seventy metres, no more. Maybe he'd hit us too. They said they simply threw the shells out by hand—ordinary mortar shells.

The noise came still nearer. Persistent, in a way homely, not at all military . . . The "corn-cob", "Russian plywood", the Germans called it. At first they had jeered at it. But later they realised the advantages it had for us—a cheap, handy and undemanding little plywood aeroplane. In the newspapers it was called a "low-powered night bomber". It buzzed just like a great beetle. There are some night beetles like that, which buzz and buzz monotonously and are never seen.

The "corn-cob" was already right overhead. He was circling, presumably to make certain of his position. The Germans started to fire at him from the other side of the hill. There were no searchlights up, but in any case you couldn't catch him in a searchlight beam—he was too low.

Now he was going to unload.

You might imagine that he was deliberately testing our patience.

The major had phoned to say that only one aeroplane would come over. He would drop bombs twice. Then he would circle for five or ten minutes to give us the chance to creep up.

The " corn-cob " made his second circle. It seemed to me that the soldier could hear my heart thumping. I was very nervous, and sick with the desire to smoke. If I'd been on my own I'd have squatted down right away and had a cigarette.

The " corn-cob " dropped his bombs. They made a clattering noise, like pop-guns. A bit too high up the hill. The German trenches were closer. But the machine-guns seemed to be up there.

One more circle . . . The whistle held tightly in my lips gave me cramp in the jaw and made the saliva run. It was with such whistles that football referees signalled goals.

The " corn-cob " dropped some more bombs. This time right on the trenches. We covered our heads. A few splinters sailed over our trench with the usual whistle. One buzzed around us for a long time, just like a bumble-bee. Then it fell close by, on the breastwork, between me and the soldier. It was so hot you couldn't pick it up. It was small and jagged. For some reason it sent cold shivers up my spine.

The " corn-cob " was firing from his machine-gun—in quick, short bursts, as though he were spitting.

The moment had come!

I gave the signal, covering the whistle slightly with my hand. I listened carefully. I could hear the lumps of clay tumbling down on the right.

Would we take it or not? We mustn't fail. I recalled the eyes of the div. commander when he said: " All right, then you'll take it."

I took my gun, and clambered downwards. The minefield was left behind. There was the big gun. It was to one side —some twenty metres. To the left of me were three more men. They knew they mustn't go there. I had warned them. I couldn't see them, but could only hear them creeping along.

The " corn-cob " was still circling. There were no rockets. The Germans were afraid of revealing their positions. That was all to the good.

But maybe he was going to drop more bombs? Maybe someone had got things muddled. Not twice, but three times . . . It happened sometimes.

155

I crept across the bottom of the ravine, hanging on to bushes, and then clambered up the opposite slope. I didn't want to run into anything by mistake . . . True, Chumák said their trenches began only beyond the bushes. Twigs were crackling to the right. People were certainly careless.

I crept on. Higher and higher, trying not to breathe, I don't know why. As though somebody might hear me breathing. Right in front of me was a star—the big, bright, unwinking Star of Bethlehem. I crept straight towards it.

Then suddenly—trrr-trrr-trrr—right above my ear. I pressed myself into the ground. I seemed even to feel the draught from the bullets. Where the devil had that machine-gun sprung up from?

I raised my head slightly, but I couldn't make out a darned thing. It seemed to be getting darker. There was silence all around. Not a crackle or a rustle. The " corn-cob " was already somewhere behind us. Now the Germans would start to light up the front line.

I wanted to sneeze, so I squeezed my nose in my fingers with all my strength and rubbed the bridge of my nose. I crept on. The bushes were now behind me. Next would be the German trenches . . . Another five or ten metres . . . There was nothing. I crept along carefully, feeling out in front with my hand. The Germans were fond of putting odd mines around. From somewhere, as though from under the earth, came the sounds of a fox-trot—a saxophone, piano and something else . . .

Trrr-trrr-trrr-trrr . .

The machine-gun again. But already behind me. What the devil? Could I possibly have crept too far? A muffled shout. A shot. Again the machine-gun. It had begun.

I threw a grenade at random—forwards, at something shadowy. I threw it with all my force and felt every muscle in my body and every nerve straining. Figures appeared for a moment in the darkness, like startled birds . . . Occasional shouts, muffled blows, gunfire, muttered curses. A trench. Crumbling earth. Machine-gun belts got mixed up with my feet. Something soft, warm and sticky. Something rose up in front of me and quickly vanished.

Night fighting is the most difficult type of fighting. It's a fight between individuals. There's no place here for the mass, self-effacing recklessness of the daytime attack. There is no " elbow feeling ". None of the " hurrahs " that relieve the strain, cover other sounds and inspire the soldier. There are no green greatcoats. No helmets or caps. No horizon. And no way back. Nobody knows where either his own men or the Germans are.

You don't see the end of the battle—you feel it. Later it's difficult to remember anything about it. You can't describe a night battle or anything that happened in it. In the morning you find yourself covered with scratches and bruises and blood. But at the time there's none of that. There's a trench . . . a corner . . . somebody . . . a blow . . . a shot . . . a rifle-butt . . . a step backwards, another blow. Then—quiet.

Who's that?—One of ours. Where are ours?—The devil only knows. Go on—Stop! Not a Jerry?—No, one of us . . .

Have we really taken the hill? It can't be. Which way are the Germans? Where have they gone to? We crept in from that direction. Where's Karnaúkhov?

"Karnaúkhov! Karnaúkhov!"

"They're over there, in front."

"Where?"

"There, by the machine-gun."

Somewhere far ahead our machine-gun was already firing away.

XI

Karnaúkhov had lost his cap. He was fumbling about in the darkness among our feet.

"It was a good one, a real cloth one. I fought the whole war in it. Pity."

"You'll find it in the morning. No one will take it."

He laughed.

"Well, what about it, comrade battalion commander? We took the hill after all."

"We took it, Karnaúkhov. We took it." And I also laughed, and for some reason I wanted to embrace him and kiss him.

In the east it was turning yellow. In an hour it would be quite light and the moon would be up.

"Send someone to the command post. Tell them to get the telephone connected."

"I've sent already. In half an hour we shall be able to talk to the major."

"Have you checked the men?"

"Yes, I've checked them. There are ten present so far. Four still missing. All the machine-gunners are here. I've already deployed the portable ones. The heavy one, it seems to me, wouldn't be bad right here. Now the second . . ."

"The second over there, to the right. Do you see where?"

"Perhaps we could go down and have a look?"

"Let's go."

We went along the trenches, leaning over to see whether there were any machine-gun pits. As far as we could see, the Germans' defences were circular. Of the Germans themselves there was nothing to be seen or heard. There was some firing away to the right and the left—on the sectors of the first and third battalions. Our eyes had already become accustomed to the darkness, and it was already possible to make out certain things. A couple of times we came across the bodies of dead Germans. Beyond the "Red October" something was still burning.

"Where's Sendétsky?"

"Here," came the voice unexpectedly in the darkness, as a figure appeared.

"Run along to the command post. Tell Kharlámov to remove men urgently from the old trenches and join up with our right flank. On the way make sure about his flank. I think it finishes just the other side of that bush. That's right, isn't it, Karnaúkhov?"

"Yes, there's nobody beyond that."

"Do you understand, Sendétsky? Go on, then. Quick as you can."

Sendétsky vanished. We found a place for the machine-gun and went back. In the darkness we ran into somebody.

"Battalion commander?"

"Yes. What is it?"

"I've found a wonderful dug-out. Come and have a look. You've never seen one like it." It was Chumák's voice.

"What are you doing here?"

"The same as you are . . ."

"But I thought you were going to take it easy?"

"What if I was?"

Chumák suddenly stopped and I couldn't help shambling into him.

"Hey . . . what's happened?"

"Listen, battalion commander . . . It turns out that you, er . . ."

158

" What?"

" I thought you were a poet . . . that you wrote verses. But it turns out . . ."

" Oh, all right. Lead on."

He made no reply. We went further. A light breeze sprang up. It was pleasant to feel it blowing your hair and getting past your collar under your tunic, right to your body. I was rather light-headed and my body felt a sort of strange lightness. It's what you feel in early spring, after the first stroll in the country. The air makes you drunk, your legs are stiff from unaccustomed exercise, your whole body aches slightly, but still you can't stop and on and on you go, quite aimlessly, coat undone, hat off, filling your lungs with the warm, stupefying, scented spring air . . .

Damn it all! We took the hill after all! And it turned out to be not so difficult. Apparently the Germans were not so very thick on the ground. They had left a covering party and gone off to the " Red October " . . . But, if I knew them, they wouldn't leave it at that. If they did not start to drive us back right away, they certainly would do so in the morning. If only we could manage to drag just one forty-five millimetre gun up and straddle the ravine . . . Kharlámov would now start getting busy, looking for things, packing things up and generally getting organised . . . The signals officer was there with him, it was true. They'd manage it together—it wasn't as difficult as all that. I still had Sinítsyn's spades with me—the men would be dug in by morning and to-morrow night we'd lay mines.

The Star of Bethlehem was now directly overhead, greenish and unblinking. It seemed to have stopped still. Thus far and no further.

The moon had crept out; it dangled just above the horizon, yellow and not yet giving light. All around was quiet, as in a field. Was it really true that a battle had been fought here?

Later we were sitting in the dug-out. It was deep, four layers down with another metre and a half of earth on top. The walls were boarded and hung with paper that looked like oil-cloths. Fanned out on a wall above a card table with a baize top and curved legs, were postcards: a sprig of fir-tree with a gutted candle, a round-eyed pug-dog that had upset an inkwell, a gnome in a red cap, and an angel sailing through the sky. A little higher was the Führer, looking exalted, with tight lips, and wearing a glistening raincoat.

On the table was a lamp with a green shade. There were about five bottles. A tin of sprats. Kid gloves thrown down on the bed.

Chumák played the host, pouring brandy into thin monogrammed glasses.

"The Führer didn't forget our stomachs anyway . . . Let's thank him . . ."

The brandy was good and strong and caught your breath.

Karnaúkhov drank up and went straight out. Chumák studied with curiosity the intertwining vines on the bottle labels. The brandy was French.

"You've got a heavy hand, you know, lieutenant. I would never have thought it."

"What hand?"

"That one there, that you're holding your cigarette with."

"I don't understand what you're talking about."

"Well, my left shoulder still feels as if it belonged to someone else."

"What left shoulder?"

"Don't you remember?" And he laughed merrily, with his head thrown back. "You don't remember clouting me with an automatic? A full swing. On the left shoulder blade."

"Wait . . . wait a minute . . . When was that?"

"When? About half an hour ago. In the trench. You took me for a Jerry. You didn't half let fly! I saw nothing but stars. And I thought you were a poet, writing poems. I even offered you a pen . . . I wanted to nark you. But when a real Jerry turned up—you certainly gave it him . . ."

I did remember actually striking someone with an automatic, but I hadn't been able to distinguish a darned thing in the darkness.

"For such a blow I can spare a watch," said Chumák, fumbling in his pocket. "A good one. With jewels."

We both laughed.

The signallers tumbled into the dug-out with boxes and coils of wire. They were breathing like steam engines.

"We only just made it. We jolly nearly dropped in on the Jerries."

"On what Jerries?"

A fair-haired, watery-eyed signaller, puffing, removed the radio that was strapped on to his back.

"Oh, they're creeping along the ravine there like cockroaches."

"Along what ravine?"

"Along the same one . . . where our front line went."

Chumák's eyes were suddenly small and sharp.

"Are you going alone or with the men?" I asked.

"Never mind the men. I'm going now . . ."

He grabbed a gun and, forgetting even to put on his jacket, disappeared through the doorway.

Could they really have cut us off?

The signallers dragged the wire in through the door.

"You're really sure that the Jerries are in the ravine?"

"Couldn't be surer," replied the fair-haired one; "we ran smack into them. There were about five of 'em creeping up. We even opened fire on 'em."

"Maybe it was our chaps, taking up new defences?"

"How could it be our chaps? Ours were still sitting in the trenches when we left. We met the platoon commander on the way, the one who goes about with a bandaged throat. He was looking for the chief of staff."

"Come on then, put me through to the battalion."

The fair-haired one fitted his mouthpiece on his head.

"Jupiter . . . Jupiter . . . Hallo . . . Jupiter . . ."

By his lifeless expression I could see that nobody was replying.

"Jupiter . . . Jupiter . . . This is Mars . . ."

A pause.

"No good. They've cut it, the bastards. Léshka, go and check it . . ."

Léshka—red-nosed, big-eared, in an out-size cap—grumbled, but went.

"They've cut it. It's a fact," said the fair one calmly and took from behind his ear a cigarette he had rolled in advance.

I took myself off outside. There was the sound of automatic gun-fire from the direction of the ravine and occasional rifle shots.

Then Chumák appeared.

"That's the way it is, bat. commander—a ring."

"We've fallen into it, you mean?"

"We have. The Jerries have taken up positions in trenches on this slope."

"Many?"

"How can you tell? They're firing from everywhere."

"Where's Karnaúkhov?"

"He's moving the machine-gun to a different place; he'll be here in a minute."

Chumák took out a green packet of cigarettes.

"Have a smoke. Jerry ones."

We lit up.

"Yes, Chumák, we're in a mess . . . That's the truth."

"We're in a mess," laughed Chumák. "Well, never mind, bat. commander. We'll get ourselves out of it somehow. My lads are also here. We've got machine-guns. We've got more supplies than we know what to do with. They left everything. There's even a hot dinner in the thermos flasks. What more do we need?"

Karnaúkhov came up. He had already taken up circular defence positions and had found two German machine-guns. There were also lots of grenades, about ten boxes. And, apart from that, they were lying about in every gun-pit and in the niches.

"The only really lousy thing is that their trenches are not under fire from our side. It's too steep."

"How many men have we got?"

"Infantry—twelve. There are a couple we still haven't found. Two fixed machine-guns. Two portable ones. And two more German ones. Six, that is."

"My lads make another three," interjected Chumák, "and there's three of us. And a couple of signallers. We can live."

"That makes twenty-six," I said.

Karnaúkhov reckoned it up in his head.

"No, twenty-two. The hand machine-gunners aren't to be counted—they're included in the twelve."

From the direction of the ravine the firing never ceased. It would flare up and then die down. It was apparently ours who were shooting—from the other side, and the Germans were replying. Tracer bullets, like threads, were flying from one side of the ravine to the other. It was awkward for the Germans to fire at us from the ravine. Their situation was also unenviable—they were pressed in from both sides.

Then firing started somewhere to the left. The Germans were pulling themselves together. They were pressing in around us. But they weren't putting up any rockets, so it was difficult to determine exactly where their front line now ran.

We went to check the fire points.

XII

The whole thing was idiotic . . . There had been no need for me to join in the attack. A battalion commander ought to direct an attack and not take part in it. Now see where I had got myself to. I had relied on the first battalion. After all, I had agreed everything with Sinítsyn: as soon as I sent up a red rocket, he was to open fire with all kinds of weapons, so as to create a small diversion and give the men I'd left behind the chance to take up new positions. Actually it seemed as though they had opened fire. That was because Kharlámov and the signals officer had got busy. The toothy captain had been quite right in his forebodings—he had asked about the flanks. He was probably furious now. Or he was gloating. I felt he was that kind of person. He was probably already telephoning in all directions: "I told him, I warned him . . . but he wouldn't even listen. He ordered me out. Now see what he's got himself into . . ."

It would have been possible, of course, to break through back to our lines. But what would have been the point of that? We would only lose the hill and get the hell of a pasting in return . . . But to sit doing nothing, using up ammunition, was also silly. Our chaps would lie there, on the other side of the ravine, with their arms folded. This was the very moment for the third battalion to come into action —cut off the bridge and join up with us.

We had enough ammunition to last a couple of days, even if we had to fend off attacks all the time. Our machine-guns had kept deliberately silent practically throughout the previous day—they had been saving bullets. We also had grenades. Only we were a bit short of men. And all of us on a pocket handkerchief. There would be no rest from German mortars.

Just after four o'clock the Germans went over to the attack, and tried to creep through unnoticed. Our machine-guns were not yet properly sighted, but we drove off that first attack fairly easily. The Germans didn't even reach the trenches.

At two points our trenches joined up with the German ones. Two long communicating ways stretched in neat zigzags in the direction of the water towers. They were deep, practically the height of a man, and from our direction they were quite out of sight. I ordered them to be dug in in several places.

More carelessness. We hadn't taken the sappers' spades with us, and we'd found only three among the captured material, though they were good steel ones with well fashioned handles.

We had only just started digging when the mortar bombardment began. First one, then two and by the evening even three batteries. Mortar shells exploded continually, one after the other. They were softening us up in a truly methodical German way. We sat in the dug-outs, with only observers posted outside.

Two men put out of action. One was wounded in the leg, the other had an eye knocked out. We bandaged them up with our personal first-aid kits—we had nothing else.

After midday the attacks began again. Three in a row, and certainly not less than two companies involved. So long as there were machine-guns this didn't scare me. With four machine-guns—we left a couple to deal with the ravine—we could hold a whole regiment. It wouldn't be so good if tanks came up. The land between us and the storage tanks was as flat as a table. And we had only two anti-tank weapons—Símonovs. Maybe our chaps would think of setting up forty-five millimetre guns on that side of the ravine.

About three o'clock our long-range gun on the other side of the river came into action. It fired for about an hour with reasonable accuracy. We even had time to get a meal. The shells exploded not very far away—about a hundred metres from our front line. One round came quite close and the splinters sailed over our heads. For a couple of hours the Germans did not bother us.

Later, just before evening, there were two more attacks—artillery raids, and that was that. Peace reigned. The first rockets flared up.

XIII

Stretched out on a wooden bed, Chumák was describing a certain Músya he had met in hospital.

Karnaúkhov and I were cleaning our revolvers.

The lamp gave an astonishingly peaceful light from beneath its green shade.

"You ought to see the sort of regulations they have down there in Kuíbyshev," said Chumák, drawing on his cigarette and spitting. "The gates are locked and there's a watchman. Like in prison. You can only stroll in the yard. And the yard's about as big as a pocket handkerchief. Walls on every side, asphalt in the middle, benches, and ice-cream on sale. The nurses are not bad. Only they're scared of the authorities. They'll sit alongside you on the bench or by your bedside, but as for anything else . . . nothing doing. Not allowed and that's that . . . So long as I was on my back, I didn't want to and I even began to get a bit concerned . . . But later, when I began to walk, I started to look around, to come to life and the blood began to surge again in my veins. It surged all right, but to no purpose: "You mustn't, comrade patient, it's not allowed. You must rest and get well." A rest, they call it! Lying on your bed or going to the cinema in the evenings. The pictures were all old ones—like *Alexander Nevsky, Pozharsky, A Girl with Character*—so they kept breaking down. And the cinema stank of plaster. Ugh!"

Karnaúkhov's lips twitched in a smile.

"Just keep to the point—you started talking about a certain Músya . . ."

"I'll get around to Músya in time. Don't interrupt. If you don't like it, don't listen. Go and check your machine-guns. I'll tell the lieutenant instead. He hasn't been in hospital yet. I must put him wise." He reached for another cigarette. "There's nothing in these things. Can't get a decent smoke . . ." And, turning ostentatiously in my direction, he continued. "So my arm was in plaster. The left radius was smashed. Trying to sleep at night, I just couldn't get comfortable. The hook just stuck out and that was that. But it was still a good thing it was broken below the elbow. The ones who had it higher up, or in the shoulder blade, were in a real mess. They had to have a great plaster case right across their chests, and their arms on a support. They call them ' aeroplanes ' in the hospital. They walk about with their arms sticking out half a yard in front. The second wound was just below my backbone—the splinter's still in there . . . It's all right now, can't feel it. But then to go to the bucket —that was a business. I was shy of Músya . . . She was just the job. Plaits as long as this. And a close-fitting smock. She would sit on my bed—I still couldn't walk—and feed me scrambled powdered egg with a spoon, while I was on tenter-hooks . . . Later we used to climb out of the window . . . It was all right to jump from the bathroom there. Couple of yards, no more. When you stood on the radiator your chin just reached the window sill. There was a captain in there with me. A cultured chap, with an education—like you! He had been chief engineer in a factory before the war. So we used to dive out together just in our pants and nightshirts with the hospital badge on them. Round the corner was a house with some people we knew, where we used to change our clothes and go off into town. The captain had been wounded in the stomach, but he was convalescing. He used to climb out first, then he'd pull me up by the plaster hook. But when they nailed the window up—the woman in charge of the passes saw us—we found a way of getting down the drain pipe. There was one chap there without legs. He would hang his crutches on one arm and be out like a monkey—only the wall plaster used to crumble . . . People adapt themselves. If you buried them in the ground they'd get out somehow."

Karnaúkhov laughed.

" When we were in Baku, people used to ' dive ' out during the cinema. You could hear them outside the window—plop, plop, plop, one after the other. When the film ended there'd be no one left in the ward except those who couldn't get out of bed."

" That's nothing," Chumák interrupted, without turning round. " In the sixth ward we made a rope ladder. All properly done, with rungs, as it should be. We used it for a couple of weeks. There was a great big tree right under the window which nobody had noticed. But then they started to clean the windows—some high-ups were expected—and they ripped our ladder off . . . The whole ward was summoned to the sister in charge . . . But what could they do? The next day we were diving out of the seventh ward."

Mice were scratching between the beams. Somewhere far

away and above us night mortars crackled every now and then.

The yellow-bearded gnome sat on his toadstool smoking a long pipe with a lid. The angel sailed through the thick, inky sky. The pug-dog stared in astonishment at the overturned inkpot. Somebody had given Hitler a beard and a luxurious "Maupassant" moustache, so that he now looked like a hairdresser's advertisement.

The wounded were lying in the neighbouring dug-out. They were constantly asking for something to drink. But water was terribly short—two German thermoses for twenty men.

During the day we had beaten off seven attacks and lost four men killed, four wounded and one machine-gun.

I smeared my revolver with oil and put it into its holster. Then I stretched myself out on the bed.

"Going to sleep, lieutenant?" asked Chúmak.

"No, I'm just going to have a lie down."

"Are you fed up with listening?"

"No, no, carry on with the story, I'm listening."

He went on talking. I lay on my side, listening to the endless tale of the hospital sister who succumbed, gazing at Chumák, vest-clad, sprawling on his bunk, at Karnaúkhov's big, oily fingers fiddling with his revolver, at the lock of hair covering his eyes . . . He kept on brushing it back with the back of his hand, so as not to get the oil on his face. And it was hardly credible that an hour or two previously we had been driving off attacks, dragging wounded along awkward, narrow trenches and that we were now occupying a small patch of ground, cut off from everybody.

"So, it was pretty good in hospital, Chumák?" I asked.

"It was all right," he replied.

"Better than here?"

"What a question! You lie on your back, you think of nothing, no 'tongues'[1], no fatigues. Just eat, sleep and go for treatment."

"Didn't you miss your men?"

"What men?"

"The men in the regiment."

"Of course I missed them. That's why I got myself discharged a month early."

"But you said it was good in hospital," laughed Karnaúkhov, " —no fatigues, you just eat and sleep."

[1] "Tongue"—an enemy soldier captured by scouts and brought back for interrogation.

167

"What are you grinning about? As if you didn't know. It's always better somewhere else. When you're here, you'd like to be in hospital, playing the fool, lying in clean sheets. But when you're there, you don't know what to do with yourself, you want to be back at the front and with the lads."

Karnaúkhov put his revolver together—he had a big, captured 'Walter' with a comfortable grip—and rammed it into its holster.

"How many times have you been in hospital, Chumák?"

"Three. Twice in field hospitals and once in a base hospital. What about you?"

"Twice."

Karnaúkhov laughed.

"All the same, it's sort of strange when you come back to the front. Didn't you find it so?—Getting used to it all over again."

"It wasn't so bad coming back from the field hospitals—you don't spend long there. But coming from the base hospital . . . It was even embarrassing—a mine pops off and there you are, ducking down."

They both laughed.

"It's an amazing thing, comrade lieutenant," said Karnaúkhov, wiping his oily hands on his padded trousers, "when you are sitting in the trenches it seems as though there's nothing better or quieter than your own dug-out. Your battalion command post is always behind the lines. As for regimental or Divisional HQ . . . The soldiers speak of all those who are stationed on the shore as being in the rear . . ."

Chumák, who couldn't sit without talking, butted in:

"Have you never come across the sort of chap who's a hundred kilometres behind the front and shoots a line like a front-line man! We had one in hospital . . ."

He stopped suddenly, with his eyes fixed on the doorway. "Where did you come from?"

Karnaúkhov also stared at the door.

Good heavens! Valéga. The man himself—with his big head and prominent forehead, in his unbelievable shoes with their turned-up toes. He stood in the doorway, wearing my greatcoat, which reached down to his heels, and squinting.

"Where did you spring from, Valéga?"

"From there. From our lines."

He saluted awkwardly. He was never very good at that. He took a sack off his back.

"I brought some tinned meat . . . and your greatcoat . . ."

"Have you taken leave of your senses?"

" Why should I have? Certainly not. Here's a message for you."

" From whom?"

" Kharlámov gave it me—the chief of staff."

" Was it he who sent you?"

" Certainly not. I came of my own accord . . ." Valéga took the tins and two loaves of bread out of the sack. " I was packing the sack and they were talking with someone from regimental HQ about having somehow to make contact with you. So I said I was just off to you. They started to look for something and then gave me this note."

From his side pocket, which, like every soldier's, was crammed full, he got a page out of a notebook folded in four. He handed it over to me. It was written in Kharlámov's precise handwriting:

" 5.10.42.   12.15.   *Command Post Hurricane.*
" Comrade lieutenant. Following orders received on the 31st I have to report that an attack will be launched by us to-day at 0400 hours with the object of linking up with you on the right flank and with the task of cutting off and destroying the enemy group that has penetrated into the ravine. I have to inform you that we have received reinforcements of 7 (seven) men and that they have telephoned from Storm to say that a new commander of our outfit has arrived in your place. We have not seen him yet. How are you getting on there, comrade lieutenant? Captain Abrósimov and several others from the big outfit came along early this morning. Hold on, comrade lieutenant. We'll get you out of it.

Kharlámov Lt."

The signature was ministerial, bold and sloping, with a splendid baroque " Kh " and a whole host of flourishes, curls and dots flying around it like birds.

I tore up the message and burnt the pieces. How could anyone think of sending such a message through the front line! Oh that Kharlámov! He was not a bad chap at bottom and even a keen one, only such a . . .

Valéga was opening a tin with a complicated German opener that had a little wheel at the end. The lop-eared devil! He crawled through the front line with those tins and brought my greatcoat with him. And brought a message at the same time. " So I said I was just off to you." As though we were just round the corner, on the second floor . . .

169

Valéga puffed away but just couldn't open the tin with the unfamiliar opener. He didn't even ask whether I was hungry. I asked no questions—I felt the proper tone might evade me. It was the others—Karnaúkhov and Chumák—who asked them. Valéga replied unwillingly.

"The greatcoat got in the way a bit, it was too big . . . Otherwise nothing special. Over there, a little to the left—there's a gap in their lines. Between the trenches. I studied it in the daytime, and at night . . . Maybe you'd like it warmed up, comrade lieutenant?"

"No, don't bother. Anyway there's nothing to warm it up on."

"You didn't forget to bring a primus, did you?" laughed Chumák.

Instead of replying Valéga drew out of the greatcoat a German pocket spirit lamp and a handful of white slabs of dry fuel that looked like lumps of sugar. Without a word or the shadow of a smile he put them down on the table.

"It isn't worth it, Valéga. We'll eat it as it is."

And all four of us finished off the tin with relish. It's certainly a wonderful thing, corned beef . . .

XIV

Our watches showed half-past three. Then a quarter to four . . . Four. We waited. Half-past four. Five. Everything quiet. Six, seven . . . First light. No good waiting any more.

So there was to be another day of it.

Throughout the first half of the day the Germans sprayed us from mortars—medium and even heavies. By three o'clock there were twelve men left out of sixteen. Of those wounded the previous day four were dying. It seemed to me they had blood poisoning. One had tetanus. That was frightful. He was dying before my eyes, a man no longer young, about forty, who had been hit by an explosive bullet in the right arm, just below the elbow. He kept worrying that his arm would be amputated. Before the war he had been a metal turner. "How will I manage without an arm?" he kept saying, carefully laying his arm, which was bound to a board from an ammunition box on his knee. "At our job you just can't do without an arm. Better be without a leg." He looked inquiringly from me to Karnaúkhov and from Karnaúkhov to me, as though our opinions were worth anything. We told him that bones grew quickly together, that the flesh would also grow, and that his nerve was intact, since he could move his fingers. This reassured him. He even began to tell us about some gadget he had invented before the war for his lathe. Later his face began to twitch. His mouth gaped open in a frightful, strained smile. His neck became rigid. Convulsions seized his whole body. He arched himself up, with only his heels and the back of his neck on the ground. He screamed. It was impossible to unbend him—his body was as stiff as iron.

"Tetanus," said Karnaúkhov. "We had a chap in the medical corps who died from that."

Two hours later he died.

His name was Fésenko. I discovered that from his army book. The name was for some reason familiar. Where had I heard it? Then I remembered. He was one of those two soldiers who had been digging at night, when I was coming back from the minefield, and who couldn't explain to the runner where the battalion commander was.

A regimental mine—a 120-millimetre one—landed on our dug-out. Theoretically the dug-out should have held firm—four layers of 25-centimetre beams with earth on top. In fact, it was put out of action: the roofing stood up, but the explosion fetched down the boarding and filled the dug-out with earth.

We moved into the next one, where the wounded were lying. There were four of them. One was delirious—he was wounded in the head. He kept talking about some tin troughs, then he would call for somebody, then he'd come back to the troughs again. His face was waxen, his eyes were closed all the time. He too would probably die.

We did not bury those who were killed. Mortar shells whistled and exploded all around without a break. In the course of one minute I counted six explosions. There were occasional breaks. But not more than six or seven minutes. In those seven minutes we had time only to gather ourselves together and make sure whether the observers were still alive.

The three of us, Karnaúkhov, Chumák and I, smoked our last cigarette—half makhorka and half bread-crumbs scraped together from all our pockets. There was no more tobacco. All the fag-ends had already been picked up.

The water was coming to an end. A shell hit one of the thermos flasks. We only noticed this when practically all the water had run out. In the other one there were only about

171

ten litres. And the wounded kept begging for something to drink. We didn't know if we ought to give them any. One was wounded in the stomach—he certainly shouldn't have any. He kept begging: "Just a drop, comrade lieutenant, just a drop, my mouth's dry . . ."—and he looked at me with such eyes that I wished I could vanish through the ground. The machine-guns also asked for water.

After three the Germans began attacking. It went on intermittently until the evening. Attack, bombardment, attack and again a bombardment.

By the time we drove off the last attack we were completely exhausted. The machine-guns were hissing away like kettles.

Where could we get some water? If we ran out, the machine-guns would pack up the next day . . .

In the evening we analysed the situation.

There were eleven of us. I, Chumák, Karnaúkhov, Valéga, two signallers, four machine-gunners—two to each gun—and one private soldier—that same Siberian with whom I had sat in the trench. He'd had the little finger of his right hand shot off, but he was putting up a good show. Apart from that there were three wounded. The one who had been delirious had died towards evening. We carried him out into a trench. That's where we put all the dead.

We had four machine-guns. Two had gone out of action. We had enough ammunition for the German ones. For our own there was just about enough for half a day.

But the most important thing was water. Without it all the bullets weren't worth a damn. Surely our chaps couldn't fail to join up with us that night? It was impossible that they wouldn't try. They knew we couldn't hold on for ever. And that, if we were knocked out, the hill could be written off.

We were giddy with longing for a smoke. Valéga found a wet, squashed cigarette in the pocket of a dead German. We took turns to smoke it, inhaling deeply, closing our eyes and burning our fingers. In a couple of hours we would long for water in the same way—there were no more than two litres in the thermos. That was the indispensable reserve for the machine-guns.

The signallers dug out from somewhere in the depths of the dug-out a dozen appetising, oily herrings wrapped in grease-proof paper. My mouth watered. They were silvery and smooth, with soft backbones and little spots of fat, like dew, below their heads. Just the sort you'd like to get your teeth into. I crawled up into the trench, threw them as far as I could in the direction of the Germans and came back.

The wounded had quietened down, but were breathing heavily. They were lying on the ground. We put greatcoats under them. The new dug-out wasn't as good as the other one. There was a sort of table made of boards roughly knocked together and covered with a newspaper—that was all. Against the damp, crumbling wall our green-shaded lamp looked preposterous. We had brought it along from the other dug-out. How it had remained unbroken was a mystery.

Karnaúkhov drew little flowers with a pencil stump on the margin of the newspaper. His face was very drawn and he had big black rings beneath his eyes. Chumák had removed his vest and was going through the seams for lice.

" We shall have to take a bath," he said, scratching his head wearily. " When we join up I'll organise a bath. We'll fetch some water from the Volga at night and we'll have a good bath. I itch all over."

" You won't get rid of 'em anyway till the war is over," Karnaúkhov consoled him. " It isn't as if the laundry ever got sterilised. It only gets washed in the Volga and what's the good of that?"

I watched Chumák's biceps quivering beneath the tight skin. He'd make a good subject for a lesson in anatomy.

Chumák stood up.

" Ach . . . I'd like a smoke . . ."

Karnaúkhov sighed:

" Yes . . . wouldn't be bad. Even a ' Motor ' at thirty-five kopecks. One for the three of us."

" ' Motor ' . . . Why a ' Motor '? If you dream, you might as well dream properly . . ."

" What did you smoke before the war, comrade lieutenant?"

" ' Belomor ' . . . and ' Labour '. You could get them in Kiev—also at two roubles."

" I smoked ' Belomor ' too. Fat and good. Especially the Leningrad ones."

" Then you don't know much about cigarettes," said Chumák. " Longing for ' Belomor ' . . . ' Kazbeck '—those are real cigarettes. I used to smoke a couple of packets a day. Those were the days."

He walked up and down the dug-out—two steps up and two steps back—stretching himself, throwing his arms back behind his head.

" I'd put on my bell-bottom trousers—thirty centimetres
173

wide—pull my cap down, take a girl on my arm and . . ."—
sticking out his chest, he seized Karnaúkhov by the arm—
" off down the Primbul."

Karnaúkhov pushed him away.

"What did you do before the war?"

" Me? I was a chauffeur. Drove a ZIS. Then I served on
the ' Red Ukraine '[1]. In the regulars. Those were the days.
Polish up my buckle with chalk, press my tunic, put on my
white bell-bottomed trousers—and off into the town."

" Did you ever think of anything except girls, Chumák?"

Chumák appeared to reflect.

" I used to think about vodka too. What else? As for
money—there was always plenty. I had no intention of
becoming a scientist." There was a pause. " And look
now . . ."

" Surely you haven't cooled off?"

Chumák didn't answer at once. His hands deep in his
pockets and his feet wide apart, he was trying to pick his
words:

" It's not that I've cooled off. I've always been fond of the
women and I always will be, but now when there's a war . . ."
Another pause. " You see, before the war I thought I was
God Almighty. I had my own gang. We drank together
and together we bashed the faces of such . . ."—he smiled
faintly and winked at me with his cunning eye—" chaps as
him. But, on the whole, that's not the point . . ."

He sat down on the edge of the table, swinging his leg.
He found it difficult to formulate his thought. It was turning
around somewhere, but he couldn't quite hit it on the head.

" At Sevastópol, for example. There was a case like this.
Right at the beginning of the siege. In December, I think, or
maybe the end of November? I can't remember . . . I had a
pal. He wasn't even a pal, he just worked with me on the
' Red Ukraine '. He too was a sailor. Later we found
ourselves together in the trenches on the shore. Near the
French cemetery. Before the war we behaved like cat and dog
to each other. He once tried to get some woman away from
me. He was a decent-looking chap, well-built, and the girls
were always after him. My fists itched to knock a couple of
his teeth out."

In the corner a wounded man started to toss and turn. He
begged for a drink. We gave him a wet rag to suck—that was
all that was now in our power. He drew his greatcoat over

[1] " Red Ukraine "—battleship of the Black Sea fleet.

174

his face and settled down. I tried not to look at where the thermos of water was standing. Chumák put the wet rag down on it and again sat on the edge of the table.

"In other words I didn't like him. And he didn't like me . . ."

Karnaúkhov sat with his head resting on his hands. He didn't take his grey eyes off Chumák. Chumák swung his leg.

"I knocked a couple of 'em out for him. And he bust a couple of my ribs. For two weeks—three maybe—I couldn't breathe properly. But that wasn't the point . . . To cut it short, the Jerries ripped up my whole back with an explosive shell. About fifteen yards from their trenches. I thought it was the end all right. And, goodness knows, I might have had it altogether . . . In the morning I woke up in our own trench. It turned out that that same Teréntyev had dragged me in."

For a few moment we sat in silence. Chumák was picking at the edge of the table with his nail. Karnaúkhov sat just as he had been sitting, with his head on his hands. The little tongue of flame flickered in the lamp. One of its ends was long and thin and licked against the glass leaving a black smear.

"He died later on, that Teréntyev. Both his legs were blown off. It was in Gagri, in hospital, that I found out. They sent me on a card from him. He'd asked them to just before he died. Anyway, Teréntyev's gone, what's the use of talking . . ."

He jumped down from the table and again started walking up and down the dug-out. Karnaúkhov, without turning his head, followed him with his eyes.

"You see, before the war, for me chaps were . . . well, how shall I put it . . . well, they kept you from being bored drinking alone. But now . . . Look, I've got a scout . . . You know him, bat. commander—the one on whose account you and I sort of quarrelled. Well, you see, for him I would bite through anybody's throat with my bare teeth . . . Or Helman, the Jew. Send him where you like he'll do anything. The Jerries slaughtered his whole family in some little village . . ."

He broke off in the middle of a word, turned sharply on his heel and left the dug-out. The steps creaked as he went up them. Karnaúkhov turned again to his drawing.

"You usedn't to be on good terms with Chumák, comrade lieutenant?" he asked discreetly, without raising his head.

"Well, there was something like that," I replied.

Karnaúkhov smiled.

"He told me about it yesterday. Over some dead Jerry or something. Wasn't that it?"

"Yes, it started with a Jerry."

"He didn't like you too much then, he said."

"What can you do? You can't please everyone."

"And now it's all right?"

"What d'you mean?"

"You've made it up?"

"But who said we quarrelled? It was just that he has an obstinate nature. He doesn't like orders. But I like people like that. I don't mean those who don't carry out orders, but those like Chumák—who aren't afraid to stand up for themselves."

"Yes, you have to give him his due."

"And not only for that."

"Well, I didn't think they were the sort you'd like."

"What kind, then?"

"Well, what shall I say . . . You are not, so to speak, birds of a feather . . ."

"But maybe . . ."

With that the conversation ended. Chumák came in.

"Where's the empty can? The one that had water in it?"

"What can?"

"You know, the thermos. Whatever it's called. It was standing by the entrance."

"Why, has it gone?"

"Yes."

"Where's it got to?"

"The devil knows . . ."

"When I went out it was standing at the entrance," said Karnaúkhov. "I even tripped over it."

"Well, now it's gone. I've searched everywhere."

"Valéga's probably taken it. To stop up the shrapnel hole."

"But where's Valéga?"

"He was here, not long ago. He was cleaning a Sten gun. What do you want him for?"

"Well, we must do something about the water. We want a drink, and so do the blasted machine-guns."

"What on earth can you do?" I asked uncomprehendingly.

"Something must be done . . . The old chap over there says he thinks something is bubbling. He's standing to the left, by the ravine. He says it's bubbling. Maybe a spring of some kind."

"How can there be a spring! It's paraffin dripping from the

trucks. You know how you hear things at night? It's only a couple of hundred metres to the tracks, no more."

"But why not have a look?"

"Have a look if you want to."

We distributed the rest of the water around the mess-tins. There was not even enough for two. With the thermos hoisted on to his back, Chumák departed. Five minutes later Valéga appeared. He sat in the corner cleaning a Sten gun, as though he had been nowhere.

"Where did you get lost?"

"I didn't get lost," he replied, cleaning the dirt from his gun with a splintering of wood.

"Did you take the can? The thermos?"

"Yes, I did."

"What the hell. We've been looking all over the place."

Valéga looked at me reproachfully.

"You said yourself there was no water."

"Well?"

"So I went to get some."

"Water?"

"Of course, water."

"Down to the Volga, or what?"

"No. I didn't go to the Volga."

"Listen, talk sense. Do you mean you've brought water?"

"I didn't bring water. I brought wine." He went on fiddling with his gun.

The picture gradually became clear. While it was still daylight he had looked for a way through. Some footpath to the right of the bridge—in the direction of the third battalion.

"Why didn't you say anything?"

"You wouldn't have let me go."

In short he didn't manage to get as far as the third battalion—he came across some German kitchen.

"There, by the embankment. They must bring it there at night time. On horses. Fine great animals. So I crept up. There was a little ditch. It was where they threw their dirty water. I got in there. Two Jerries were sitting nearby, smoking. In the darkness you could only see the glow of the cigarettes. They were talking quietly in their own way— hau, hau, hau . . . Then one of them lit a cigarette lighter and I saw some thermoses standing by the stove. Just like this one. About five steps away. Probably tea or coffee, I thought. They kept on chattering away. Then one of them went out and the other stayed. He sat and smoked. So I waited. I

177

hung on for about ten minutes. I was soaked in dirty water up to the belly. Then he went to relieve himself—behind the kitchen. So I took a thermos and left him ours—the empty one. They'll be cross."

Valéga smiled—just the slightest smile, at the corner of his mouth. He very rarely did that.

" It's lousy wine, sour . . . Just right for the machine-gun."

We drank it up, half a glass each. In little sips, prolonging the pleasure, cleaning out our mouths. Then we went to sleep.

For some reason I dreamt of the Black Sea. I was diving from the cliffs into the transparent water, quivering with needles of sunlight. And all round were jelly-fish—big and small, just like umbrellas.

XV

Our attack was not successful. We stood in the trenches and watched the gun battle. The Germans fired away with their machine-guns without any break at all. The bursts collided with one another, crossed each other and flew up high into the sky. Here and there on the other side of the ravine were flashes of mortar fire. Then they fell silent. There remained only the regular ones, with their steady fire. We went back into the dug-out.

We didn't sleep the remainder of the night. The conversation flagged. Having no tobacco made us irritable. The wounded kept on begging for something to drink. Towards morning another of them died.

At seven the " crate " arrived. It droned and droned away endlessly, twisting and turning and reflecting the sun on its windows. Then—without the slightest preparation—the Germans went and launched an attack.

We met their fire with four machine-guns. Two of them were manned by machine-gunners. At the other two were Chumák and Karnaúkhov, and Valéga and myself. The signallers and the old man covered our flanks.

The sun shone from behind our backs. It was good for shooting.

Then came the bombardment. We withdrew the machine-guns and squatted right down. Shrapnel sailed over our heads. It was only then that I noticed how much weight Valéga had lost. His cheeks had fallen in and were covered with spots. His eyes were big and serious. He sat with his knees practically touching his ears.

A mine exploded in the passage a few steps away from us.

" Bastards!" said Valéga.

" Bastard," said I.

The bombardment lasted some twenty minutes. It was very exhausting. Then we dragged the machine-gun out on to its platform and waited.

Chumák waved his hand. I could see only his head and hand.

" The two on the left have had it," he shouted.

We were left with three machine-guns.

We drove off one more attack. My machine-gun got stuck. It was a German one and I didn't understand it very well. I shouted to Chumák.

He ran along the trench. A piece of shrapnel had got him in a soft part of the body. There was a hole through his cap over his right ear.

" Those two are dead all right," he said, as he extracted the bolt. " Only rags left."

I did not reply. Chumák did something tricky with the bolt and pushed it back. He fired a burst. It was all right.

" Got enough ammunition, bat. commander?"

" For the time being."

" There's another box lying there near the dug-out. I think it's the last."

" A mortar hit it."

He looked me straight in the eyes. I could see my own image in his pupils.

" Shall we get out of here, lieutenant?" his lips hardly moved. They were dry and quite white.

" No," I said.

He stretched out his hand. I squeezed it with all my strength. Yet another one—the old Siberian—was put out of action. Again we opened fire. The machine-gun shook as though in a fever.

I could feel little streams of sweat running down my chest, my back and under my arms.

In front was the flat, repellent grey earth. There was just one crooked bush, looking like a hand with gouty fingers. Then it too vanished, cut down by a machine-gun.

I could no longer remember how many times the Germans had come in. Once, twice, ten, twenty times. My head was buzzing. Or maybe that was aeroplanes overhead? Chumák

shouted something. I couldn't make out anything. Valéga
handed me one belt after another. How quickly they were
emptied! All around were shell-cases—there was nowhere
to put your foot . . .

" Give me some more! More . . . more, Valéga!"

He dragged up a box . . . Sweat ran into my eyes, sticky
and warm . . .

" Come on, come on!"

Then there was a face—red, without a cap, shiny.

" Allow me, comrade lieutenant."

" Go to hell!"

" But you're wounded."

" Go to hell!"

The face vanished and in its place there was something
white, or yellow or red. Circles going round and round. They
spread and paled. Then they suddenly disappeared and there
was a face again. A golden forelock, an open collar and
laughing blue eyes. Shiryáev's eyes. And Shiryáev's forelock.
And the lamp with the green shade. And it stank of ammonia
enough to make you cry.

" D'you recognise me, engineer?"

The voice was Shiryáev's. And somebody was shaking and
embracing me, and somebody's collar was getting into my
mouth—rough and prickly.

Our dug-out. And Valéga. And Kharlámov. And Shiryáev.
Real, live, tangible, golden-haired Shiryáev.

" Well, d'you recognise me?"

" Good Lord alive, of course I do."

" Well, thank God for that."

" Thank God."

We shook each other by the hand and laughed and didn't
know quite what to say. And everybody around was laughing
for some reason.

" You be careful, comrade senior lieutenant, he's wounded.
You'll shake him to pieces."

That was, of course, Valéga. Shiryáev waved him aside:

" That's no wound! Took the skin off, that's all . . . It'll
heal by to-morrow."

I felt weak and dizzy. Especially when I turned my head.

" Want a drink?"

I had no time to answer—a rather bitter-tasting tin was
between my teeth and something cold and pleasant spread
through my whole body.

" Where did you spring from, Shiryáev?"

" Dropped from the moon."

180

" No, but seriously?"

" What do you mean, where from? Got posted, that's all. Battalion commander in your battalion . . . Do you object?"

He hadn't changed a bit. He hadn't even got thinner. He was just as strong and broad-shouldered and upstanding, with his cap still over one eye.

" You've had—sort of—bad luck," he said, and the broad, white smile just wouldn't leave his face. " You don't seem to have had a lot of rest."

" Yes, as far as rest goes, it hasn't been so good . . . But wait, wait . . . Where have you come from?"

" What d'you care? We've come, that's all."

" But the Jerries?"

" The Jerries are all right. They beat it out of the ravine. Even left a couple of prisoners."

" Are there a lot of you?"

" What shall I say? Couple of battalions. Yours and the third. About fifty men."

" You're kidding?"

Again he laughed. And everybody around laughed.

" Why should I? Is that such a lot?"

" What d'you think?"

" Well . . ."

" Wait . . . The bridge? How's the bridge?"

" There's still about five men there," Kharlámov put in, " but they haven't got long to go."

" Wonderful. Simply wonderful . . . And Chumák and Karnaúkhov?"

" Alive."

" Well, thank God. Give me a drop more water."

I drank another half mug. Shiryáev stood up.

" Tidy yourself up, and I'll have a look at what's going on there. We'll have a talk this evening—we'll talk about Oskól and Petropávlovka. Do you remember how we sat together on the shore?" He stretched out his hand. " Remember Filátov? The machine-gunner. Middle-aged, a grouser."

" I remember."

" Got flattened out by a German tank. He wouldn't leave his machine-gun. So they got flattened out together."

" Pity about the old chap."

" It was a shame. He was a wonderful chap."

For a few moments we were silent.

" Well, I'm off."

" Off you go. Till this evening, then."

He went off, his cap cocked over his left eye.

181

In the evening Shiryáev and I sat in the battalion command post—in a hole at the bottom of the embankment.

My wound was trifling—it had taken some skin off my forehead and some hair off my head. I could even drink. Not much, it was true. We drank some frightful-smelling stuff that was either spirit or home-made vodka. We ate herrings, the very herrings I had thrown out on the hillock. Valéga, of course, had not put up with that.

"How could you throw it away? The last time you had a drink you say yourself: 'Could do with some herring, Valéga . . .'" And he laid it out in neat little slices, without bones, on a newspaper stolen from Kharlámov's files. This was a constant source of quarrels between them.

We sat and drank and recalled June and July, the first days of the retreat and the farm buildings in which we parted. After that Shiryáev had lost almost the whole of his battalion. The Germans surrounded them near Kantemírovka. He nearly got taken prisoner himself. Then with his four remaining men he tried to get to Véshenskaya. There they nearly got caught by the Germans again. But they managed to extricate themselves and get themselves across the Don. On the other side of the Don they got into some division made up of the remains of those that had been routed. They were in action before Kalách. He had been slightly wounded. He fetched up in Stalingrad—in the front-line reserve, and there he hung around for about a month and had only just received the appointment as battalion commander in our regiment.

Lying on the bed made of boards knocked together I studied Shiryáev. I tried to find at least some little change in him. But no, everything was the same, even down to the blue triangle of vest peeping out from his unbuttoned collar.

"You didn't hear anything about Maxímov?" I asked.

"No . . . Somebody, I can't remember who, thought he'd seen him somewhere on this side of the Don. But it's not very likely. I've been everywhere on this side and I've not come across him."

"Who did you come across of our chaps?"

"Of ours?" Shiryáev wrinkled his nose. "One of the company commanders. The intelligence officer Goglídze. He went past in a car. Waved his hand. Now, who else? Girls from the medical unit . . . Kostríchny, the Party organiser . . . Yes!" He slapped the table with the palm of his hand. "What's his name, that friend of yours, the gas officer . . . what did you call him?"

"Igor? Where?" I even raised myself up.

" On this side. About five days back."

" You're kidding!"

" There you go again. At the ' Red October '. He's in the thirty-ninth."

" The thirty-ninth?"

" And he's not an anti-gas officer for some reason, but an engineer, like you. Minefields, landmines and that kind of nonsense."

" And what were you doing in the thirty-ninth?"

" Nothing. I just happened to be there by chance. I was looking for army HQ. Some fool told me it was in the Bánnaya ravine. So I popped over. And do you know what was going on there? Couldn't see a damned thing three yards away. Smoke, dust, the devil knows what . . . Just at that moment the Jerries attacked. I shot into a trench. Then I saw a wooden door. I got behind it, for shelter. Later, when the Jerries had gone, somebody took me by the hand. I looked—there was your Igor. I didn't even know him at first. He had shaved off his moustache. He was all black, covered with soot. I only recognised him by his eyes."

" Alive and fit?"

" Alive and fit. Of course, he asked about you. But what could I say? I didn't know. We said how sorry we were and then he said he had an idea you were in the one-eighty-fourth. Only he was afraid he'd mixed up the number. But I wrote it down all the same. I thought I must get in touch with you. Lots of vacancies in the division now, as you know. So I asked at army HQ to be put into the one-eighty-fourth. They were delighted. And in the division I found out which regiment you were in."

" You're a lad, I must say."

" Well, that's the way it worked out." Shiryáev reached out his hand for the bottle. " Let's have another one, shall we?"

We drank another shot apiece.

" You haven't seen Sedykh?"

" No. And I forgot to ask. We only spoke for about ten minutes altogether."

" I've still got his cigarette case. He gave it me as a parting gift."

I took the celluloid case out of my pocket.

" It's a good one," said Shiryáev.

" It is good. We made them ourselves. At the tractor plant. You've no idea how much of this celluloid there was there."

"It's jolly well made. Did you really make them yourselves?"

"We did."

"Who did the scratching on the lid?"

"I did. That's a monogram. I just scratched it on with a knife."

"Jolly good. You've only got one?"

"Yes. I gave mine away. This belonged to Sedykh—a parting gift. He was a fine lad."

Shiryáev poured out some more drink.

"I ought not to have any more," I said. "My head is going round."

Later Abrósimov, the regimental chief of staff, came in, pale and out of humour. He said the divisional commander had nearly removed him because he had called off an attack last night—not to-night, but last night. But what could he do: they were again preparing to transfer the regiment. Then they withdrew the order.

He and Shiryáev went off to the front line, while Kharlámov and I prepared documents for the handing over of the battalion.

About twelve o'clock Shiryáev returned. I handed over the battalion and as the moon rose Valéga and I set off for the shore. Karnaúkhov and Chumák were still at the front line, so I didn't say good-bye to them.

Kharlámov stretched out his hand:

"If you get bored, drop in and see us." He looked at me with his kindly Armenian eyes.

I felt a bit miserable. I'd got used to the battalion. The soldier at the entrance—he had some long and complicated surname I couldn't remember—even saluted, switching his rifle quickly from his right to his left hand.

"Are you leaving us, comrade battalion commander?"

"Yes."

He coughed and again saluted, this time taking leave.

"Come and see us, don't forget us."

"Surely, surely," I said. Leaning on Valéga, I scrambled out of the trench. The soldier with the difficult name gave me a discreet push in the rear.

XVI

For three days I did nothing. Just ate, slept and read. Lisagórs' new dug-out was excellent—a miracle of underground skill. A seven-metre tunnel straight into the side of the hill. At the end on the right there was a room. Really a room. Only it had no windows. It was all neatly lined with thin, carefully fitted boards. A floor, a ceiling, two bunks and a little table between them. Above the table was an oval Empire mirror with a thick-necked Cupid. In the corner were a primus and a stove. Mattresses, pillows and blankets. What more could you ask for? Opposite, across the little corridor, the sappers were still hacking away. That was for himself.

"We'll live like gods," said Lisagór. "We'll make double-decker bunks, a pyramid for rifles and tools, a table, a bench and a kitchen corner. In the corridor there'll be places to store the explosives. Do you realise how much earth there is above us? Fourteen metres! And all clay. As hard as granite. It's a good job and made to last."

I liked that. A good, safe place to live and work at the front was, if not half, at any rate a quarter of the way to success. And for three days I enjoyed that little quarter.

In the morning Valéga fed me a thick, greasy macaroni soup—you could hardly turn the spoon in it—and then tea from our own samovar. It made a homely noise in the corner. I lay with a pillow tucked under my back, did the crosswords in the back number of the *Red Army Man* and enjoyed myself reading the Moscow papers.

All was quiet around the globe.

In New Zealand a new army call-up had been announced. British patrols were active on the Egyptian front. We had established diplomatic relations with Cuba and Luxembourg. Allied aircraft had carried out small raids on Laet, Salamaya, Buna in New Guinea and on the island of Timor. Battles with the Japanese in the Owen-Stanley sector had become rather more fierce.

In Madagascar British troops were advancing on somewhere, occupying something, fighting with someone, it was difficult to understand with whom, but they were fighting and even taking prisoners.

Dubrowski was on at the Bolshoi Theatre, Korneichúk's

Front at the Maly, and *Helen of Troy* at the Nemiróvich-Dánchenko.

Meanwhile there, at a depth of fourteen metres, a kilometre and a half from the front line, about which the whole world was then talking, I was as cosy and peaceful as though I were back home. Could there possibly be a more peaceful place? Brightly lit streets, trams, trolley-buses and taps which you could turn and water ran out. How strange . . .

I lay, with my eyes fixed on the ceiling, thinking of most high-falutin matters, of how everything in the world is relative, of the fact that my ideal for the moment was this very dug-out and the pot of noodle soup, so long as it was really hot, while before the war I needed suits and striped ties and I made a fuss at the baker's if the bread for two-seventy wasn't properly baked. And was it really possible that after the war and after all those raids we should once again . . . and so forth, in that mood.

Later I got bored with staring at the ceiling and thinking about the future. I clambered up outside.

Aeroplanes were still attacking the " Red October " as before, mines were still exploding over the Volga, boats were scurrying along the river and the Germans were firing at them. But there were few who paid any attention to that. Even when a couple of stray Messerschmitts shot up the shore or some Junkers dropped bombs for a change, not on the " Red October " but on us, nobody got particularly alarmed. The men would scramble in somewhere under a beam or in a trench and peep out like field-mice. Then they'd come out and if anybody had been killed they'd bury him right there on the shore in the bomb craters. The wounded were led off to the first-aid post. And it would all pass off calmly, with smokes and jokes in between.

I found myself a spot on a pipe, of whose origin I had no idea, and sat swinging my legs. I smoked a smashing, breath-taking mixture, enjoying the last rays of the sun, the blue sky and the little church on the other bank and thinking . . . No, I suppose I wasn't really thinking of anything. I was smoking and swinging my legs.

Garkúsha came up—the assistant platoon commander with a moustache. I showed him my watch—it had stopped for some reason. He inspected it, shook it, pronounced it to be junk—a cylinder movement—and straight away began to repair it at my feet, on a little board put across his knees. His movements were astonishingly delicate and precise, although it looked as though the watch should be crushed and crumpled at one touch of those powerful, horny hands.

What his profession was before the war I couldn't quite make out. He was 26, but he had already managed to be a watchmaker, a plumber, a diver on underwater construction work, and even an acrobat in a circus, and to have been married three times and he maintained a regular correspondence with all three, although two of them already had fresh husbands.

In conversation he was restrained, but answered questions freely. I asked him a lot out of boredom. He would reply carefully, as though he were filling up a questionnaire. His concentration on the watch did not slacken for a single minute. Only once he went off into the tunnel to check up on the sappers.

Then Astáfyev appeared—the assistant chief of staff for operations, or ACS-1 as we called him. Young, elegant, with Onegin[1] sideburns and a metallic look. He spoke with a slight burr, in the French way. He apparently thought that it suited him. We had known each other a couple of days, but he for some reason already considered me his friend and called me Georges. His name was Ippolit. It seemed to me very appropriate. Something indefinable about him recalled the fat Ippolit Kurágin[2]. Just as stupid and self-assured. He was a reader in history at Sverdlóvsk university. When he smoked a cigarette he stuck out his little finger and puffed out the smoke through lips rounded like a pipe.

He was devoted to his profession and was already gathering material for a future history.

" Do you realise how interesting it all is, Georges?" he said, leaning elegantly against the pipe after carefully brushing the dust off it. " It is precisely now, in the stress of the moment, that it must not be forgotten. Especially by those of us, participants in these events, who are men of culture. When the years have passed they'll pay thousands for some half-decayed fire card made out by your platoon commander and study it through a microscope. Isn't that true?"

He took hold of one of my buttons and twisted it lightly between his first finger and thumb.

" And you'll help me, Georges, won't you? It's no use counting on Abrósimov and others like him—you realise that. Apart from carrying out orders or seizing some hillock, they're not interested in anything."

1 Eugene Onegin: hero of Pushkin's poem, a dandy.
2 Ippolít Kurágin: character from Tolstóy's *War and Peace*.

He half smiled with the air of a man who was perfectly certain that it was impossible not to agree with him.

The devil only knew . . . Maybe he was right. But it didn't interest me for the moment. On the whole he annoyed me. His sideburns, and " Georges ", and his pink fingernails which he kept cleaning all the time with a pocket knife.

A line of yellow-winged Junkers appeared above the ravine. Giving them a sidelong glance, Astáfyev made a gracious gesture with his hand.

" Well, I'm on my way . . . Forms are piling up. Twenty of them a day. They've gone completely mad at Div. HQ. Drop in, Georges." And he disappeared into his shelter.

The Junkers formed up in a line and dived on the " Red October ".

Garkúsha, the tip of his tongue sticking out, was carefully pushing some little wheel back into my watch with a pair of pincers.

From the officers' kitchen could be heard the banging of knives. We must be having cutlets for dinner.

XVII

Towards the end of the third day I was summoned to HQ. The engineering equipment had arrived. I received a thousand mines. Fixe hundred anti-tank YAM-5's—strong six-kilogram boxes made from unfinished boards—and the same number of small anti-personnel PMD-7's with two-hundred-gram cores of TNT. Forty rolls of American wire. About two hundred spades and thirty picks. Both spades and picks were rubbishy. Especially the spades. They were made of iron, which bent, and the handles were not properly finished.

All this wealth was stacked on the shore immediately opposite the entrance to our tunnel. The sappers took it in turn to guard it—one could hardly rely on the honesty of our neighbours.

In the morning we found ourselves short of twenty spades and ten picks. Tugíyev, the guard, a round-faced, tough-looking fellow, blinked with surprise. His fingers, held stiffly down at his sides, trembled with tension.

" I only went to relieve myself, comrade lieutenant. Honestly. And I went no distance."

"Whether you relieved yourself or not does not concern us," said Lisagór, his voice and look so threatening that Tugíyev's fingers began to tremble even more. "See that everything's back here by the evening."

In the evening, when we had the inspction, there turned out to be two hundred and nine spades and thirty-five picks. Tugíyev was beaming.

"That's training for you!" said Lisagór cheerfully and, getting the men together on the shore, he read them a long lecture to the effect that a spade was just the same as a rifle, and if, God forbid, anyone should lose a spade, a pick or even a pair of wire cutters, he'd be court-martialled straight away. The men listened with concentration and carved their names on the handles. They slept with their spades under their heads . . .

Meanwhile I was busy with diagrams. I drew a big map of our defences on tracing paper, finished it off with coloured pencils and went to see the divisional engineer.

He lived some three or four hundred metres from us, also on the shore in a sapper's battalion. His name was Ustínov. A captain. He was no longer young—approaching fifty, and with glasses. Polite. By the look of it he was at the front for the first time. As he talked he would turn a yellow, beautifully sharpened pencil in his fingers. Every thought that was formulated he recorded on paper in microscopic, round handwriting—firstly, secondly, thirdly.

On the table in the dug-out was a pile of books—Ushákov's *Fortification*, Gerbanóvsky's *Fortification of an Area*, manuals, reference books and regulations, pamphlets in coloured covers put out by the War-Engineering Academy and even a fat little *Hütte*.

Ustínov's plans for fortifying the front line were phenomenal—in the scale of them, the variety of means to be used and the detail in which the whole scheme had been worked out.

He took out a map completely covered with all sorts of coloured brackets, hoops, crosses, squares and zigzags. It wasn't even a map, but a sort of carpet. He unrolled it carefully on the table.

"I shall not attempt to explain to you how important all this is. I think you understand that yourself. From the history of wars you and I know very well that in positional warfare—and that is exactly the kind of warfare we are aiming at now—the quantity, quality and careful planning of

189

the engineering works play a prominent, I would say even the primary role."

He swallowed and looked at me over his glasses with heavy-lidded eyes.

"Eighty-seven years ago it was for that very reason that Sevastópol held, because our colleagues, the sappers, and Totleben himself had managed to build an almost impenetrable belt of engineering works and obstacles. The French and British and even the Sardinians devoted tremendous attention to this question. We know, for example, that before Malákhov hill . . ."

To crown it all he told me in detail, with a whole mass of figures, about the Sevastópol defences, then skipped over to the Russo-Japanese war, to Verdun and the famous barbed-wire defences at Kakhóvka.

Then he carefully put away the diagrams of the disposition of the Sevastópol *retranchements* and approaches in a file labelled "Historical examples" . . .

"You can see there's no end to the work we've got to do. And the sooner we can get it done the better."

He wrote the figure 1 down on a sheet of paper and put a ring round it.

"That's the first thing, Secondly: I must beg you to let me have every day by 0700 hours a report on the works done during the night. A—by your own sappers, B—by the divisional sappers, C—by the army sappers, if there are any, and I hope there will be, and D—by the infantry units. Apart from that . . ."

Again the paper became dotted with figures—Roman, Arabic, in circles, hoops, squares or with nothing at all.

When he said good-bye he stretched out a slender, intellectual's hand, with gouty swellings on the joints.

"I would ask you especially not to forget every fourth and twenty-fourth of the month to send the forms 1, 1b, 13 and 14. And the monthly report by the thirtieth. Even better, by the twenty-ninth. And every week a cumulative summary of the work done. That's very important . . ."

That night over a tin of fish Lisagór laughed happily and loud:

"Well, lieutenant, you're right in the soup! You'll have to open a complete designing bureau. You didn't ask where he came from   He isn't from the Engineering Academy, is he?"

XVIII

Days passed.

The guns went on firing. Small, short-barrelled, regimental —straight, point-blank, from the front line. Slightly bigger ones—divisional—from the steep cliff above the shore, tucked in somewhere between a stove and a broken bed. And really big ones, with long barrels projecting from beneath netting, from the other side, across the Volga. The heavies also came into action. They were transported on tractors: the barrel separately from the gun-carriage. The finance officer who came across from the other side to give us our pay, an agreeable, lively and keenly interested chap called Lazar—everybody in the regiment called him Lazar—said there wasn't room to spit on the other shore, with a gun under every bush.

The Germans continued as before to have fun with mortars. They fired at the ferry from the six-barrelled ones, and for a long time afterwards the Volga would glisten from the silver bellies of stunned fish.

Aircraft buzzed away—German in the daytime and our "corn-cobs" at night. It was true that the Germans had also acquired some "night birds" so that at night you couldn't quite make out which were ours and which theirs. We went on digging, laying mines and writing long reports: "Completed in the course of the night—so many rifle trenches, so many mortar positions, dug-outs, minefields, losses—so and so, destroyed in the same period—this and this . . ."

Workshops were opened up on our part of the shore. Two sappers on the sick-list were turning a wooden drum: they were making Bruno spirals—something half-way between a concertina and a sausage made of barbed wire. Later the divisional sappers stretched them out along the front line in front of the trenches. Every evening a platoon from the second company of the sapper battalion came along. My men laid mines and took charge of the second line of defences. Also working on them were the so-called "loafers"—the tailors, barbers, pioneers and the flame-thrower men who had not yet received their weapons. Also working on mine-laying, of course, were Garkúsha and the section commander Agnívtsev, an energetic and capable chap, whose rudeness did not endear him to the men.

Lisagór was just as busy as ever. He always had some urgent job for the regimental commander—the construction of a transport store, or an armament workshops, or something like that. He smelt of vodka like a barrel, but he bore himself well on the whole.

In daytime we rested, fitting out the dug-outs and caulking the boats. As the first stars came out we took up picks and shovels and set off for the front line . . . There were now very few fires. The path was lit by Verey lights.

After work I used to sit with Shiryáev and Karnaúkhov smoking makhorka—mostly I was to be found in the second battalion, in a crowded, over-heated dug-out, where we cursed the soldier's life and envied the chaps in the rear. Sometimes we played chess and Karnaúkhov regularly checkmated me. I was no good at the game.

In the morning, by the first light of dawn, we would set off home. The mornings were already cold. The ground frost did not go away before ten o'clock. In the dug-out there would be tea waiting, the left-overs from the previous evening's tinned food and a little stove crackling away in a homely way in the corner . . .

In the language of the official reports all that meant was that " our units had exchanged fire with the enemy and forti-fied their positions." The words " fierce " and " heavy " had not found their way into the reports for some ten days, although the Germans were shelling us from morning to night as before, and were firing at us and mounting attacks, now in one place, now in another. But by now they didn't seem to have the same bravado and self-confidence in them and it was rarer and rarer for them to drop clouds of leaflets on our heads with appeals to surrender and abandon all hope of Zhúkov's driving down from the north.

November started with steadily hardening morning frosts and the winter uniforms were issued to us at last. Fur hats, padded jackets and breeches, foot-cloths, rabbit-fur gloves. In a few days, they said, there would be felt boots and fur waistcoats. We transferred our little red stars from our caps on to the grey fur hats, and we switched over to a winter programme—we no longer went and washed in the Volga and we began to reckon up how long it was to spring.

Ustínov overwhelmed me with a whole flood of papers. They were small, carefully folded and stuck down, invariably marked " Top Secret " and " For Kérzhentsev only " in the top right-hand corner. They demanded from me, insistently and in varied language, forms I hadn't sent or a report that was overdue, or they warned me of the need to prepare the minefields for winter conditions—to smear the detonating fuse with grease and paint the badly camouflaged mines with white paint.

The papers were brought by a cheerful, freckled and terribly snub-nosed sapper who was Ustínov's runner. From outside the doorway he would shout in his young, ringing voice:

"Open up, comrade lieutenant! The morning post!"

Valéga and he were on good terms, and they would inevitably smoke a cigarette together, squatting near the entrance, and discuss their own and other people's officers.

"Mine is always writing and writing . . ." the voice of the runner came through the door. "The minute he's up he gets hold of a pencil. I don't think he even goes to the lavatory. He's terribly scared of mines. He ordered a shield of beams to be put across the entrance and the lavatory to be reinforced with rails."

"Mine doesn't like writing at all," said Valéga in his deep voice. "He's always cursing yours for sending so many letters. But he loves books. Reads everything. When he eats his food he's always got one eye on a book or a newspaper. He's a very educated man!"

"Not more than mine, certainly," the runner said in an offended tone. "Have you seen how many books there are lying on our table? In one of them—I looked myself—there are five hundred pages. And all so finely printed that you can't make it out without glasses."

"And does yours spend any time at the front line?" asked Valéga suddenly.

"You can't expect him to. He's pretty old. And he can't see anything at night."

Valéga maintained a triumphant silence. The runner took my reports and departed.

Sometimes Chumák dropped in on us—he lived close by, ten yards away. He would bring his cards and we would play nap.

Sometimes Lisagór and I would call on him and listen to the gramophone.

From time to time Lazar, the finance officer, would arrive from the other side and spend the night with us. Valéga would lay out his greatcoat between the bunks and find himself a place near the stove. Lazar would tell us the news from the left bank. They were apparently proposing to withdraw us for re-forming. Possibly to Léninsk or even to Siberia. We knew that this was all nonsense and that we wouldn't be withdrawn anywhere, but we pretended to believe it—believing was far more pleasant than not believing—and made plans for a peaceful life in Krasnoufimsk or Tomsk. The principal place in all these dreams was taken up by pelmeni, sour cream and, of course, the female sex.

On one occasion a Messerschmitt fell within the area of our regiment. Who shot it down nobody knew, but in the evening reports of all three battalions there appeared: "By accurate rifle and machine-gun fire units of our battalion shot down an enemy aircraft." It fell near the Meat Plant, and, despite the gunfire and the shouts of the officers, a real pilgrimage started to go and look at it. Half an hour after it had fallen Chumák brought along a beautiful watch with luminous hands and a big lump of perspex. A week later we were all flaunting enormous transparent cigarette holders of Garkúsha's manufacture. Even the major, who had three pipes and who never smoked a cigarette, ordered a special one with a metal edge for himself.

XIX

On the evening of the sixth Shiryáev called me on the telephone:

"The Jerries are not stirring. I'm bored. I've got some chops to-day. And to-morrow's a holiday. Come on over."

I didn't waste any time. I went. Later Farber and Karnaúkhov came along.

"Do you remember," said Shiryáev, "how we drank together near Kúpyansk? On the last night . . . Down in my cellar. And we had fried potatoes. My armourer Philip was there to fry the spuds. Do you remember Philip? I lost him. Near Kantemírovka. He wasn't a bad chap . . ."

He turned his glass in his hands.

"What were you thinking about then? Eh, Yurka? As we sat on the river bank? The regiment had gone and we were sitting and watching the rockets. What were you thinking about then?"

"Well, I don't know how to put it . . ."

"You don't have to say . . . I know. We felt pretty bad, awful. Didn't we? And then in one village, do you remember, an old chap gave us a drink of water. You don't want to fight, he said. You're fit, but you don't want to. And we didn't know what to say. I'd like to have him here now, that toothless old man."

Suddenly he stopped and his eyes became narrow and sharp. They looked as they did when he found out that two of his men had deserted.

"Tell me, engineer, did it ever happen to you during the retreat? You know, the feeling that this is the end . . . that everything's gone to pieces . . . Nothing left. It did to me once. When we were crossing the Don. Do you remember what a mess there was? Everybody was on top of everybody else. I and a captain—he was a sapper too: his battalion had fixed up the crossing—tried to get some order into things. The pontoon bridge was very shaky and full of holes and patches after the bombing. The lorries got across one by one, up to their bellies in water. We got things going somehow. Made them form a queue. Then suddenly some major in a tank helmet drove up in a jeep. He got right up to the bridge in his jeep, drew himself up to his full height and started to bawl at me: "Why the devil don't you let us through? German tanks are only three kilometres off! And you're trying to boss people about!" You know, I was sort of struck dumb. There he was, with his pistol in his hand, his face red and his eyes popping out. Well, I thought, if majors are talking like that, that means it's bad . . . Meanwhile the lorries were piling one on top of the other. I could see that my captain was knocked right over . . . And then goodness knows what happened—something must have come over me. I leapt up on to the jeep and gave it to him —one, two, three, straight in his lousy face. I ripped the pistol off him and put all eight into him . . . It turned out there wasn't a trace of any tanks. And the driver hid himself somewhere. Maybe they were Jerries, provocateurs, eh?"

"Maybe they were Jerries," I replied.

Shiryáev fell silent. He stared at a point in front of him. Somebody could be heard swearing into the telephone.

"Play something, Karnaúkhov," said Shiryáev. "The guitar's hanging there doing nothing, it's lonely."

Karnaúkhov took the guitar down from the wall. The battalion scouts had found it yesterday in one of the ruined houses. It had a blue silk ribbon with an inscription burnt on it: "A souvenir for dear Vitya from Volya."

"Let's have something nice and soulful."

Shiryáev made himself more comfortable on his bed, stretching out his legs in their tightly fitting polished boots.

195

"How is it there on the front line, Leshka? Quiet?"

"All quiet, comrade senior lieutenant," replied the lop-eared Leshka, especially brightly, lest anyone should think he had fallen asleep. "They've brought supper up to the fifth. They're grousing about it being too watery . . ."

"I'll tear a real strip off that sergeant-major one of these days. If he comes at night-time, wake me up. Right, let's have it, Karnaúkhov."

Karnaúkhov struck a chord. He turned out to have a very pleasant, resonant voice, half-way between a baritone and a tenor, and a remarkable ear. He sang quietly, but with feeling, sometimes even closing his eyes. The songs were all Russian, and pensive, and many of them I was hearing for the first time. He sang well. And he had a good face. It was rather coarse, but somehow clear and straightforward. He had shaggy eyebrows and blue eyes, intelligent and quiet, and a sort of deep smile that never left them. Even there, on the hill, they had still smiled.

Farber sat with his hand covering his eyes. Fair, curly hair came through his fingers. What was he thinking about? I hadn't the slightest idea. About his wife, about his children, about integrals and infinitesimal quantities? Or did nothing at all in the world interest him? It sometimes seemed to me that even death didn't frighten him, to judge by the absent, bored way he would smoke during a bombardment.

Karnaúkhov was tired, or else he was tired of singing, and he hung the guitar on a nail. For some time we sat in silence. Then Shiryáev raised himself on one elbow.

"Farber . . . Were you like this before the war?"

Farber raised his head.

"Like what?"

"Like you are now."

"And what am I like now?"

"Goodness knows what you are . . . I don't understand you. You don't like drinking, you don't like swearing, you don't like women . . . Just look at our engineer here. After all, he's also got a higher education."

Farber smiled faintly.

"I don't quite follow the connection between wine and women and higher education."

"It's not a question of connection." Shiryáev sat on the bed, with his legs spread apart. "I just can't understand how it's possible to live at the front without vodka. And without swearing. Now, how do you manage without it? Karnaúkhov is a quiet, modest chap—don't you listen, Karnaúkhov—

196

but sometimes he uses language that would stagger you."

"Yes, in that field I'm not very strong," replied Farber.

Shiryáev laughed.

"Don't get the idea that I want to corrupt you. Or to teach you to swear. God forbid. I just don't understand how it can happen . . . Do you know how to swim?"

"Swim? No, I don't."

"Can you ride a bicycle?"

"No, I can't ride a bicycle either."

"Well, did you ever clout someone in the face?"

"Why do you keep on at a chap so?" Karnaúkhov interrupted. "Go and talk to Chumák about that. He'll tell you some stories."

"I have struck someone in the face," said Farber quietly and stood up.

"You did? Who?"

"I'm going." Farber did not answer the question and buttoned up his greatcoat.

"No, whom did you hit?"

"It's of no interest . . . Allow me to go . . ."

He went.

"Strange chap," said Shiryáev, standing up.

Karnaúkhov smiled. He had two little dimples on his cheeks, like a child's.

"I dropped in on him yesterday, when I came up from the shore. He was sitting there writing. Must have been a letter. He was finishing the fourth page of an exercise book. In tiny, tiny writing. I was bursting to read it."

Shiryáev directed a scarcely noticeable wink at me.

"Maybe it wasn't a letter?"

"What, then?"

"Maybe it was poetry."

Karnaúkhov blushed.

"What are you blushing for?"

"I'm not blushing," and he blushed all the more.

Shiryáev remained silent, restraining a smile. He did not take his eyes off Karnaúkhov.

"Well, and what about yours?"

"My what?"

"Poems, of course."

"What poems?"

"Do you think we don't know? In that oil-cloth notebook. What did he have there, Kérzhentsev, do you remember?"

Kornaúkhov was driven into a corner.

" Oh, that was . . . to pass the time."

" To pass the time . . . You're all like that—passing the time. Pushkin also probably wrote to pass the time. I drink vodka to pass the time, and you write verses. You probably write to your girl—own up!"

" We better have a drink." And Karnaúkhov measured with his finger a third of the vodka remaining in the bottle and poured it into a mug.

In half an hour Karnaúkhov and I left. At the signal post we parted: he to the right and I to the left.

" All the same you'll read us your poems," I said as I took leave of him.

" Maybe," he replied uncertainly and vanished in the darkness.

XX

The night was dark. No stars to be seen. Only here and there were dim, diffused patches of light. All around was quiet, except for some desultory firing on the hill.

Somebody was sitting near the ruined bridge. The lighted end of a cigarette flared up.

" Who the devil's smoking?"

" It doesn't matter, it can't be seen from here," came a rather toneless voice in reply. It was Farber's voice.

" What are you doing here?"

" I'm getting some air."

I went closer and for some reason sat down. Farber said nothing more. He sat and smoked. I also lit a cigarette. We stayed silent. I didn't know what I could talk to him about.

" They'll be starting the concert now," said Farber suddenly.

" I don't think so," I replied. " Their ' ishaki ' have been quiet for two days now for some reason."

" No, I'm talking about a real concert. They've set up a loudspeaker on the other side. There's a news bulletin now. Then there'll be a concert. It was at this time yesterday evening."

" From Moscow?"

" I suppose so."

Some of our men went past. About ten of them, one after the other, in a line. They were carrying mines and ammunition. You could hear the gravel slipping away under their feet and their swearing as they stumbled. Twenty minutes later they returned. In another half an hour they would come past again, stumbling and swearing at the darkness, the bits of iron strewn about, Hitler, and the sergeant-major who had made them carry four battalion mortars apiece. In the course of the night they would make six or eight trips. In the daytime the whole lot would be used up. But as soon as the sun went down they'd be off again to the shore, from the shore to the front line and from the front line to the shore again.

" How are things in the company?" I inquired.

" All right," replied Farber indifferently. " Nothing much changed."

" How many men have you got now?"

" Same as before. Never adds up to more than eighteen or twenty. There's practically no one left of the old ones who first landed."

" What about the reinforcements!"

" Some reinforcements!"

" Too young?"

" It's the first time they've seen a rifle. One was killed yesterday. A grenade blew up in his hands."

" Mm—yes," I said. " It's a lousy business, war."

Farber did not reply. He took a box of tobacco from his pocket, rolled a cigarette and lit it from his own fag-end. For a moment the light fell on his thin face, with its sunken cheeks, angular nose and deep folds round his mouth.

" Have you thought that life itself is a senseless business?" Farber asked. He couldn't get his cigarette going—the fag-end was small and falling apart.

" Life or war?" I asked.

" No, life."

" That's a complicated question . . . There's a lot that's senseless, of course. But what were you thinking of in particular?"

" Nothing in particular . . . I was just philosophising. Summing up, as it were."

" Isn't it a bit early for that?"

" Of course it's early, but you can draw a few conclusions."

He slowly ground out his cigarette end with his heel. " Do you ever start thinking about your past life?"

" What about it?"

" Does it ever strike you that in some ways you and I have been living like ostriches?"

" Ostriches?"

" That's the nearest parallel, I think. We practically never poked our noses out of the sand."

" Can you put that a bit more simply?"

" I'm talking about war. About us and about war. By ' us ' I mean you, me—people like ourselves who are not directly concerned with war in peacetime. Did you know there would be a war?"

" I suppose I knew."

" You don't suppose—you knew. And you knew you'd be involved in it."

He took several deep puffs and noisily expelled the smoke.

" Before the war you were a reserve officer. That's right, isn't it? V.U.S.[1] 34 . . . Advanced territorial training, or something like that."

" V.U.S. 34 . . . V.V.P. . . . commander of a reserve platoon!"

I had never once heard Farber talk so much. Apparently the vodka was having an effect on him.

" Once a week you had a military day. You all did your best to dodge it. In the summer there was a camp. Right turn, left turn, quick march. The officers insisted on sharp turns and cheerful songs. On tactical exercises you hid in the bushes, slept, smoked and looked at your watches—to see how long it was to dinner. I reckon I'm not far wrong."

" Frankly, no."

" Well, that's just the snag . . . We relied on other people. During the May First parades we stood on the pavement, our hands in our pockets, and watched the tanks going by, the aeroplanes overhead and the troops marching along in ranks . . . Oh, how fine, oh, what strength! And that was all we thought about it then. Isn't that true? That *we* should ever have to march, and not on asphalt, but on a dusty road, with a pack on our shoulders, or that *we* should be responsible for the lives of, well, not hundreds, but at least tens of people, did we ever think about that?"

Farber spoke slowly, even lazily, pausing, taking a puff after every sentence. Outwardly he was completely calm, but from something elusive, from the frequent puffs, from the unbalanced pauses, from the wrinkled forehead lit up by the cigarette—you could sense that he had long been wanting to talk about all this, but that there had been no one to talk to, or no occasion to say it, or no time, or goodness knows what! It was clear to me that he was very worked up about it all, but that, as with many people of his

[1] V.U.S.—military training speciality.

sort, reserved and untalkative, his concern found scarcely any outward expression but, on the contrary, made him even more restrained.

I remained silent, listening and smoking. Farber continued:

" On the fourth day of the war they lined up thirty young chaps in front of me in two ranks—carpenters, fitters, blacksmiths, tractor-drivers—and said: take command, teach them. That was in a reserve battalion."

" A sapper battalion?"

" In a sapper battalion."

" Are you really a sapper?"

" I'm a sapper. Or rather, I was a sapper."

" Why did you suddenly become a gunner?"

" Oh, even before that I was a mortar man. But after the Khárkov excursion I had to become a gunner."

" I didn't know. That means you're a colleague."

" A colleague," Farber smiled and went on: " So, take command, they said, and teach 'em. On the programme it said: demolition work—four hours, fortification—four hours, roads and bridges—four hours. There they stood, shuffling from one foot to the other, glancing at their rucksacks lying under a tree. They stood and waited for me to tell them. And what could I tell them? I only knew that TNT looked like soap, that dynamite was like jelly, that trenches were of complete or incomplete profile, and that, if they were to ask me how many parts there were to a rifle, I should scratch my head for a long time and then blurt out the first figure that came into it."

He paused. He felt in his pocket for the tobacco box. I hadn't noticed before that he smoked so much—one after the other.

" Whose fault was that? Uncle's . . .—as my sergeant-major says? No, not uncle's . . . I myself was to blame. I just wasn't interested in military things before the war. I regarded the camps as a necessary but extremely unpleasant imposition. Nothing you can do about it, but definitely an imposition . . . That was not, you see, my calling. My business was mathematics and things like that. Science . . ."

Farber fumbled in his pockets.

" What can we use for matches?" he said. " Mine are finished."

" Is your fag-end out?"

" Yes."

" You'll have to wait for some troops. They're on their way to the shore now."

" I'll have to."

" And we waited. After a short silence Farber continued in the same quiet, tired voice:

" I taught them for four months. Can you imagine what sort of training it was? And what could I teach them? Our whole battalion had only one book of instructions on demolition work. That was all. No other reading matter at all. I read it up at night. And in the morning I told the men how a demolition charge was constructed, without ever having had one in my hands . . . Br-r . . . I get the shivers just from thinking about it."

Some troops went by. We asked them for a light. One of the men squatted down and struck up a light with his flint lighter. We took a light in turn from the wick. Then the troops went away. One after the other their awkward figures, with greatcoats over their jerseys, disappeared in the darkness.

Farber turned his head.

" A moaner, eh?" he said quietly.

So far he had spoken without turning round, but staring out somewhere into the space in front of him. Now, in the darkness, I could feel his short-sighted eyes peering at me.

" Who's a moaner?" I asked.

" Me. That's what you probably think. He grumbles and complains. True?"

I did not at once know what to answer. Much that he said was true. But was it worth talking about what was past? To analyse the past, or rather what was wrong in the past, made sense if the analysis helped to better the present or prepare for the future.

" It seems to me it's difficult to live if you keep thinking of your past mistakes and cursing yourself. Cursing won't help. And I reckon now you understand the rifle and can teach the troops to handle it . . ."

" I suppose you're right . . ." A pause. " But, you know, if I'd met, say, even Shiryáev, before the war, I'd never have believed that I would come to envy him."

" And do you envy him?"

" I do." Another pause. " I'm not bad at higher mathematics. After all, I studied it for eight years. But something elementary like having to catch out a sergeant-major who is stealing food from the men is for me a practically insurmountable obstacle."

" You are inclined to self-criticism," I said.

"Maybe. I dare say you are too, only you don't talk about it."

"All the same, why do you envy Shiryáev?"

"Why?" He stood up, walked a few steps and then sat down again. All around it was surprisingly quiet. Only somewhere far away, beyond the "Red October" plant, a machine-gun would splutter away from time to time, without much enthusiasm.

"Because, when I look at him, I feel particularly conscious of my own inadequacy. That seems funny to you. But that's the way it is. He is a simple, integrated fellow, whom it costs nothing to ask me whether I can swim or ride a bicycle. He doesn't realise he's hitting the nail on the head. You know, I lied when I said I'd bashed somebody's face. I've never bashed anybody. I never liked fighting and I never liked physical exercise. And now . . ."

He stopped short suddenly. He breathed heavily through his nose. That was apparently a nervous habit. I was gradually beginning to understand him—his restraint, his reserve, his taciturnity.

"Never mind," I said, trying to think of something comforting to say. I recalled how I shouted at him when he was battalion commander. "War's tough on everybody."

"Good God alive! Surely you haven't taken me that way?" His voice even trembled and failed from emotion. "You see, they offered me quite a decent staff job at the HQ at the front. I know languages. They offered me a job in the intelligence section, dealing with prisoners. And you say it's tough on everyone in wartime."

I realised I'd really said something wrong.

"Are you married?" I asked him.

"Yes, what about it?"

"Oh, nothing. I was just interested."

"Well, I am."

"Have you any children?"

"No children."

"How old are you?"

"Twenty-eight."

"Twenty-eight. I'm also twenty-eight. Did you have friends before the war?"

"I had, but . . ." He stopped.

"You don't have to answer if you don't want to. This isn't a questionnaire. Only . . . You seem to me to be so very lonely, somehow."

" Oh, you mean that . . ."

" Yes, that. We've known each other for almost six weeks. And this is the first time in all those weeks that we've really talked, so to speak."

" Yes . . ."

" I get the impression that you keep yourself to yourself, you avoid people."

" Maybe . . ." And then, after a silence: " I'm not very gregarious usually. Or, rather, people find me difficult. I've got nothing much to interest them as a person. I don't like vodka, I can't sing songs and I'm not a very good dancer . . ."

" You're wrong to believe that."

" You just ask Shiryáev."

" Shiryáev certainly doesn't have a bad opinion of you."

" It's not a matter of opinion . . . Anyway this is not very interesting."

" But I think it is interesting. I'll tell you frankly—the first time I saw you—you remember where it was, on the bank at night, after the landing?"

" Wait." Farber stopped me with a movement of his hand. " Do you hear?"

I strained my ears. Sounds of flutes and violins, a little hoarse-voiced, floated solemnly, from across the Volga, seeming now nearer, now further away, sometimes interrupted by the wind. They wailed over the river, over the ruined and now silent city, over us, over the Germans, beyond the trenches, beyond the front line and beyond Mamai Hill.

" Do you recognise it?"

" Goodness knows . . . Something familiar . . . Terribly familiar . . . It's not Tchaikovsky?"

" Tchaikovsky. From the Fifth Symphony. Second movement. Andante cantabile."

We listened in silence. Behind us a machine-gun began to hammer away, insistently, like a sewing-machine. Then it stopped.

" That's the place . . ." said Farber, touching my knee with his hand. " It's like a shriek. Isn't it? It's not like that in the finale. The melody is the same but it's not like that. Do you like the Fifth?"

" I love it."

" So do I . . . Even more than the Sixth. Although the Sixth is considered—Now it'll be the waltz. Let's keep quiet."

And we were silent. We stayed silent to the very end. Again I recalled Kiev, the chestnuts, the lime-trees, Lusia, the bright flowers and the conductor with something white in his buttonhole . . .

Then a bomber flew over—a heavy night bomber, with three engines. For some reason we used to call it the TB. Monotonously, drearily, it droned away above our heads. One of ours.

"It's funny, isn't it?" said Farber, rising.

"What's funny?"

"All this . . . Tchaikovsky, the greatcoat, the TB."

We stood up and went in the direction of Farber's dug-out. The bomber was dawdling about in one place. From beyond Mamai Hill the long fingers of the searchlights stretched out.

I stayed with Farber for the night.

XXI

On the evening of the seventh the newspapers arrived with Stalin's speech. We had long been waiting for it. We had not been able to pick it up on the radio—there was too much interference. The only sentence we had managed to make out was: "We too will have our day."

This sentence was being discussed in all the dug-outs and trenches.

"There's going to be an offensive," announced Lisagór authoritatively, as he always spoke about everything. "You just see. Lazar must have been right when he said last time—remember?—that there are some divisions moving up by night."

Stalin spoke on the sixth of November.

On the seventh the Allies landed in Algiers and Oran. On the tenth they entered Tunis and Casablanca.

On the eleventh of November, at seven in the morning, military operations in North Africa came to an end. An agreement was signed between Darlan and Eisenhower. On the same day and at the same hour German troops, on Hitler's orders, crossed the demarcation line at Chalon-sur-Saône and advanced on Lyons. At 1500 hours Italian troops entered Nice. On the twelfth of November the Germans occupied Marseilles and landed in Tunis.

On the thirteenth of November the Germans bombed Stalingrad for the last time. Forty-two Ju-87s came over in three waves, dropping bombs on the positions of our heavy artillery in the area of Krásnaya Slobodá on the right bank of the Volga. They went off. There was a curious, unusual and quite astonishing silence.

After eighty-two days of impenetrable din and smoke, after uninterrupted bombing—from seven in the morning till seven at night—something very curious happened. The cloud over the " Red October " disappeared. There was no need to crane one's neck every minute and seek those repulsive triangles in the cloudless sky. Only the " crate " appeared with its usual punctuality in the mornings and before sunset, and sometimes the Messerschmitts would zoom overhead only to disappear almost at once.

Clearly, the Jerries were exhausted . . . And in the trenches there were lively discussions going, why and for what reasons and whether the events in Africa could be regarded as a second front. Political officers were in great demand. The regimental agitator,[1] Sénichla Lozovóy, small and black like a little beetle and always excited, was completely overwhelmed. He hardly put in an appearance on the shore—he would pop into HQ for a minute to listen to the radio and rush straight back. There, on the front line, you could hear nothing but: " Sénichka, come here! Sénichka, come to us! " They all called him that—Sénichka. The men and officers alike. The commissar had already told him off:

" What is this, Lozovóy? You a lieutenant and everyone calling you ' Sénichka '? It won't do."

But he only smiled in embarrassment:

" Well, what can I do? They're used to it. How many times have I told them. But they forget . . . And I forget."

And so he remained for us—Sénichka. The commissar dismissed the matter with a gesture:

" He works like the devil . . . How can I shout at him?"

Sénichka really did work like the devil. He had so much initiative and imagination that you couldn't imagine where it all went in such a small and puny fellow. At one time he was always fussing with a trumpet. The sappers made him an enormous megaphone out of tin and he would spend whole days with this megaphone and interpreters lecturing the Germans. The Germans would get annoyed and start firing at him, and he would tuck his trumpet under his arm and move to another place. Later he got taken up with leaflets and cartoons of Hitler. They turned out quite well. It was just at that time that the regiment received a supply of

[1] Official propagandist.

leaflet shells and mortars. When they were used up, he spent a long time trying to construct something out of empty tins and even made a catapult out of rubber. But nothing came of this enterprise—the tins did not reach the Germans. Then he set about making a scarecrow. After he had done it they started making similar scarecrows in all the divisions. It was great fun for the troops. Out of rags and a German uniform he made a likeness of Hitler, with moustache and forelock of dyed rope, and he hung on it a notice: "Shoot at me!" and with the scouts he somehow set it up at night in the no-man's-land between us and the Germans. They got furious and put machine-gun fire on their Führer all day long and at night stole the scarecrow. They stole it all right, but they lost three men doing it. The troops simply split their sides with laughter.

"Good old Sénichka!"

The men were very fond of him.

Unfortunately he was soon taken away from us. As the best agitator in the division, they sent him to Moscow for training. We waited a long time for a letter from him, and when at last it came they spent a whole day at the first battalion command post—where he had been most often—getting out a reply. In the end the text came to not more than a couple of pages, and they were mostly questions ("nothing new—a little bit of fighting"), but the signatures would only just go on to four pages—there were close on a hundred of them.

The troops remembered him for a long time.

"When's his training going to finish, then?" they would ask, and they all imagined that Sénichka would come back to our regiment. But he never returned—he got to the Northern Front, apparently.

XXII

The nineteenth of November is a date that sticks in my memory. It is my birthday. In childhood it was marked by pies and presents, later by parties and drinks. But, one way or the other, it was always celebrated. Even the previous year, in the reserve regiment, on that day we had drunk home-made spirit and had eaten sour milk out of a vast enamel bowl. This time Valéga and Lisagór were up to something again.

The night before Valéga made me go to the bath-house—a

207

tumble-down, roofless shack on the banks of the Volga—gave me clean, and even ironed, underwear, and then vanished somewhere for the whole day, popping in only for a minute —with a worried look, hunting for something, and with mysterious packages under his arm. Lisagór smiled enigmatically. I didn't interfere.

Towards evening I went out to see Ustínov. He had invited me three days running. First he had just " suggested ", then he " ordered " and finally " for the last time I order you to come or there'll be trouble." I knew in advance what was the matter. I had not sent in the plan of engineering works for strengthening the defences, the current inventory of engineering equipment with losses and acquisitions for the last week or the design for the disposition of the planned command posts. I could expect a long, tedious lecture, full of historical examples, Verdun, Port Arthur, Totleben and Clausewitz. It couldn't possibly take less than an hour.

Ustínov greeted me with unusual formality. He loved form and ritual. On the whole brain-workers who find themselves at the front can be divided basically into two categories. Some are oppressed and tortured by army drill—everything fits them like a sack, their tunics are full of creases, their belt buckle is on one side, their boots are three sizes too big, their greatcoat sticks out and they are tongue-tied. But others, on the contrary, like all the outward side of military life—they salute with pleasure, even with a sort of relish ; every minute they inject " comrade lieutenant " or " comrade captain " into the conversation ; and they parade their knowledge of the regulations and the types of German and of our own aircraft. When they listen to the flight of a mortar or a shell, they have to say: " That's a regimental one " or " They've found a one-five-two." They can't talk about themselves except as " we front-liners " or " with us, at the front."

Ustínov belonged to the second category. You could tell that he was rather proud of his precise manner and his literal observations of all the regulations. And he didn't do it badly, despite his advanced years, his spectacles and his love of writing. No matter whom he greeted he invariably rose to his feet. When he addressed someone senior he kept his arms to his sides.

On this occasion he met me with unusual solemnity. His expression was withdrawn, his brows were knit and he waved me to a stool with a flowing, stagy gesture. All this suggested that the conversation would not be restricted to tables and diagrams.

I sat on the stool. He sat facing me. For some time we were silent. Then he raised his eyes and gazed at me over his glasses.

" Have you been informed about the latest events, comrade lieutenant?"

" What events?"

" What? Don't you know anything?" His eyebrows rose in surprise. " Didn't the CRR tell you anything?" In the informer's language which he loved " CRR " stood for " Commander of Rifle Regiment "—in this case Major Borodín.

" No, nothing."

Slowly, as though hesitating, his eyebrows dropped and took up their usual position. His fingers twiddled a long, carefully sharpened pencil with a cap.

" At 0600 hours to-morrow we go over to the offensive."

The pencil described a little circle on the paper and, to underline the importance of the sentence, put a full stop in the middle.

" What offensive?"

" An offensive along the whole front." He spelt it out slowly, savouring every word. " You realise what that means?"

So far I understood only one thing: that there remained ten hours to the opening of the offensive, and that the rest time I'd promised the men—the first in the last fortnight—would be hopelessly upset.

" The task of our division is limited but important," he went on. " We have to take possession of the storage tanks. You realise what responsibility rests on us? At four thirty the artillery preparation will begin. All the front artillery will open up, the whole left bank. We have at our disposal—it is now seven minutes past eight—a very limited period of time: some ten hours. Your regiment will have a company from the sapper battalion transferred to it. You will have to give each rifle battalion one platoon from that company for engineering reconnaissance and clearing the enemy mine-fields. You will put the regimental sappers in the gaps in your own fields."

The sheet of paper lying in front of him was slowly being filled with carefully drawn, even lines.

" Don't for a minute forget about records. Every mine removed must be recorded, every minefield discovered must be identified and related to a landmark, and it must be a permanent one—not oil drums or gun but something permanent. You must send reports on the work carried out every three hours by special runner."

He went on talking long and verbosely, without omitting a single detail, practically dividing up my whole time into hours and minutes. I silently made note. The divisional sappers were already preparing for the job—cleaning their tools, fixing charges and mending fuses.

I listened, made notes and glanced at the clock. At nine o'clock I left. I agreed with the commander of the second company that had been transferred to me—it was the same company as had been working with me all the time—that they would come to me at two in the morning.

Lisagór greeted me, bad-tempered and dishevelled. His little eyes were glistening.

"How do you like that, eh? Lieutenant?"

He was almost choking with excitement and couldn't sit still—he kept jumping up and striding up and down the dug-out.

"We dug ourselves in, laid a mass of mines, enough to stop the devil himself. We got everything fixed . . . Now they have to have an offensive. Make paths through, remove the wire entanglements. All our work goes west . . . They could have sat in the trenches and fired away, now the Germans don't attack. What else do they need?"

He was beginning to get on my nerves.

"Let's stop this idiotic talk. If you don't like it, don't fight, that's your business . . ."

But Lisagór wouldn't give up. A plaintive note crept into his voice.

"But it's a shame, damn it! Just you look at the table. Once in a blue moon we were about to celebrate a birthday in a civilised way and now everything goes to the devil."

The table was really unrecognisable. In the middle were four open half-litre bottles of vodka, thin elliptical slices of sausage, a packet of "Pushkin" biscuits, chocolate in a brown and gold-lined wrapping, smoked herring and—the centre of the whole feast—meat steaming away in a pot and filling the whole dug-out with its aroma.

"Do you realise that Valéga got hold of a hare—a real hare? He went across to the other side specially for it. Chumák was supposed to turn up. There's condensed milk, your favourite . . . Well, what are we going to do? Keep it for the New Year? Is that it?"

210

Frankly speaking, I would also have been a lot happier to sit down and eat hare and wash it down with wine than to busy myself with preparations for the offensive . . . But what could you do . . .

We poured ourselves each half a glass and drank it down without a toast. We followed it with some hare. It was a bit tough, but that, after all, hardly mattered. What mattered was that it was hare. Our mood improved somewhat. Lisagór even winked:

"Hurry up, lieutenant, before you get called out . . . You've already been sent for twice."

A minute later a runner appeared from HQ. Abrósimov wanted me.

The major and Abrósimov were sitting over a map. In the dug-out there wasn't room to turn—battalion commanders, staff officers and commanders of special units. Chumák was there in his usual forage cap, his tunic unbuttoned and his vest gleaming white.

"Well, engineer, it fell through, did it?"

"Yes, it did."

"Never mind . . . Hide it in the cupboard . . . We'll come back and give you a hand," and he laughed happily, his eyes sparkling.

I squeezed my way through to the table. There was no comfort there. Before the beginning of the offensive a new command post had to be made for the regimental commander. The old one was no good—the tanks could not be seen. I knew it. Well, and, of course, clearing the minefields, making ways through and safeguarding the infantry operations.

"Watch out, engineer, don't make any mistakes." Borodín puffed on his pipe. "You've sown your own potatoes there on the front line and nobody but you can sort them out . . . Otherwise our men will be blown to bits. And every man counts, as you know very well."

You could tell he was excited, but he was trying to conceal it. His pipe kept going out, and the matches just wouldn't light—the sides of the boxes were no good.

"Cover the command post with rails. And see there's a stove in it. My rheumatism has started up again. At 0500 on the very dot I'll be there. If you don't finish it I'll rip your legs off. Understand? Now get going."

I went off.

Lisagór was sitting, changing his foot-cloths.

" Well?"

" Take a detachment and see that there's a new command post ready by 0500 hours."

" A new one? By five? You've gone off your head."

" Off my head or not, you've got seven hours to play with."

Lisagór stuffed his foot into his boot in such a temper that he pulled off the tongue.

" If you go hunting you must feed the dogs. I said that the tanks would not be visible from that post. Never mind, they said, they won't give the tanks to us but to the forty-fifth. We are further to the left. Now there's your further to the left."

" All right. You can grouse to-morrow, but don't waste time now. You can use the scouts' observation post. You can put the scouts in with the gunners. You can say Borodín ordered it. Clear?"

" Everything's clear . . . And, of course, he ordered rails to be put on it? Yes?"

" You are to put rails on it and fix up a stove. Only let the pipe come out on our side. Reduce the size of the embrasure, and the left-hand one you can close right up."

" Didn't he order it to be lined with smooth planks?"

" That's your business. You can even put a divan in it if you want. Take Novokhátko and his detachment with you."

" He's as blind as a bat."

" He'll do for the command post. Garkúsha will go with Agnívtsev to do the throughways."

" Then let him stay here and look after the spades."

" As you wish. So long as the command post's ready at five."

Lisagór pulled on his other boot. He grunted.

" Who the devil invented this war? I could lie on the stove now and chew sunflower seeds."

And, picking up half the sausage which lay on the table, and stuffing it into his mouth, he departed.

I remained to await the divisional sappers.

XXIII

Towards four o'clock I went to the front line. As though they sensed something was going to happen, the Germans kept up practically incessant fire from machine-guns, which lit up the front area.

I had a look round the battalions. Agnívtsev and Garkúsha had finished the throughways, and were warming themselves and smoking in the dug-outs. I went to the command post. A long way from it I could hear Lisagór's obscene whispering. Sitting on top of the dug-out, he and Tugíyev were fixing the rails as a covering. They were both grunting and swearing. German bullets were whistling almost over their very heads. The machine-gun was some fifty metres away, so that the bullets overshot and landed somewhere far behind.

I scrambled into the dug-out. The signallers were already there, and the regimental commander's adjutant. The embrasure was covered with a blanket, so that no light should be seen. A smoking cartridge case was standing right on the floor. One of the signallers was stoking up the stove with extra mortar charges. He apparently found pleasure in watching the powder flare up—he kept throwing little handfuls of it on to the stove.

Ten minutes later Lisagór tumbled in. His whole face was beaded with sweat. His hands were red from rust and clay.

"Have a look at your watch, engineer."

"Twenty past four."

"That's speed for you: ready on the dot for the beginning of the artillery preparation. Got any tobacco?"

I gave him a smoke. He wiped his face with his sleeve. It became striped, like a mattress.

"He's a bear, that Tugíyev. He'll take half a rail on his shoulder without a word. Do you know where we carted them from? Practically all the way from the Meat Plant. We cut them up with TNT and then carted them on our own shoulders. Here, feel it, just like a pillow it's become. A nice cure at a health resort, that's what we need—Sóchi or Matsesta . . ."

"How many layers did you put?"

"Two of rails, and then there's the old wooden one still there."

213

" Did it make a mound?"

" Do you know how many mounds there are? Wherever you step it's either a mound or a dug-out, and if it's not a dug-out it's a mound."

" No wounded?"

" Tugíyev's greatcoat—three little holes. But he's worth his weight in gold. He should be mentioned. Just as if he was digging the garden at home. Wait . . . It's begun, hasn't it?"

We listened carefully. From across the Volga the first volleys could be heard. I looked at my watch. Four thirty.

" Into your trenches!" shouted Lisagór. " 'Sights at zero five, get your own alive.' Shout down to the sappers, signaller, and tell 'em to come up here."

The sappers squeezed themselves into the strong-point. They lit up cigarettes and got themselves mixed up in one another's rifles and spades.

" Where's Tugíyev?"

" Still up there on top."

" What do you know? He's covering it over with sand. Making a good job of it. Get him down here, Sedélnikov. Or he'll get his head knocked off by a shell."

The bombardment got heavier. Through the badly fitting door shells could be heard whistling over the dug-out. The rumbling of the explosions smothered the sound of the firing. The dug-out trembled, and earth fell from the roof.

Lisagór dug me in the side.

" Well? What about it? Shall we send 'em all home? Before it's too late. Or else Abrósimov will arrive and that'll be that. He'll send everybody into the attack."

It seemed as though they would really have to be sent away while the softening up was going on and the Germans were silent. And that's what we did.

They had hardly left when the major, Abrósimov and the head of intelligence appeared. The major was breathing heavily—his heart was probably not good.

" Well, how is it, engineer? We shan't get ourselves buried here?" he inquired in a kindly tone, the wrinkles gathering around his eyes. He was already feeling for his pipe.

" I don't think so, comrade major."

" There you go, thinking again . . . I shall fine you. Five roubles for every ' think '. Did you put rails over?"

" I did. Two lots of them."

Abrósimov came up. His teeth were clenched and his eyes screwed up.

"Where's Lisagór?"

"He's gone to rest. With his men."

"To rest? He should have been left here. What a time to rest . . ."

I didn't reply. A good thing I had sent them off to the shore in good time.

"And where are the others?"

"In their battalions."

"What are they doing?"

"Making pathways through the minefields."

"Have you checked up on them?"

"I have."

"What are the divisional men doing?"

"On reconnaissance."

"Why didn't they do their reconnoitring yesterday?"

"Because they got the order to-day."

Abrósimov bit his lips. His eyes, cold and sharp, did not look very friendly. The left corner of his mouth was twitching slightly.

"You watch out, lieutenant: if they get blown up, it'll be bad for you."

I didn't like his tone. I replied that the paths through the fields were marked with pegs and that the battalion commanders had been informed. Abrósimov said no more. He called the first battalion on the telephone.

The guns thundered away louder than ever. The explosions and detonations ran together into one unbroken rumble that did not stop for a minute. The door kept banging. Then someone tied it up with wire.

"They're doing a good job," said the major.

Somewhere quite close a shell exploded. Earth crumbled from the roof. The lamp nearly went out.

"No kidding, it's a good job," said the intelligence officer with a forced smile. "Yesterday a one-twenty-two nearly landed right in Pozhársky's dug-out—the artillery commander."

The major also smiled. So did I. But it wasn't very pleasant. The German front line was about fifty metres from us—a fairly normal area of spread for long-range artillery.

We sat and smoked. At such times it is difficult not to smoke.

Later the divisional sapper-scout arrived. They had discovered and removed eighteen "S" mines. They had unscrewed the detonators and left the mines where they were. He left.

Abrósimov could not let his phone alone.

Could the Germans really hold on after such a softening-up?

It started to get hot. The sides of the stove were orange-red. I undid my tunic.

"Don't put any more on," said the major to the signaller. "It's getting light and they'll fire at the smoke."

The signaller crept away into his corner.

Towards six the bombardment died down. Every minute we looked at our watches. Quarter to . . . Ten to . . . Five to . . .

Abrósimov was stuck to his phone.

"Get ready!"

The last scattered shells. And then—quiet. A frightening and unnatural quiet. Our chaps had finished. The Germans had not yet begun.

"Get going!" Abrósimov shouted into the phone. He was pale and the corner of his mouth kept twitching.

I stood at the embrasure. Against the grey dawn sky stood out the water-tanks, some sort of pipes, German trenches, a knocked-out tank. Further to the right were our dug-outs. A bird flew, slowly flapping its wings. They say birds are not afraid of war.

The major was to my left. He was also at the embrasure, sucking his pipe. For some reason I shivered. My hands trembled and I felt goose-flesh up my back. It must have been from excitement. Lack of anything to do is the most frightful thing of all.

Shapes appeared above our trenches. They were running. Hurrah . . . Straight for the tanks . . . A-a-a-a.

I didn't even hear the German machine-gun start firing. I only saw the shapes falling. The white puffs of smoke as mines exploded. Then another machine-gun. To the left.

There were more explosions. A white smoke, like cottom wool, spread across the ground. Then slowly it dispersed. On the grey, bare earth were men. There were a lot of them. Some were crawling, others were lying still. No one was running.

The major sucked on his pipe and coughed.

"They didn't put a damned thing out of action . . . not a damned thing . . ."

Abrósimov phoned to the second and third battalions. The same thing. They had taken cover. Machine-guns and mortars wouldn't let them raise their heads.

The major went away from the embrasure. His face seemed swollen and tired.

"For an hour and a half they blazed away and still we can't take it . . . Blast them. They're pretty tough, the devils."

Abrósimov stood with the phone to his ear, his foot on a box, running his nervous, dry fingers over the wire.

"Have a look out of the embrasure, engineer . . . Are there many dead? Or have they got themselves into the craters?"

I had a look. There were some twenty men lying. They must be dead. Their hands and legs were spread out. The others were not to be seen. A machine-gun was firing right at the breastworks—nothing but clouds of dust rising. Things were bad.

"Kérzhentsev," said the major very quietly.

"Yes, sir."

"There's nothing for you to do here. Go over to your previous battalion, to Shiryáev. Give him a hand . . ." And then, after a suck on his pipe: "There you've got German communication trenches. Shiryáev worked out how to take them. Set up a machine-gun and fire on the Jerries' flank!"

I turned on my heel.

"What are you up to—sending him to Shiryáev?" asked Abrósimov, without moving from the telephone.

"Let him go. There's nothing for him to do here. We can't take them frontally in any case."

"We'll take them!" said Abrósimov in an unnatural screech and threw down the phone. The signaller skilfully caught it in mid-air and adjusted it on his head. "We'll take 'em frontally if we don't hide in holes. Go on, Kérzhentsev, to the second battalion—get things organised there, or they won't make any sense. Just fancy! The fire's heavy, so we can't get up! . . ."

His usually quiet, cold eyes were now round and bloodshot. His lips were trembling.

"Get 'em up, get 'em up! They've been lying there too long. They can't get off their arses . . ."

"Listen, don't get so worked up, Abrósimov," said the major quietly and waved me on.

I departed. I ran full tilt to Shiryáev's command post, weaving my way between the shell bursts. The Germans had lost their tempers and were firing indiscriminately, just for the sake of firing. Shiryáev was not there; he was at the front line, so I ran up there, and bumped right into him at the entrance to a dug-out—the very same one we sat in when we were surrounded.

"How are things?"

Shiryáev shrugged. "Half the battalion is missing."

"Killed?"

"Goodness only knows . . . They're taking cover . . . Go and fight with Abrósimov!"

"What do you mean?"

The veins on Shiryáev's neck were standing out:

"I mean that the major wants one thing and Abrósimov another . . . I thought I'd got things agreed with the major. I told him honestly how things were. I've got common communication trenches with the Germans."

"I know. What about it?"

"Well, I got everything ready at night. I laid charges, so as to break a way through . . . The very one that you filled in. I put my sappers in position. Then—bang! Abrósimov called up—no break-throughs, but lead into the attack . . . I explained that there are machine-guns there. 'No matter—the artillery will suppress them, and the Germans are scared of the bayonet . . .' So there you are."

"How many men have you got?"

"Infantry—something over sixty. I sent thirty into the attack and kept thirty. That'll be something else for Abrósimov to swear about. 'Make a massed attack,' he said. 'Keep only machine-gunners and mortar-men back. Put the sappers in too . . .'"

"Does the major know all this?"

"How do I know . . .?"

Shiryáev flopped on to a stool with all his weight. It nearly collapsed.

"Well, what are we to do now? Half the men are killed, the other half will be missing until evening—the Jerries won't let them get up. And he'll be on the phone again any minute now."

I told Shiryáev what the major had said to me. His eyes lit up. He jumped up, seized me by the shoulders and shook me violently.

"Wonderful! You just sit here and I'll have a word with Karnaúkhov and Farber . . . If only we can winkle the men out of those craters . . ."

He grabbed his cap.

"If the phone goes, say nothing! Let the signaller answer. Leshka—you say I'm at the front line. Get me? That's if Abrósimov phones."

Leshka nodded his head in understanding.

218

Shiryáev had no sooner slammed the door than Abrósimov phoned. Leshka winked slyly.

"He's gone out, comrade captain . . . Only just left. Yes, both of them . . . They came and went."

Covering the mouthpiece with his hand, he laughed.

"He's swearing . . . Why didn't they phone him when they arrived?"

Half an hour later Shiryáev had everything ready. In three places our trenches linked up with the German ones—on the hill and in the ravine. In each of them there were two mined obstructions. During the night Shiryáev and the sappers attached to him had connected fuse wires to them. The trenches from us to the Germans had been checked and about ten mines removed.

Everything was in order. Shiryáev slapped his knee.

"Thirteen of the lads have crawled back. We're doing fine! Let 'em rest for the time being and keep watch. The remainder, in groups of ten, we'll put into the break-through. It's not too bad, eh?"

His eyes were shining. His shaggy white cap was down over one ear and his hair was stuck to his forehead.

"I'll send Karnaúkhov and Farber to the hill and I'll go along the ravine."

"And who's going to direct the operation?"

"You will."

"Stop kidding. I'm not a battalion commander any longer, I'm an engineer, a representative from HQ."

"Well, what about it? You're the representative, so go ahead and take command."

"Why don't you send Sendétsky into the ravine? He's a brave lad. What about it?" ?

"Sendétsky? He's rather young. But still . . ."

We were standing in the trench at the entrance to the dug-out. Suddenly Shiryáev's eyes screwed up and his nose wrinkled. He seized my arm.

"For goodness' sake . . . He's here already."

"Who?"

Abrósimov was scrambling up the side of the ravine, hanging on to the bushes. Behind him was a runner.

Shiryáev spat and pushed his cap over his forehead.

Abrósimov shouted while still far off:

"What the devil do you think I sent you over here for? Just to gossip?"

He was out of breath and his tunic was undone.

"I phoned and phoned . . . Someone could at least answer . . . Are you thinking of fighting or not?"

He was breathing heavily. He wetted his dry lips with his tongue.

"I'm asking you—do you propose to fight or not?"

"We do," Shiryáev replied calmly.

"Then fight, blast you . . . What the devil are you standing about for? And the engineer too . . . And I have to run around like an errand boy . . ."

"Allow me to explain," said Shiryáev, in just the same calm and restrained manner, although his nostrils were quivering.

Abrósimov turned purple.

"I'll give you 'explain'!"

He reached for his holster.

"Quick march, into the attack!"

I felt something boiling up inside me. Shiryáev stood breathing heavily, his head stuck forward. His fists were clenched.

"Quick march, into the attack! Do you hear? I shan't say it again . . ."

He had a revolver in his hand. His fingers were white, bloodless.

"I'm not going into any attack until you have heard me out," Shiryáev said slowly, through clenched teeth.

For a few seconds they stared each other in the face. Another moment and they would be at each other. I had never yet seen Abrósimov like that.

"The major ordered me to take those trenches. I agreed with him . . ."

"In the army you don't make agreements, you carry out orders," Abrósimov broke in. "What did I order you to do in the morning?"

"Kérzhentsev has just confirmed to me . . ."

"What did I order you to do this morning?"

"To attack."

"Where is your attack?"

"It broke down, because . . ."

"I didn't ask why . . ." Suddenly flying into a temper again, he waved his revolver. "Quick march into the attack! I'll shoot you as cowards! For not carrying out orders!"

I thought he was going to fall down in a fit.

"All officers in front. And you yourself too. I'll teach you to try and save your own skin . . . Some scheme about trenches you've thought up . . . It's three hours since the order was given."

I couldn't listen to any more. I turned on my heel and walked away.

XXIV

Machine-guns fetched us all to the ground at once. A soldier running past fell flat, his arms stretched wide before him. I jumped full tilt into a fresh crater, still smelling of the explosion. Earth fell all around. Somebody leapt over me. He also fell. Quickly pawing the ground he scrambed somewhere to one side. Bullets whistled just above the ground, struck the sand and screeched. Somewhere quite near mines were going off.

I lay on my side, rolled up into a ball with my knees under my chin and a revolver in my right hand. It was covered with sand. Valéga had smeared it with oil the night before. I had forgotten to clean it off in the morning.

Nobody was shouting hurrah any more.

Where was Shiryáev? We had jumped out of the trenches almost at the same time. I had tripped and grabbed at some piece of iron sticking out of the ground. Then I saw his greatcoat ahead, a little to the right. It had a big yellow stain on it—it caught my eye at once.

The German machine-guns were not silent for a minute. You could tell exactly how the gunner swung his gun: fanning round, from right to left and left to right.

I pressed myself as close as I could to the ground. The crater was fairly large, but it seemed to me that my left shoulder was still sticking out. I dug away with my hands. The soil was soft from the explosion and easy to move. But that was only the top surface—below it was clay. I scratched at the earth feverishly, like a dog.

Tr-rak! A mortar-shell. I was covered with earth.

Tr-rak! Another one. Then a third and a fourth. I closed my eyes and stopped digging. They must have seen me throwing the earth out.

I lay still, holding my breath. Over to the left somebody was groaning. A-a-a-a . . . Nothing else, just: a-a-a-a . . . Evenly, without any intonation, on one note. I don't know how long I lay there. I was scared to budge an inch. My mouth was full of earth. It grated between my teeth. And all around was earth. I could see nothing but earth. On top it was grey and soft, like powder, and below it was clay— reddish-brown, hard and crisp. No grass, not a twig. Nothing but dust and clay. If at least I could have seen a worm. If I turned my head I could see the sky. That too was somehow bare, grey and unfriendly. It was probably going to rain or snow. Snow, more likely—my toes were freezing.

The machine-gun began to fire irregularly, but still low down, just above the earth. I could not begin to understand why I was still in one piece, not wounded and not dead. To go straight into a machine-gun at fifty metres was certain death. The first to leap out had been Shiryáev, Karnaúkhov, Sendétsky and myself. And one other, a platoon commander, one of the new ones. I remembered only that he had a white tuft of hair sticking out from under his cap. I didn't catch sight of Farber at all.

Apparently I had not run far but had flattened out at once. I couldn't remember what had made me lie down. I had a feeling of empty space all around me. There had been a lot of people and then suddenly nobody at all. It must have been instinct. It was frightening being all alone. Actually I didn't remember whether I had been frightened. I couldn't even remember how and why I had turned up in that crater.

I got a cramp in my right leg from lying in an awkward position. First it was in my calf, then in my foot, and then in the tendon that goes up from behind the knee and along the thigh. I turned over and tried to stretch my leg. But there was nowhere to stretch it—I was scared to put it outside the crater. I rubbed it and worked it with my fingers. The calf would not come round—the top of the boot prevented it.

The wounded man was still groaning. Without any break, but rather quieter now.

The Germans transferred their fire into the depth of our defences. Shells were bursting far behind. The bullets flew much higher. They were leaving us in peace. I pushed my cap a little way out of the crater. They didn't fire at it. A little further. Still no fire. I raised myself on my arms and peered out. The Germans were close by. You could have thrown a stone to the gun rests standing in front of their trenches. There was a machine-gun right opposite me.

I scooped up some earth and made a little barrier on the side of the Germans. Now I could look around and back— they couldn't see me.

I was closer to the German trenches than to ours. Ours were thirty metres away, possibly more. Someone was running along them, bent double—you could only see the ear-flaps sticking up. He vanished. The soldier who had been running at my side was still lying with his arms outstretched. His face was turned towards me. His eyes were open. He looked as if he had put his ear to the ground and was listening to something. A few paces further on was another. Only his legs in thick cloth puttees and yellow boots could be seen.

I counted fourteen bodies altogether. Some had probably been there since the morning attack. Neither Shiryáev nor Karnaúkhov were among them. I would have recognised them at once. There were lots of craters, big and small, all around. In one of them, something moved then vanished.

The wounded man kept groaning. He lay a few paces from my crater, face downwards, his head towards me. His cap was alongside. The hair was dark and wavy and terribly familiar. His arms were bent up close to his body. He was crawling. Slowly, slowly he crawled, without raising his head. He only used his elbows. His legs dragged along helplessly. And all the time he groaned. But now very quietly.

I didn't take my eyes off him. I couldn't think how to help him. I did not even have a personal first-aid packet with me. He was now quite close. I could reach him.

" Come on, come on in here," I whispered and stretched out my hand.

The head rose up. Big, black eyes, already covered with a deathly glaze. Kharlámov, my former chief of staff . . . He looked at me but without recognising me. There was no suffering on his face. Only a sort of stupefaction. His forehead, teeth and cheeks were covered with earth. His mouth was half open. His lips were white.

" Come on, come on in here . . ."

Supporting himself on his elbows, he crawled right up to the creater. He rested his face on the ground. I got my hands under his arms and dragged him into the crater. He was somehow soft and boneless. He slithered down head forward. His legs were completely lifeless.

I got him in with difficulty. It was tight for two in the crater. I had to put his legs on top of mine. He lay with his head thrown back staring at the sky, breathing slowly and heavily. His tunic and the top of his breeches were covered with blood. I undid his belt and pulled up his shirt. There were two clean little holes on the right side of his stomach. I realised that he must die.

He turned his head towards me. His lips moved and he was saying something. I could make out only: "Comrade lieutenant . . . comrade lieutenant . . ." It appeared that he had recognised me after all. Then he let his head fall and did not raise it again. He died quite peacefully. He simply stopped breathing.

I closed his eyes, put his cap over his stern and immediately rigid face.

Snow began to fall. At first in small and then in big, fluffy flakes. Everything around suddenly became white—the earth, the prostrate figures and the breastworks of the trenches. My hands and legs began to freeze. Ears too. I turned my collar up.

The Germans opened fire. Our men fired back. Bullets whistled overhead.

And so we lay—I and Kharlámov cold and stiff, with snow-flakes not melting on his hands. My watch had stopped. I could not be certain how long we had lain. My legs and arms were going numb. I got cramp again. How long could I lie like that? Perhaps I should just jump up and run for it? Thirty metres to our trench—five seconds at the most before the machine-gunner realised what was happening. After all, thirteen men ran out of it in the morning . . .

In the next crater someone was moving about. Against the background of the white, already melting snow, the grey patch of a cap was moving. A head appeared for a second. It vanished. Then it appeared again. Then suddenly a man shot up out of the crater and ran. Very quickly, his hands close to his sides, bent down, and lifting his feet very high.

He covered three-quarters of the distance. There were only some eight or ten metres left between him and the trenches. Then a machine-gun cut him down. He made a few more steps and fell headlong. And so he remained lying three paces from our trenches. For some time his greatcoat showed up black against the snow, then it too turned white. The snow kept on falling . . .

Later another three ran for it. One was in a short jersey. He must have got rid of his greatcoat so as to run more easily. He was killed practically on our breastworks. The second—a few paces away from him. The third managed to jump into the trench. From the German side the machine-gun went on for a long time putting bullet after bullet into the place where he had vanished.

I deepened the crater with my heels so that I could stretch

my legs. Then some more digging for Kharlámov's legs. They were already stiff and would not bend at the knees, but I somehow managed to push them in. Now we were lying side by side, stretched full length, I on my side, he on his back. He looked as if he were asleep and had covered his face with his cap to keep off the snow.

The work warmed me up a little. I arranged myself on my left side, so as not to see Kharlámov. I dug a little underneath my hip so as to lie in greater comfort. Now it was all right. So long as our long-range gunners didn't open fire on the German front line . . . And I'd have liked a smoke . . . even a couple of puffs. I had left my tobacco in Shiryáev's dug-out. Only matches rattled in my pocket.

I felt drowsy. The snow around me was melting. The grey dust was turning to mud. My knees were soaked. And my head was freezing. I took Kharlámov's cap and covered his face with a handkerchief. I cleaned my revolver—that was to keep myself awake. It turned out to have only four bullets in it and I had no spare cartridge clip.

What time could it be? Probably past twelve . . . But it wouldn't get dark till six. Another six hours to lie there . . . an eternity . . .

I let my ear-flaps down and closed my eyes. To hell with them!

Sleep wouldn't come. I kept imagining Kharlámov was moving about behind me. I remembered that I ought to remove his documents from him . . . That wasn't so easy— he had them in his back trousers pocket. I had seen him take his membership card out of his back pocket when he paid his dues. It took me a long time—Kharlámov had got heavy, as though he'd grown into the ground. But I got them in the end. In a little folder carefully folded and held together by a safety-pin were his membership card, two letters, some almost completely faded certificate in ink that had run, and some photographs. The photographs were done up separately. I had never thought that Kharlámov would be so careful. When he was on my staff he was always losing and forgetting things.

I looked at the pictures. One was of Kharlámov and a woman with a child in her arms. She had long, wavy hair and wide-set eyes. It must have been his wife. The child had the same big, black eyes as its father. Another was of the same woman, alone, and wearing a beret. A third was of a group of people on the bank of a river. They were laughing. There was a chap with a guitar. Kharlámov was in his pants, lying

on his stomach. In the distance was a field and a haystack . . .
On the back was written: " Cherikízovo, June 1939, Mura
is second from left."

I wrapped it all up in the oilskin folder, fastened it and put
it in my pocket.

A little lump of clay hit me in the ear. I started. Another
one fell nearby, by my knee. Someone was throwing them at
me. I raised my head slightly. A broad unshaven face peered
out of the neighbouring crater.

" Got any matches, chum? Or a lighter?"

" I have."

" Chuck 'em over, for God's sake."

" Can you let me have a fag?"

" Sure."

I threw the box, but it fell a couple of yards short. Oh,
blast . . . The man in the crater stretched his hand out. No,
he couldn't reach . . . Neither of us could take his eyes off
the box. Small and dark-sided, it lay in the snow and seemed
to laugh at us. Then a rifle made its appearance. Slowly
and carefully it was pushed out of the crater, moved along the
snow and touched the box. This whole operation lasted an
eternity. The matchbox slipped off, moved away and just
didn't want to hook on to the foresight. The mouth of the
owner of the rifle opened wide from the effort. But in the
end he hooked on to it. The head and the rifle disappeared.
A thin cloud of smoke appeared over the crater.

" Take care . . ." I whispered, but I had the feeling he
couldn't hear me.

He smoked for a good half-hour, certainly not less. I was
quite giddy with longing and envy. Then the box returned
to me with a very small wet cigarette end inside it. I sucked
and sucked as long as I could, burning my lips with it.

" Soldier! Have you got a watch?" I asked in a whisper.

" Quarter to twelve," came from the crater.

I couldn't believe my ears. I had thought it must be two
or three, and it was not yet twelve. And to cap it all, the
shelling began again. Whether it was ours or the Germans',
the devil only knew. Shells were bursting quite nearby. Ten
or fifteen minutes. Then a break. Then another attack.

I should have to run for it. To wait meant another six
hours. I wouldn't be able to stand it. If they killed me, they
killed me, you had to die some time.

Again the hoarse voice from the crater:

" Friend . . . Hey . . . Friend . . "

"What do you want?"

"Let's run for it."

He couldn't stand it either.

"Let's," I replied.

We thought up a little dodge. The last three had been killed almost at the breastwork. What we had to do was to flatten out before reaching our trenches just before the machine-gun burst—then straight into the trenches in one rush. We might be lucky. I turned in the direction of our trenches. So long as I didn't get another cramp. The ground ahead was flat—only one small crater and a dead man beside it.

"Well, are you ready?"

"Ready."

I rested on my left leg, the right one bent at the knee. I took a last look at Kharlámov. He was lying peacefully, with his knees bent, and his hands on his stomach. There was nothing more he needed . . .

"Let's go!"

"Right!"

Snow . . . A crater . . . A dead man . . . Again snow . . . I threw myself on the ground . . . And almost at once . . . Ta-ta-ta-ta-ta . . . I didn't breathe . . . Ta-ta-ta-ta-ta . . . I lay still . . . Ta-ta-ta-ta-ta.

"You alive?"

"Alive."

I lay with my face in the snow. My hands were stretched out. My left leg was beneath my stomach—it would be easier to jump up. It was five or six steps to the trenches. I devoured that little bit of ground with my eyes.

We'd have to wait two or three minutes, for the machine-gunners to relax. He couldn't get us even as we were then—we were too low.

We could hear moving about in the trenches and talking. The words weren't audible . . . Now it was time . . .

"Get ready," I said into the snow, without raising my head.

"Ready," came the answer from my left.

I tensed. My temples throbbed.

"Let's go!"

I pushed myself off. Three long strides and I in the trench.

After that we sat for a long time, right in the mud at the bottom of the trench and laughed. Somebody gave us a fag-end.

It turned out to be already five o'clock. The soldier's watch had also stopped. We had lain in the crater from seven to five—ten hours. It was only then that I felt that I was madly, supernaturally hungry.

In the morning we buried our comrades—Kharlámov, Sendétsky and the platoon commander with the white tuft of hair. During the night medical orderlies carried their bodies from the battlefield. Karnaúkhov was not found at all. They said he had been seen with four soldiers leaping into the German trenches. There he must have died.

Shiryáev crawled in, covered in blood and with one arm hanging helplessly at his side. He dragged himself over the breastwork and at once lost consciousness. He was sent off to the medical unit. I went to look him up but he had just been taken to the field hospital on the other side.

Not counting the wounded the battalion lost twenty-six men—practically half.

Farber took over the command. He alone of all the officers had not taken part in the attack. Abrósimov had kept him at his side.

We buried our comrades on the very edge of the Volga in plain coffins made of rough pine planks. Heavy leaden clouds coursed overhead. The wind flapped the skirts of our greatcoats. Wet snow worked its way disgustingly inside our collars. Ice was floating down the Volga—autumn sludge.

The three graves stood out dark.

Everything was very simple there at the front. Yesterday he was here—to-day he isn't. And to-morrow maybe you won't be here. And the earth will fall just as dully on the lid of your coffin. Or maybe there'll be no coffin, and you'll be covered up with snow and you'll lie with your face in the ground until the war's over.

Three little brown mounds rose over the Volga. Three grey fur caps. Three pegs. A salute—the dry, fine rattle of an automatic. The rumble of long-range guns from across the Volga came like an echo. A minute's silence. The sappers gathered up their spades and tidied up the graves.

And that was all.

We moved away.

Not one of them was more than twenty-four years old; Karnaúkhov, possibly twenty-five. We couldn't even bury him; his body was over there on the German side.

And so he never read me his poems. I kept them in my pocket—along with my mother's letter and Lusia's photo. Simple, clear and clean—just as he had been himself:

You are so far from this mean dug-out,
You might be in another world.
Yet to me you seem so near
That I can almost reach out and touch you.

I can see the branches quivering
And hear the rustling of the young birch leaves,
While the wind tangles up your hair
And binds me closer to you.

I hung the portrait of Jack London over the table, below the mirror. They were even a little alike—London and Karnaúkhov.

I had spoken to Karnaúkhov for the last time only three minutes before the beginning of the attack. He was squatting down in the corner of a trench and fixing capsules to grenades. I asked him something—I forget what. He raised his head and for the first time I missed the smile I had always seen deep down in the very depths of his eyes—that quiet smile which I liked so much. He made some reply and I went away. I never saw him again.

I lay for a long time with my face pressed into the pillow. Lisagór came in. He sat down on his bed, drew up his legs, and puffed at a cigarette. He smoked in silence, with his chin resting on his knee.

"They say Abrósimov's going to be court-martialled," he said glumly, spitting between his legs on the floor.

"Who said?"

"Ladygin, the clerk, heard it."

"He's a liar."

"Not always. He hangs around the commanding officers—he might have heard."

"Have you been to HQ then?"

"Yes."

"What's going on up there?"

"Nothing. As usual. Astáfyev is drawing diagrams. He asked how many men we've got. I lied—I said twelve. You have to be careful what you say to him. He's another bureaucrat."

"Didn't you see the major?"

"I popped in for a minute. He was gloomy, depressed. He took the list of losses from Ladygin . . ."

"I could do with a drink . . ."

In the evening the major stopped me in the officers' mess. "Get yourself ready for to-morrow, engineer."

I didn't understand.

" For what?"

The major puffed on his pipe and didn't hear. His face was pinched and pale.

" For what?" I repeated.

He slowly raised his head.

" You'll have to tell how it all happened . . . there, on the hill," and he went off, leaning on his stick. He was still limping.

I asked no more. It was all clear.

Ladygin—the staff clerk and the principal gossip in the regiment—was saying that the major and Abrósimov had been summoned to Div. HQ and had been there three whole hours. Abrósimov had then shut himself in his dug-out and had not left it since. He had sent his meals back.

" His runner was trying to get hold of something at the ration stores. Then he raced back to the dug-out—holding on to his pockets. They'd received supplies of vodka that morning."

And he winked his insolent green eye.

XXV

I was late getting to the court-martial. As I arrived the major was already speaking. In the second battalion's dug-out—the roomiest place on our sector—it was so full of smoke that you could hardly make out the faces. Abrósimov was sitting by the wall. His lips were tightly closed, white and dry. His eyes were to the wall.

Astáfyev, the secretary, was shuffling papers, arranging them and trying his pen on a corner of a page. Beside him were two others—the intelligence officer and the commander of an anti-tank company. It was a court of honour. The major was standing, leaning with his hands on the table. In the last twenty-four hours he had aged by some ten years. From time to time he raised a glass of tea to his lips and took little nervous sips. He spoke quietly. So quietly that he could not be heard at the far end of the dug-out. I pushed my way forward.

" In wartime you can't do without trust," he was saying. " Courage is not enough, knowledge is not enough, there has to be faith. Faith in the people with whom you are fighting. Without that it's quite impossible . . ."

230

He undid his collar. It was hot in the dug-out. I thought his fingers shook slightly as he undid the hooks.

"I have travelled a long way with Abrósimov—Orel, Kastornaya, Vorónezh . . . and now here . . . And I trusted him. I knew he was young, inexperienced, that maybe he was learning as he went along, in the course of the war, and I knew that he might make mistakes—who doesn't—but as for trusting—I trusted him. You have to trust your chief of staff."

Turning his head, he gave Abrósimov a long, grave look.

"I know it's my own fault. It's I who am responsible for the men, not the chief of staff. And I'm responsible for this operation. And when to-day the divisional commander shouted at Abrósimov, I knew he was shouting at me too. And he was right." The major ran his hand through his hair and looked around at us with a tired expression. "There's no war without casualties. That's war. But what happened in the second battalion yesterday—that is certainly not war. That was a massacre. Abrósimov exceeded his authority. He countermanded my order. And he did it twice. In the morning, by telephone, and then personally, driving the men into attack . . ."

"The order was to attack the tanks," Abrósimov interrupted in a dry, wooden voice, without taking his eyes off the wall. "And the men did not attack . . ."

"You lie!" The major struck the table with his fist so hard that the spoon rattled in the glass. Then he pulled himself together. He took a sip from the glass. "The men went into the attack . . . But not the way you wanted them to. The men used their heads, they thought it out. But what did you do? You had seen what the first attack led to. But on that occasion it was impossible to do anything else. We counted on the artillery preparation. We had to strike at once, without giving the enemy a chance to come round. And it didn't come off. The enemy turned out to be stronger and smarter than we had thought. We had not succeeded in suppressing his fire points. I sent the engineer to the second battalion. Shiryáev was there—a fellow with a head on his shoulders. He had got everything ready at night to seize the German trenches. And he did it in a very intelligent way. But you . . . What did Abrósimov do?"

Abrósimov's lip began to tremble.

Borodín's face, usually kindly and soft, turned red and his cheeks trembled.

"I know how you shouted . . . how you waved a revolver."

231

He drank some more tea from the glass.

"At war an order is sacred. Failure to carry out an order is a crime. And it's always the last order that's carried out. And the men carried it out and are now lying outside our trenches. But Abrósimov is sitting here. He deceived his regimental commander. He exceeded his authority. And men died . . . That's all. That's enough, I think."

The major sat down heavily.

Abrósimov continued to sit as before—his hands on his knees, his eyes to the wall. Astáfyev, his head on one side, was writing earnestly and quickly.

Several other people spoke. Then came my turn. After me—Abrósimov. He was brief. He considered that the tanks could be taken only by a massed attack. That was all. And he had demanded that that attack should be carried out. Battalion commanders were out to save their men, so did not like attacks. It was not his fault that people had taken fright and failed to do their duty . . .

"Taken fright?" came from somewhere in the depths of the dug-out.

Everybody turned round. Clumsy, head and shoulders taller than the rest, wearing a greatcoat ridiculously short for him, Farber pushed his way through to the table.

"Taken fright, did you say? Did Shiryáev take fright? Did Karnaúkhov take fright? Are you talking about them?"

Farber was out of breath; he blinked and screwed up his shortsighted eyes—he had lost his glasses the day before.

"I saw everything . . . With my own eyes I saw it . . . How Shiryáev went . . . And Karnaúkhov and . . . everybody. I'm no good at talking . . . I've known them for a long time, Karnaúkhov and the others . . . How can you bring yourself to say such things! Courage doesn't mean rushing at machine-guns with your bare fists . . . Abrósimov . . . Captain Abrósimov said that the order was to attack the tanks. Not attack, but take. The trenches weren't thought up by Shiryáev out of cowardice. It was a device, and it was a correct device. He would have saved men . . . Saved them so that they could fight again. Now they're gone . . . And I consider . . ." His voice broke, he fumbled for the glass, failed to find it and made an impatient gesture. "I consider that such people . . . such people should not be in command."

Farber could not find words, he broke off, blushed, looked for the glass again; then suddenly blurted out:

"You are a coward yourself. You didn't go into the attack. And you kept me next to you. I saw everything . . ." He jerked his shoulder and, catching the hooks of his greatcoat in his neighbours' clothes, pushed his way back.

I followed him outside. He was leaning up against the dug-out.

"You spoke well, Farber."

He started.

"No, it was no good. Everything got mixed up in my head. When I look at him, you know . . . And he goes on sitting there calmly and even snaps at us. No . . . It's not what I meant to say."

He breathed heavily.

"He killed off my last two old men—Yermák and Perevérzev. Do you remember them? One was a sailor, the other worked a combine harvester, I think. They were inseparable. They slept, drank and ate together. You knew them . . . One of them was good at tricks."

"That young platoon commander, I've forgotten his name, with the white tuft of hair—was he yours?"

"Kalábin? Commander of a machine-gun company. He was only a boy. He hadn't been with us a week. He'd come out of hospital and he was always telling how they fed them on semolina."

"They haven't sent any new commanders yet?"

"They've sent company commanders from the first and third battalions. Meanwhile I've put sergeants in charge of platoons. There's no senior adjutant so far."

"It's a bit difficult without an adjutant," I granted.

For some reason I was now completely happy about Farber. There was a new firmness in his manner and his tone. It had not been there before.

"And what about Shiryáev? How bad is he? Do you know?"

"It's not very serious, apparently. His skull is undamaged, but I don't know about his arm. There wasn't much blood, but it was flapping about like a rag."

"The right one?"

"No, the left."

"That's a good thing . . ."

"He didn't want to be taken away. He cursed. You'll see, he said, I'll be back. Whether you like it or not. And I'll find Abrósimov if I have to go to the ends of the earth."

"I don't envy Abrósimov—Shiryáev's got quite a fist."

We chatted for a bit longer and then Farber returned to the dug-out. I went back to my place. I didn't want any more of the court-martial.

233

Valéga was frying bread in a frying-pan. The samovar was buzzing away in the corner.

I took off my boots and tunic and stretched out on my bed.

"Tea or coffee?" asked Valéga.

"Coffee with what?"

"With American milk."

"Coffee then."

Valéga went off to grind the coffee. The fat spluttered in the frying-pan. I took Karnaúkhov's poems out and read them through.

Then Lisagór came in. He slammed the door, glanced into the frying-pan and finished up near me.

"Well?" I asked.

"Application for reduction in rank and to be sent to a penal battalion . . ."

"That's not much."

"Never mind. Let him crawl about on his stomach. It'll do him good. Is Valéga getting supper ready?"

"He's gone to do the coffee."

We spoke no more of Abrósimov. The next day he departed without taking leave of anyone, with a pack on his back.

I never saw or heard of him again.

XXVI

That night the tanks came up. Six old, patched and re-patched T-34s. For a long time they snorted about and clattered their tracks along the shore and then camouflaged themselves. Everything seemed to get more cheerful all at once.

We had been waiting for them a long time. For ten days there had been rumours. They said a whole tank division was coming up from the rear, straight from the factory. And all that actually arrived were six old things that had seen their best days—and not from the rear, but from the "Red October" plant where they had been in battle practically since the very first day of the defence. But still, they were tanks—modern equipment . . . And they certainly had a pretty awesome appearance.

By the morning they were due to be right on the front line. The major ordered me to look out and prepare a pathway for them. Two railway wagons blocking the way at the rail crossing would have to be blown up. I sent Lisagór and Agnívtsev there.

Three tank men dropped in on me to warm up—two lieutenants and a sergeant, black, dirty and covered in oil from head to foot.

" Nothing to eat?" asked the senior of them, whose face was patterned with scars—he must have been burnt. " We haven't had a bite since morning."

With a disgruntled look Valéga brought out the remains of the birthday hare. They stuffed it into their mouths with relish.

" Well, how's it going? Are you fighting?" they asked.

" We fight from time to time," I replied.

" You haven't managed to take the tanks yet?"

" No, we haven't . . . You can't take a damned thing with your bare hands."

The tank men exchanged smiles.

" Are you relying on us?"

" Who else? It's the age of machines, after all . . ."

The lieutenant laughed. He had a thick unkempt beard practically up to his eyes.

" Have you any idea how many places this machinery has been in?"

" I can see from the way they look that they've done some pretty hard work. Were they on the South-Western?"

" Just ask where they haven't been."

" Were they at Khárkov?"

" Why, were you there?"

" I was."

" Do you know Nepokrytaya and Ternyvaya?"

" I certainly do. We attacked there."

" So did we . . . Because of your footsloggers we missed Khárkov. We were already at the Tractor plant . . . Is there no more hare?"

" That's the lot. Only the skin left."

" That's a pity, as it so happens we've got some spirit."

" Oh, we'll fix something."

I sent Valéga to Chumák.

" Tell him to come over. And to bring something to eat with him. How much spirit have you got?"

" It'll be enough. Don't worry."

Valéga departed. So did the sergeant.

" But you live like gods," said the lieutenant with the scars, looking towards the fat Cupid on the mirror, " like aristocrats."

" Yes, we can't grumble about accommodation."

" And you read books?"

" Sometimes . . . "

He flicked through *Martin Eden.*

" I can't remember when I last read something. In Premysl, was it? The Saturday before the war. I've probably forgotten how to read," he laughed. " After the war I'll have to learn all over again."

Chumák arrived. Sleepy, scratching his head, and with feathers in his hair.

" Call yourself an engineer . . . Drinking vodka in the middle of the night . . . What an idea. Here you are."

He took out from under his jacket two lumps of sausage and a loaf of bread.

" Your Valéga has gone for my sergeant-major. They'll bring some tinned meat."

He looked at the tank men.

" Those your boxes on the shore?"

" Who else's?"

" I'd be ashamed to get into them. They won't get as far as the front line, they'll fall to pieces."

The bearded one took offence.

" That's our business."

" Sure, it's not mine. My business is to drink vodka and swear at tank men for fighting badly."

" And who are you?"

" I? You ask the engineer. He'll tell you."

" Must be a scout. Can tell by your face."

" What about my face?" Chumák clenched his fists.

" Take it easy, little one. Whose spirit are you going to drink?"

" What? Yours?"

" Ours."

" All right, then. I'll shut up. And I take back what I said about tanks. You take the storage tanks to-morrow. With such machines—how could you fail?"

The tank men laughed. Chumák stretched himself and cracked his fingers. The bearded officer looked at his watch.

" Where the devil's that Prikhódko got to?"

" He must be untying the barrels. Or looking for glasses. Do you have water, by the way, engineer? Because it's strong —ninety-six . . ."

" There won't be any hold-up over water. The Volga's right beside us."

"Are you going into the attack to-morrow?" asked Chumák.

"The order is to wait in our initial positions and see what happens."

"It'll hardly be to-morrow. They've told us nothing."

"They'll tell you yet."

"If it's not to-morrow," said Chumák pensively, digging at the table with his knife, "do you realise how the Jerries will knock you to pieces with direct hits?"

"They say there's a hill there—that we can't be seen."

"They say, they say . . . And what are the Messerschmitts for?"

"Have the Jerries got a lot of anti-tank artillery?" asked the bearded one cautiously.

"Enough to deal with you."

Something went flying with a crash in the corridor. Someone cursed. Then the sergeant tumbled in, laden with bottles.

"Who the devil left those spades lying about there? I nearly smashed all these bottles."

He put the bottles down on the bed. Then he turned round—radiant and happy.

"What do I get for some news?"

"What news?"

"Wonderful news. Say what I get and I'll tell you."

"One good shot extra." Chumák made a face as he tried the spirit on his tongue. "It's strong, damn it."

"Not enough."

"Then keep it to yourself. You'll start talking anyway after the first glass. Let's have the mugs, engineer."

I gave out the mugs. There were only two. We'd have to use them in turns. Chumák poured out. He added water from the kettle.'

"Well, what's the news?" asked the scarred lieutenant.

"I told you it was wonderful . . . I just heard a bulletin on the sixteenth machine."

"Is Hitler dead or something?"

"Better still . . ."

"Is the war over?"

"On the contrary . . . it's only just begun . . ."—and he sustained a pause: "Our forces have taken Kalách! And then, what do you call it, Kriváya . . . Kriváya . . ."

"Kriváya Muzgá?"

"Muzgá . . . Muzgá. And then somewhere else . . . begins with a G . . ."

237

"Could it be Abganérovo?"

"That's it . . . Abganérovo . . ."

"You're not lying?"

"Why should I lie? Thirteen thousand prisoners . . .
Fourteen thousand dead!"

"Wonderful!"

"When did this happen?"

"In these last three days . . . Kalách, Abganérovo and
somewhere else. A whole bunch of names."

"That's it, then. The Jerries have had it."

Chumák slapped me so hard between my shoulder blades
that I nearly swallowed my tongue.

"To the rot with the Jerries, lads!"

And we all drank at once—from mugs, from bottles and
chasers straight from the spout of the teapot.

"Fine goings on! Boozing!"

In the doorway stood Lisagór. His mouth had dropped
open with surprise.

"I'm blowing up the trucks up there while they are
swigging vodka."

I handed him a mug. He knocked it down in one gulp, then
closed his eyes and shuddered. He felt for a crust of bread
and quickly put it to his nose.

"Here you are, going to pieces, and the offensive's at five
o'clock . . . Do you realise the battalions have already had
their breakfast brought up?"

"Blast . . ."

"Have a look at what's going on on the shore."

The tank men dashed off, without finishing the sausage.

"As it is, Shiryáev is cursing because we are behind with
the throughways."

"Which Shiryáev?"

"What do you mean, which? The chief of staff. The senior
lieutenant."

"Goodness . . . where did he spring from?"

"You'll miss the whole war like that," laughed Lisagór.
"He skipped from the field hospital. He's killing himself down
there on the shore."

Chumák ran out of the door.

I pulled on my boots, looked for my revolver and looked
at my watch. Quarter to three.

"Have you made the throughways?"

"Yes."

"The full width?"

"Yes. They'll go through beautifully."

The tank men were already starting up their engines and fussing about. The whole shore was white. There had been more snow. Somewhere to the left could be heard Shiryáev's voice. He was shouting at someone.

"He's to come to me in five minutes and report. Understand? Off you go . . ."

Chumák came running up, doing up his jacket as he ran. "The new chief of staff's a terror. Just watch yourself, engineer . . ."

Shiryáev stood at the entrance to the staff dug-out. His arm was bandaged and in a sling. A white bandage showed beneath his cap. When he saw me he waved his good arm.

"Get up to the front line fast, Yurka! Help the tank men . . . Nobody knows where your throughways are."

"How's your arm?" I said.

"Later . . . later. Get moving . . . There's only a couple of hours left."

"Very good, comrade senior lieutenant. May I go?"

"Get going, you silly devil . . . And send Lisagór to me . . ."

I saluted, turned left about, clicked my heels and whipped my hand down at my first step.

"Repeat! Two hours square drill for you!"

A cold firm snowball caught me right in the back of the neck. It broke up and went down under my collar.

I hopped on to the first tank. Valéga was already there— fixing a bottle to his belt.

One after the other the tanks made their way along the river bank. They passed the level-crossing and the blown-up wagons, and came out on the cobbled roadway. That was where the Germans would open fire—the tanks roared furiously.

The snowflakes fell, twirling slowly in the air.

Mamai Hill stood out in front, an enormous, heavy mass. There was an hour and forty minutes left before the attack.

XXVII

The attack was fixed for five. At twenty to five Garkúsha ran up, out of breath.

"Comrade lieutenant . . ."

"What's the matter now?"

He breathed heavily, wiping his wet forehead with the palm of his hand.

"The scouts have come back."

"Well?"

"They've come across some mines . . ."

"What sort of mines?"

"German. Right opposite the left throughway. About fifty metres. Some strange ones . . ."

"Oh, blast . . . What the devil did they look for yesterday?"

"They say they weren't there yesterday."

"They weren't . . . Where's that Bukhvóstov?"

"He's down in the anti-tank men's dug-out."

"Shiryáev! Phone HQ and tell 'em to hold up the signal. I'll go . . ."

Bukhvóstov—the terribly pock-marked, tiny commander of the reconnaissance of the sapper battalion—threw up his hands.

"The Jerries laid them last night. Honestly, last night. Yesterday evening I tested everywhere with my own hands—there was nothing. Honestly . . ."

"Honestly, honestly . . . Why didn't you report it sooner. Always at the last minute. Are there a lot of them?"

"Oh, about ten. And they're different ones, I've never seen them before. Something like our infantry mines, but not quite. The detonator's somewhere at the side . . ."

"Garkúsha, bring the camouflage capes. You'll have to lead in."

It was our good fortune that there was no moon. We crawled through the tank passage, marked with pegs. The pock-marked sergeant, Garkúsha, and I. The bottom of Garkúsha's boots, with their steel studs, shone in front of my nose, as we crawled beyond the line of our own minefields. All around was as white as white. The line of the German trenches stood out dark ahead. The sergeant stopped. He pointed silently with his gauntlet at something black in the

240

ow . . . A mine. The most ordinary of mines with a ser-
rated case, a detonator and a short wire. Beside it was an
additional peg so that it held more firmly. And he had
taken it for the detonator. A useless creature, not a scout.

Lying on his stomach, Garkúsha skilfully removed the
detonators one after the other. My hands were frozen and it
was only with difficulty that I undid two. The sergeant puffed.

Psh-sh-sh . . . A Verey light . . .

We lay dead still. Instantly my mouth went dry. My heart
started to beat furiously. They'll see us, the bastards . . .

Psh-sh-sh . . . Another one. Out of the corner of my eye
I saw that the sergeant had already crawled away from me
about ten metres. What a man! The Germans would see him
any moment.

There was a short burst from a machine-gun.

They had seen him.

Another burst . . .

Something hit me with terrible force in the left arm and
then in the leg. I pushed my face into the snow. It was cold
and pleasant and got into my mouth, nose and ears . . . How
pleasant it was . . . It was crisp between the teeth, like ice-
cream . . . And he said they weren't mines. The most ordinary
pomzas. It was only a peg at the side. That sergeant's an
odd fellow, that's all there is to it. Only snow between my
teeth.

XXVIII

"Well, what are you doing, Yurka? Since that note from
the army hospital two months have passed without a word.
Disgusting behaviour! If you had been wounded in the right
arm as well there would be an excuse, but it was the left. It's
not right, honestly, it's not right. I get asked about you every
day, I tell them you're getting fat on hospital rations, you're
having affairs with the nurses and haven't got time for your
old friends! But they don't forget you, you useless dog.
Chumák is saving up some sort of wonderful brandy (six
star!) that he captured and won't let anybody try. I've
snooped around everywhere but can't find it.

"On the whole, we're fed up. Fed up with stopping here.
Fed to the teeth. The others are attacking, pushing towards the
West, while we're still in the very same trenches and the very
same dug-outs. It's true the Jerries aren't quite what they

used to be. But even so it was fairly tough last month. A.
you got bust up we went into another attack with tanks, bu
we didn't take the storage tanks and then the tanks were
sent to another sector. The Jerries knocked one of them out
and we had to fight over it for a good month. The divisional
commander ordered us to set up a fire-point near it. And the
Jerry div. commander apparently decided the same—and so we
fought for the tank . . . It was no good frontally—there are
only five or six able-bodied men with bayonets in the battalions. We had to dig our way up to it. But the earth
was like stone and we had no explosives. For two weeks
the Volga just wouldn't freeze up. The " corn-cobs " dropped
biscuits and concentrated rations.

" All the same, we took the tank in the end. We dug a tunnel
twenty-two metres long, put in about a hundred kilograms of
TNT and let her go! Then we attacked through the crater.
You see what sort of chaps we are! I put Tugíyev, Agnívtsev
(he's now in the field hospital, wounded) and your Valéga up
for a ' Star '—they're wonderful lads—and the rest for the
' Courage '. Farber has now got his machine-gun under the
tank and is strafing the Jerries mercilessly. But they've still
got the storage tanks. They've dug into the ground like
rabbits and you can't approach them from any direction . . .
We are fighting mainly with artillery. They've brought all
of it, except the heavies, over to the right bank. They've set
up a battery of divisionals right next to our dug-out—they
don't let us sleep. Rodímtsev and the 92nd have been put
to the right of us, in the area of Tramway street. Meanwhile
the 39th are doing fine—cleaned up the ' Red October '
almost completely.

" There are now three of us in the platoon—I, Garkúsha and
Valéga. Tugíyev is with the horses on the left bank, instead
of Kuleshóv. Kuleshóv was caught stealing oats and got sent
to a penal unit. Chepúrny, Timóshka and that little fellow
who was always chewing—I forget his name—we lost on
Mamai. We held a defensive position there for a couple of
weeks along with the anti-gas men and the scouts. We buried
two of them, but of Timóshka we found only his hat. We
miss him. His concertina is lying about doing nothing.
Urázov was blown up by a mine and lost his foot. And
three others were sent off to the field hospital, new ones that
you don't know. Of the staff officers, the anti-gas man
Túrin, and the interpreter were killed. The Jerries got your
' favourite ' Astáfyev right in the backside with a piece of
shrapnel (how he got it I just can't understand—he never

ιt the dug-out), and he's now lying on his belly sorting out his archives.

"Now we're building command posts all the time. Every day a new one. We've already made five and the major is still not satisfied: you know him. We made one in the factory chimney, near the chemical factory, where there's plenty of tin. Another on the roof, like a pigeon loft. It was a good look-out point, but the major said ' Cold and draughty ' and ordered us to make one in the village near the cutting where the Dzerzhínsky locomotive stands. But the gunners of the 270th got their cannons in there and drew the Jerries' fire. Shells are bursting right `alongside—how can we get the major along there?

"Anyway, come back soon—we'll look for a good spot together. And you can help with the digging (ha, ha), for I'm getting such corns on my hands that I can't pick up a spade. Your Ustínov—the div. engineer—is on to me all the time: demanding diagram after diagram, and that's death to me, as you know. Shiryáev sends his greetings: his arm is quite better now.

" Oh, yes . . . In the second battalion there's a new medical orderly. In place of Burlyúk, who's gone for a course. When you come, you'll see. Chumák hangs around there all day long and cleans his webbing every day with whitening. Anyway, hurry back. We are waiting for you.

Your A. Lisagór

" P.S. I have found at last the LZZ detonator, the delayed-action one that you were always longing for. I can't sort it out without you. We've now got quite a decent collection of captured material. An ' S ' mine and a ' TMI-43 ', and five absolutely new types of detonators in wonderful boxes (they will make tobacco pouches) and excellent Jerry fuses with sieve-like detonators.

A.L."

On the back was an addition in big, curling, drooping letters:

" Good morning or evening, comrade leftenant. I have to inform you that I am so far alive and kicking and I wish you the same. Comrade leftenant your books are all right I put them away in the case. The comrade platoon commander

got two occumulators and now there's light in our dug-o
Senior leftenant Shiryáev wants to take it for the H(
Comrade leftenant hurry back soon. Everybody sends his
best greetings, as I do too.

Your batman A. Volegóv

I stuffed the letter into my brief-case, pulled on my dressing-gown and went to see the chief medical officer. He was a decent little chap with whom it was always possible to come to terms. Then to the man in charge of the stores to draw a new tunic. The sleeve had been ripped off mine . . .

Next morning, in squeaky boots, and a new soldier's great-coat and with a bunch of letters in my pockets, I took leave of my friends and set off for Stalingrad.

They accompanied me to the gate.

"Our greetings to Paulus!"

"Of course."

"You won't forget what I asked you to do, will you?"

"All right, all right.'

"It's right nearby. The second ravine from yours. Where the knocked-out 'Katyúsha' stands."

"If you see Marúsya, say I've got something interesting to tell her when we meet. It wouldn't do in a letter."

"All right . . . So long . . . Take that copy of the *Researches* to the sixth ward. My greetings to the PT instructress."

"Right—greetings."

"Well, good-bye."

"Don't forget to write."

The driver was already waving to me.

"Get it over with, lieutenant."

I shook hands and ran to the car.

XXIX

We got as far as the village of Burkóvsky by evening. In Burkóvsky we found the divisions' rear services and Lazar, the paymaster. I spent the night with him in a tiny little hovel full of old folk, children and some clerks.

"Well, how is it back there?" they asked.

"Normal."

"Were you in hospital in Léninsk?"

"Yes, in Léninsk. Not much of a hospital. Not to be compared with my dug-out on the river bank."

Lazar laughed.

"You won't recognise your dug-out now—electricity, gramophone, about fifty records and the walls hung with Jerry blankets. Beautiful."

"How long since you were there?"

"I only got back yesterday. I issued the pay."

"Are the Jerries still there?"

"What do you mean! They've already skipped from Mamai Hill and have dug in on the other side of the Long Ravine. They've practically had it. They've got nothing to eat, no ammunition and there are bare horses' bones lying in their dug-outs. Kaput, in other words . . ."

It took me a long time to get to sleep that night. I kept turning from side to side.

Early next morning I carried on further in a staff car.

We drove right up to the banks of the Volga without any attempt at concealment. The river was vast, white and dazzlingly bright. Something dark could be made out on the other side—probably the control point. There was a little flag against the white background. How time had flown, damn it . . . Only a short time ago, it seemed like yesterday, that same Volga, now so blindingly bright, had been black and red from smoke and fires, broken up by explosions and scattered with pieces of floating wood and wreckage. And now! The road across the ice, marked with stakes, shot like an arrow to the opposite bank. Transport was rushing backwards and forwards—lorries, jeeps and many-coloured, camouflaged small passenger cars. Here and there were occasional dark patches where mortar-shells had exploded, about a hundred metres from one another. They were already old traces. The traffic controller with ginger moustaches and a yellow flag said it was a couple of weeks since the crossing had been bombarded—the Germans were exhausted.

We drove past the control point.

"Your documents."

"Can't I get through without them?"

"Sorry, comrade lieutenant. Must observe the rules."

Amazing . . . All round Chúikov's headquarters was a barbed-wire fence, with guards standing at ease at the entrance, the pathways cleared and a number over each dug-out—well-made, black, on a special board.

A signal on a striped post said " Borodín's department—300 metres ", and, written in red pencil: " First street on the left ". That meant we had gone past it. The street to the left was apparently the ravine where the Div. HQ had been.

I was excited—really excited! As one always is on returning home. As you return from holiday or somewhere, the nearer you get to your home the quicker your steps become. And you notice everything as you walk, every little detail, every little change. A pavement that has been newly asphalted, a cigarette shop that has appeared on the corner, the tram stop that has been moved nearer to the chemist's, the storey added to the house at number twenty-six. You see everything and you notice everything . . .

That was the place where we landed on that memorable September morning. That was the road along which we dragged the gun. That was the white pump-house. A bomb had hit it and killed thirty wounded soldiers lying in it. It had been rebuilt and there was a sort of smithy in it. And over there had been the trench in which Valéga and I had once taken shelter from a bombardment. They must have filled it in: there was no trace of it. And there someone had built some steps—no need to scramble up the slope any more. Really cultured—there were even properly finished hand-rails.

The ravine was deserted. A pile of German mines lay on the snow. Some rolls of wire, a broken-down bench for making the Bruno coils. I recognised it as our bench: Garkúsha had made it. Near the latrines were some twenty Jerries—dirty, unshaven, wrapped up in bits of rag and towelling. On seeing me they all stood up.

"Who are you looking for, comrade lieutenant?" came a voice from somewhere above.

A sort of whirlwind surrounded by a cloud of snow hit me and nearly knocked me over.

"Are you fit and well, comrade lieutenant?"

A cheerful red face. Laughing and utterly child-like eyes. Sedykh! Blow me down . . . Sedykh . . .

"Where the devil did you come from!"

He made no reply. He just beamed—beamed from head to foot. And I beamed. And we stood facing each other and shook each other by the hand. I had the feeling of being slightly drunk.

"Everything's been shifted, comrade lieutenant. We're chasing the Germans out fast. Our command post is here, in the ravine. They are all at the front line. But I got scratched and they left me here to look after the Jerries . . ."

"What about Igor?"

"He's fit and well."

246

"Thank God for that!"

"Come along to-morrow and have a drink of vodka. There's a whole barrel. Goodness, they'll be pleased. You're just out of hospital? Yes, the lads told me."

"Yes, out of hospital. Don't keep turning round, let me have a good look at you."

He hadn't changed in the slightest! He had, though—he'd grown up a bit. Little curly hairs showed on his chin. His cheeks had slightly sunk. But he was just as rosy-faced, and just as tough as before and his eyes were unchanged—happy, mischievous, with long, curling lashes like a girl's.

"Wait, wait! What's that you've got there shining under your jacket?"

Sedykh hung his head, and started to pick at the callus on his hand—his old habit.

"Now, you rascal! And not a word . . . Give me your fist . . . What did you get it for?"

He blushed even more. My fingers nearly cracked in his huge paw.

"You won't be ashamed now to go back to the collective farm?"

"Why should I be ashamed?" He was still picking at the palm of his hand. "What about that . . . er . . . cigarette case of mine, did you keep it, or . . ."

"But of course! Here it is, have a smoke . . . Have you got a light?"

"Hans—a light for the lieutenant! Quickly now! *Feuer, Feuer*. Or whatever you call it."

A puny little German in horn-rimmed glasses, who must have been an officer, jumped up at once and struck a revolver-shaped lighter.

"*Bitte, Kamarad.*"

Sedykh grabbed the lighter.

"All right, bitty, we'll manage ourselves," and he offered the light. "What junk merchants. All their pockets are stuffed with junk. They give themselves up and straight away offer a cigarette lighter. I've got about twenty of 'em already . . . Do you want a couple?"

"Oh, never mind, I've got time yet. I'd sooner you gave me the news. After all, four months is a fair bit of time."

"What is there to tell, comrade lieutenant? The same old thing . . ." All the same he told the usual front-line soldier's story known to us all, yet always listened to with interest . . . On one occasion they were mined and nearly everybody got killed, and on another they spent twenty-four hours in a trench

—a sniper wouldn't let them move—he got three bullet ho[...]
in his cap, and then they were surrounded for a couple [...]
weeks, in the foundry, and the Germans bombed them, and
there was nothing to eat or, worst of all, to drink, and he had
gone four times to the Volga for water, and then . . . then
they had been mined again and they had cleared the mines
and fixed up a " Bruno " . . .

" In general, you know how it is . . ." He smiled his
frank, warm smile.

" You did all right, in other words. I knew you would. Let's
smoke another cigarette each and then I'll go and look for
our chaps. Do you know where they are, by any chance?"

" Everybody's up there . . . at the front line. On the other
side of the Long Ravine, they must be. Only I stayed behind,
sick."

" Nobody else?"

" One of your staff officers as well. He's in that dug-out
there. Wounded."

" Is it Astáfyev?"

" I don't know, honestly. A senior lieutenant."

" In that dug-out, did you say?" I went in the direction
of the dug-out.

" So we'll expect you this evening, comrade lieutenant!"
Sedykh shouted after me. " I won't say anything to Igor
Vladímirovich. The second dug-out round the corner. On
the left. Three steps and a blue handle on the door."

Astáfyev lay on his bed with a pillow beneath his stomach
and was writing something. Beside him on a stool was a
telephone.

" Georges! My dear! So you're back!" He broke into a
smile and stretched out his soft, pudgy hand. " Fit as a bull?"

" As you can see."

" And I have no luck. The regiment's chasing the Germans,
while I'm a telephone boy, writing reports."

" What about it—it's not so bad. It makes it easier to
write history."

" I'm not sure . . . Listen, sit down, put the telephone on the
floor and tell me all about it." He tried to turn over, but
screwed his face up and swore. " The sciatic nerve is damaged
and it hurts like hell."

" That's war, nothing you can do about it . . . Where are
our chaps?"

" In the town, Georges, in the town, in the very centre.
The first battalion is forcing its way through to the station.
Farber just phoned to say that they're blocking the hotel near

e mill. About fifty SS-men have occupied it and won't give
n . . . But sit down."

"Thanks. And where are Shiryáev and Lisagór?"

"They're there too. They're all there. They went over to
the attack this morning. Don't you want to smoke? They
are German, captured ones . . ." He offered a neat green
box of cigarettes.

"I don't like them. They irritate my throat. And what's
that—more loot?" On the table was a huge accordion, bright
with mother-of-pearl.

"Yes, loot. Chumák made a present of it to Shiryáev . . .
You've no idea how many there are of them over there . . ,"

"Well, I'll be on my way."

"Stay a bit. Tell me what it's like in the rear?"

"Some other time, perhaps. I need Shiryáev."

Astáfyev smiled.

XXX

By evening I was quite drunk. Drunk with fresh sun, walking,
meeting people, drunk with impressions and sheer joy. And
with brandy. It was the same as Chumák's—six-star . . .

Chumák poured out glass after glass.

We were lying in some ruined house—I could no longer
remember how we got there—I, Chumák, Lisagór and
Valéga, of course. We were lying on some straw. Valéga
was in a corner, smoking his pipe, cross and scowling. He was
definitely displeased with my behaviour. What was the idea—
leaving a good, re-tailored officer's greatcoat, with gold
buttons, in the hospital, and bringing back instead some
soldier's coat, that didn't reach below my knees. What's the
use of that . . . And canvas boots, with wide tops and rubber
soles.

"I got you chrome leather ones," he announced gloomily
when we met, having inspected me disapprovingly from head
to foot. "Out there in the dug-out. Only the instep is rather
small."

I excused myself as best I could. But I had not, apparently,
been forgiven.

"Drink up, engineer." Chumák poured out some more.
"Don't be shy."

Lisagór seized hold of the mug.

"Don't you make him drunk. We've been invited to the

249

thirty-ninth to-day. Eat more butter, Yurka. Come on, ta some more."

I took some more.

Through the broken-down wall could be seen the Mamai Hill, and a chimney of the " Red October "—the only one still standing. The sky was full of rockets. Red, blue, yellow, green . . . A whole sea of rockets . . . And shooting. The whole day long there had been firing. From revolvers, Sten guns, rifles, anything that came to hand. Tra-ta-ta-ta, tra-ta-ta-ta, tra-ta-ta-ta.

Well and what a day, my God! Flopped out on the straw, I stared at the sky and hadn't the strength to think of anything. I was too full, satiated. I counted the rockets. I was still able to do that. Red, green, green again, four green in a row . . .

Chumák said something. I wasn't listening.

" Go away."

" Come on, it won't hurt you . . . Do what you're asked. Don't be a pig."

" Go away, I tell you, why do you keep pestering me?"

" Come on, read it . . . Just ten lines."

" Ten lines of what?"

" Of this. His big speech. It's interesting . . . Honestly, it's interesting . . ."

He pushed right into my face a dirty scrap of some German newspaper.

" What rubbish is that?"

" You just read it."

The letters jumped about before my eyes—unfamiliar, Gothic letters. Hitler's degenerate face—tight lips, heavy eyelids, and a silly, huge, peaked cap.

" *Volkischer Beobachter*."

The Führer's speech in Munich on November 9th, 1942 —nearly three months ago.

" Stalingrad is ours! The Russians are still holding out in a few houses. Let them sit there. That's their private affair. Our job is done. The city bearing Stalin's name is in our hands. The greatest Russian artery—the Volga—is paralysed. And no force in the world can shift us from the place.

" It is I who tell you this—a man who has never once deceived you, a man on whom providence has placed the burden and the responsibility for this greatest war in the history of mankind. I know—believe me, for you can be sure—and I repeat it with a full sense of my responsibility fore God and history—we shall never leave Stalingrad. However much the Bolsheviks might wish it . . ."

Chumák shook with laughter.

"Oh dear, Adolf. What a lad! Honestly, he's a lad. It has worked out just as it was written. Valéga, fill up again for that."

Valéga filled the glasses. Chumák turned over on his stomach and rested his head on his hands.

"But why, engineer? Why? Explain it to me."

"Why what?"

"Why did it turn out like that? Eh? Do you remember how they plastered us in September? Yet they didn't bring it off. Why? Why didn't they shove us into the Volga?"

My head was turning round—I was still weak from the hospital.

"Lisagór, explain to him why. And I'll take a little walk."

I stood up and, swaying, went out through the opening that had once presumably been a door.

There was such a high, transparent sky, as clear as clear, with not a cloud or an aeroplane. Only rockets. And a pale, lonely little star among them. And the Volga—wide, calm, smooth, with only one place—opposite the pump-house—where it had not frozen. They said it never froze just there.

The greatest Russian artery . . . Paralysed, he said . . . What a fool! What a fool! "The Russians are still holding out in a few houses. Let them sit there. That's their private affair . . ."

There they were—those few houses. There it was—Mamai Hill—squat and unbeautiful . . . And just like pimples—two pimples on the top—the tanks. What a lot of trouble they had given us! Even now it was revolting to look at them . . . And behind those red ruins there—of which only the walls remained, looking like a sieve—was the beginning of Rodímtsev's positions, a strip two hundred metres wide . . . Just imagine —two hundred metres, two hundred wretched metres . . . To cross the whole of Byelorussia and the Ukraine and the Donbass and the Kalmyk steppes and still not cover those two hundred metres . . .

Chumák asked why. Not just anybody, but Chumák. That pleased me more than anything. Maybe Shiryáev or Farber would yet ask me why. Or that old chap, the machinegunner, who lay three days at his gun, cut off from everybody, and went on firing until his ammunition finished? And then

251

crawled back to the river bank with the gun. And even dragg
the empty ammunition boxes along with him. "Why thro
good stuff away—it'll come in handy." I didn't even remember his name. I could recall only his face—bearded, with
little slit-eyes and his cap straight across his head. Maybe
he would also ask me why? Or that Siberian lad, who was
always chewing smolka.[1] If he were still alive, he would also
probably ask why. Lisagór told me how he died. I knew
him only a few days—they sent him along shortly before I was
wounded. He was a cheerful, bright lad who liked a good
joke. He took a couple of anti-tank grenades in his hands and
ran straight up to a wrecked tank and threw both in through
the gun-port . . .

"Hey, Chumák, Chumák—you old sailor—why do you ask
such silly questions? You're coming towards me with a bottle
in your hand and you don't understand a blasted thing, not
a thing . . . Come here, come on. Let's embrace. People
always embrace when they're drunk. It's got nothing to do
with being sentimental, God forbid . . . And Valéga, come
here. Come on, come on . . . Drink up, old chum . . . Drink
to victory. Do you see what the Jerries have done to the
town? Bricks and nothing else . . . But we're alive. As for
the town . . . we'll build another. Is that right, Valéga? The
Jerries are kaput. There they go—look—carrying their rucksacks and their blankets . . . They're thinking about Berlin and
their Fraus. D'you want to get to Berlin, Valéga? I do.
I want it terribly . . . And we'll be there together—you'll
see. We shall definitely be there. Only on the way we'll
drop into Kiev for a minute, to have a look at my old
people. They're fine people, my old folks, honestly . . . Let's
drink to them—is there any left there, Chumák?"

So we drank again. We drank to the old folks, to Kiev, to
Berlin and to something else, I don't remember what. And
all around they kept on firing and firing, so that the sky
was quite mauve, and the rockets screeched, and somewhere very nearby someone was playing a fool dance on a
balalaika.

"Comrade lieutenant, may I speak to you, please?"
"What's the matter?"
"The chief of staff is asking for you."
"And who are you?"
"Staff runner."
"Well?"

[1] Smolka—a plant (viscaria) which Siberians dry and chew.

" The order is for everybody to parade at 1800 hours in the command post in the ravine."

" He's taken leave of his senses. It's a day off to-day, a holiday."

" It's not my business, comrade lieutenant. The chief of staff gave the order and I have informed you."

" Now, you just explain a little. What's this—ordering and informing? Is he summoning us to a banquet or something? To celebrate the victory?"

The runner laughed.

" I heard that they will finish the northern group off to-morrow at the 'Barricades'. Ours and the thirty-ninth are to be shifted over there . . ."

So that was it!

Chumák looked for his jacket and belt in the darkness. He felt about the ground. Lisagór shook the straw from his greatcoat.

" Valéga, gather up our things and find Garkúsha quick. In the second house from here, in the cellar . . . Off you go!"

Valéga dashed off.

" Mind he doesn't forget the spades!" And, turning to me: " Well, engineer, let's go and build a command post. Off we go at the gallop."

" Are there enough spades?"

" Yes. One each. Me, you, Garkúsha and Valéga . . . We'll do it in one night for sure . . . And maybe in a house somewhere we'll fix ourselves up a position near a window. Let's go."

Outside Chumák was roaring:

" In columns of four . . . Fa-a-a-ll in. With a song . . . Quick . . . march!"

Actually he had only three men in his platoon . . .

Lisagór slapped me on the shoulder:

" So you didn't manage to drop in on your friend Igor. That's always the way with you and me . . . Maybe to-morrow. God willing, if we're still alive."

Somewhere high up in the sky a " corn-cob " droned away —the night patrol. Over the " Barricades " the " lanterns " were lighting up. Our " lanterns ", not the Germans'. The Germans no longer had anybody to light them. And it was pointless for them anyhow . . .

They were winding their way towards the Volga in a long, green line. They were silent. At their rear was a sergeant

—young, snub-nosed, with a long, curved pipe in his mouth with a tassel dangling from it. He winked as he went past.

"Just taking a few tourists along. They want to have a look at the Volga . . ."

He laughed gaily, infectiously.

THE END